A
STUDY
IN THE
THEORY AND
PRACTICE OF
GERMAN LIBERALISM

Eduard Lasker, 1829-1884

James F. Harris

UNIVERSITY
PRESS OF
AMERICA

LANHAM • NEW YORK • LONDON

Copyright © 1984 by

University Press of America,™ Inc.

4720 Boston Way
Lanham, MD 20706

3 Henrietta Street
London WC2E 8LU England

Printed in the United States of America

ISBN (Perfect): 0-8191-4175-5
ISBN   (Cloth): 0-8191-4174-7

All University Press of America books are produced on acid-free
paper which exceeds the minimum standards set by the National
Historical Publications and Records Commission.

For

Ronald F. and Eileen E. Harris

Contents

Illustrations ix

Tables xi

Preface xiii

Abbreviations xv

I. From Jarotschin to New York 1

II. The Patriot 17

III. The Rise of the National Liberal Party 33

IV. The Role of Law 45

V. The Power of the Constitution 61

VI. The Crisis of Liberal Economics 87

VII. Lasker and the Collapse of the National Liberal Party 107

VIII. Eduard Lasker and German Liberalism 115

Appendix A. The Executive Committee of the National Liberal Reichstag
Faktion, 1871–1878 122

Appendix B. Occupational Distribution of Reichstag Members, 1871–1884 124

Appendix C. Absenteeism in the Reichstag and in the National Liberal
Fraktion, 1867–1884 126

Appendix D. Absenteeism among Members of the National Liberal
Executive Committee in the Reichstag, 1867–1884 127

Appendix E. National Liberal and Liberale Vereinigung Roll-Call
Wins and Losses in the Reichstag, 1867–1884 128

Appendix F. National Liberal Roll-Call Wins and Losses in the Prussian
Landtag, 1867–1884 129

Notes 131

viii

Bibliographical Note 153

Index 155

Illustrations

Eduard Lasker (ca. 1873) xvi

"The North German Parliamentary Bill with Surprises" . . . . .Between pp. 10 and 11

"Cabinet Question and Answer Game" .Between pp. 10 and 11

"The Best Hated and the Best Protected" . . . . .Between pp. 10 and 11

"That Would be the Result" . . . . .Between pp. 10 and 11

Tables

3.1   Number of Seats Held by Major Parties in the Reichstag, 1867–1881 34

3.2   Popular Vote (in thousands) for Major Parties in Reichstag Elections,
      1871–1881 35

3.3   Number of Seats Held by Major Parties in Reichstag Elections,
      1871–1881 36

3.4   National Liberal (NL) Reichstag Executive Committee, 1871–1878 37

4.1   Reichstag Roll-Call Votes on Bills Relating to the Death Penalty, 1870 57

4.2   Reichstag Roll-Call Votes on Bills Relating to Agitation, 1870 58

4.3   Reichstag Roll-Call Votes on Bills Relating to Press Offenses,
      1874–1876 59

5.1   Reichstag Roll-Call Votes on Bills Relating to the *Diäten*, 1867–1881 71

5.2   Reichstag Roll Call Votes on Bills Relating to Parliamentary Immunity,
      1868–1875 74

5.3   Final Reichstag Roll-Call Votes on Military Budget Bills,
      1867–1880 75

5.4   Reichstag Roll-Call Votes on Bills Relating to Ministerial Responsibility,
      1867–1869 78

5.5   Reichstag Roll-Call Votes on Bills to Weaken the Federal Executive,
      1868–1881 80

5.6   Prussian Landtag Roll-Call Votes on Bills to Grant Secret Funds to the
      Government, 1866–1877 82

6.1   Reichstag Roll-Call Votes on Bills Relating to Worker Freedom,
      1867–1869 91

6.2   Reichstag Roll-Call Votes on Bills Relating to the Iron Tariff,
      1873–1879 100

6.3   Reichstag Roll-Call Votes on Bills Relating to Agricultural Tariffs,
      1879–1883 101–02

6.4   Reichstag Roll-Call Votes on Bills Relating to Workers' Insurance,
      1881–1883 105

8.1   Reichstag and National Liberal Party Voting Records on Ten Important
      Roll-Call Votes, 1867–1878 118–19

Preface

This work grew out of an interest in the early development of political life in nineteenth-century Germany and the problems faced by the new politicians in a dynamically changing state. In that context Eduard Lasker was both normal and unusual and therefore doubly attractive as a subject. He was normal in most of his political views but unusual in that he was a Jew from the east. Among the most diminutive of legislators physically, his formidable political stature derived from his parliamentary ability and his nearly boundless ambition. For most of his career he was a National Liberal and gained fame as a practitioner of liberal politics. He clashed with a wide variety of opponents and faced a series of important problems during one of the most exciting eras in German history. His reactions and initiatives tell us much about the man and even more about the times.

Yet this work is not a biography in the traditional sense. Partly because the personal idiosyncrasies seem less important in Lasker's case and partly because the sources are inadequate to describe his private life well enough to be meaningful, my focus is largely on Eduard Lasker's public career. The major features of his personal life are described in Chapter I so that the reader can understand his personal background as well as his political role.

Lasker's career makes it clear that German political development, especially liberal development, was anything but a quick and easy surrender to a Bismarckian or nationalistic *Zeitgeist* after the setbacks of 1848 and 1866. Whether he won or lost, Lasker fought a good and often bitter fight—as Bismarck himself recognized! Lasker's enduring victories on significant issues in the legislative world were few and are largely forgotten. What is important is that he worked hard, using all honorable means available, both compromise and opposition, to further his liberal goals. Some of those goals may appear rather more conservative today, but Lasker was content to be a liberal and a German nationalist and made no excuse for either stand.

Sources for the study of Eduard Lasker are scattered across Germany and the United States. The University of Wisconsin and the American Philosophical Society made travel to Boston, New York and Germany possible. At a key early stage in the development of the manuscript the University of Wisconsin Center System funded a summer devoted to writing. The Graduate Research Board of the University of Maryland provided a summer of research in Germany, and a later sabbatical leave greatly assisted in completing the manuscript. The Graduate School of the University of Maryland contributed to the costs of publication and I am happy to have this opportunity to thank all of these institutions.

Many libraries and archives made materials available. I am especially indebted to the Leo Baeck Institute in New York City, the Brandeis Library in Waltham, Massachusetts, and the Zentrales Staatsarchiv, Potsdam, in the German Democratic Republic. The libraries of the University of Wisconsin and the University of Maryland, particularly their interlibrary loan divisions, were of great help in pursuing this research. The Library of Congress made its vast collection available. I would like to thank also the many libraries and archives in Germany, England, and Israel that contributed their help; they are too numerous to mention here (most are cited in the notes or in the bibliographical essay), but all were greatly appreciated.

On a personal level I must first thank Professor T. S. Hamerow of the University of Wisconsin, who supervised this project at its inception and encouraged and supported it always. I am likewise indebted to Stanley Zucker, James Cockburn, and Gabriel Spiegel for reading the manuscript at various stages. Vernon Lidtke's cogent criticisms improved several parts of the work. My friend and colleague John McCusker, tangentially interested in German history, contributed significantly through equal measures of criticism and encouragement. Gretchen Oberfranc aided greatly in improving the style of the manuscript. Gail Rauch-Tilstra performed nobly in the new field of word-processing. My wife, Cathy, and my children, Jeanne and Mark, watched the manuscript evolve over a series of years and are responsible for its appearance as a book. Despite these valuable contributions, whatever errors remain are, naturally, my own.

Abbreviations

ABRB   Hermann Oncken, ed., "Aus den Briefen Rudolf von Bennigsens," *Deutsche Revue* (1904–1909, in 35 separate segments).

AELN   Wilhelm Cahn, ed., *Aus Eduard Laskers Nachlass* (Berlin, 1902).

ALN   Wilhelm Cahn, ed., "Aus Eduard Laskers Nachlass. Sein Briefwechsel in den Jahren 1870–71," *Deutsche Revue* 15 (March-December 1892).

HW   Julius Heyderhoff and Paul Wentzcke, eds., *Deutscher Liberalismus im Zeitalter Bismarcks. Eine politische Briefsammlung.* Vol I, Julius Heyderhoff, ed., *Die Sturmjahre der preussisch-deutschen Einigung 1859–1870. Politische Briefe aus dem Nachlass liberaler Parteiführer* (1925; reprint Osnabrück, 1967). Vol. II, Paul Wentzcke, ed., *Im neuen Reich* (1925; reprint Osnabrück, 1967).

LNB   Lasker Nachlass, Brandeis University: Watham, Massachusetts.

LNP   Lasker Nachlass, Zentrales Staatsarchiv (Formally the Deutsches Zentralarchiv), Potsdam.

LT   *Wörtlicher Berichte über die Verhandlungen des preussischen Abgeordnetenhauses* (Berlin, 1865, *et seq.*). This was the Prussian Landtag and is cited as LT, followed by the date of the speech or document, the volume number in the year cited, and the page numbers.

RT   *Stenographische Berichte über die Verhandlungen des Reichstages* (Berlin, 1867, *et seq.*). Cited as RT, followed by the date of the speech or document, the volume number in the year cited, and the page numbers.

Nach einer Photographie.   Stich u. Druck v. Weger, Leipzig.

Eduard Lasker.

Verlag der Dürr'schen Buchh.

Steel engraving of Eduard Lasker (ca. 1873) by Weger of Leipzig from a photograph. Courtesy of the Germanisches Nationalmuseum, Nürnberg.

I

From Jarotschin to New York

> "I . . . was born on the furthest borders
> of the monarchy, among a linguistically
> mixed population, in a social class unac-
> customed to the rays of the sun of favor, at
> a time when my co-religionists were still
> not guaranteed the most essential rights."
>
> Eduard Lasker
> January 25, 1882

Eduard Lasker's death in New York on January 5, 1884, at the age of fifty-four, ended a long and distinguished political career in Prussia and Germany. A German Jew from a largely Polish area of East Prussia, Lasker had risen to a powerful political position in both the Prussian Landtag (state assembly) and the German Reichstag. Tireless and fervent in pursuit of his goals, he was frequently a source of contention and controversy. Even his death became a political event when the United States House of Representatives passed a resolution commending him for his "devotion to free and liberal ideas" that had "materially advanced the social, political and economic conditions of these people [Germans] . . . ." Thomas Peck Ochiltree, author of the resolution and representative of the Texas district where Lasker's brother resided, intended his commendation to mark only the normal formalities accorded the death of a distinguished foreign statesman. However, German Chancellor Otto von Bismarck interpreted Ochiltree's resolution as an attack on the emperor and himself, and refused to transmit the resolution to the Reichstag. The result was an outburst of criticism that embarrassed Bismarck.[1]

For hosts of Germans there were other major achievements to be remembered in the career of the doughty statesman. Lasker had fought for liberal goals in such diverse areas as legal and judicial reform, constitutional development, and economic policy. For many Germans, his greatest deed was to expose the corruption in the railroad industry in 1872 and 1873. The achievements that Lasker himself held dearest involved his activities as a leader of the National Liberal party in fighting for the unification of Germany and in working for the construction of the Second Reich. Doubtless it was his role in this crucial event of nineteenth-century German growth that he would have viewed as the summit of a life begun obscurely in a far corner of Prussia in 1829.

Lasker was born in Jarotschin (in Polish, Jaroczyn), a small city of about two thousand in the Prussian province of Posen (Poznan). Before the advent of the railroad, Jarotschin was a sleepy country town lying only a few kilometers from the Polish border. Most of the inhabitants were Polish and Catholic, but Jews constituted about 25 percent of the population. Jarotschin functioned as a cattle market for the surrounding farm land and thus served as something of a trade center for the region, attracting Jewish families there to engage in the commercial life.[2]

In 1835, when Eduard was six, the Jewish *Gemeinde* (community) in Jarotschin numbered 160 families, about 560 people. Jizchok (Eduard's Yiddish name) belonged to a large family; he had three sisters and two brothers, and he grew to boyhood with several advantages. His father, Daniel, owned a nail shop and had interests in a glass store and a potash refinery. Modest commercial success enabled him to support the local synagogue, as he did in 1835 by giving the *Gemeinde* an interest-free loan of 100 taler, and to tithe himself annually to help the poor. A strong-minded man with an active interest in learning, Daniel possessed a library in which his children could find both the sources of traditional Judaism and more enlightened works. He also employed a tutor for his son. The boy's mother, Rebecca, had a fine mind and a passionate nature, and Jizchok may well have taken after her, although she died when he was only ten.[3]

Young Jizchok was gifted intellectually, and family expectations for him were high. The latter were reinforced when a famous rabbi of Posen, Akiba Eger, predicted future greatness based on a horoscope cast for Jizchok at age seven. His tutor, Dr. Löwenthal, who taught him Talmud, declared that Jizchok, by the age of ten, had exhausted his store of knowledge. An impression of the boy's combination of precocity and innate stubbornness is conveyed in a story told by Eduard much later. In 1841 the community began to build a new synagogue. All the boys were to carry the stones, but Eduard refused. According to his brother Max, the young prodigy argued from Talmud that such work was a *Mitzwe*, or good deed, and that therefore all should perform such labor, including the leaders of the community. When his father imposed a light punishment for such presumption, the boy responded by talking his older brother into running away with him. They managed to escape detection for ten days and may actually have reached Breslau; eventually they were found and returned home. The coachman who drove for Daniel in search of the runaways told the boys not to worry, that their father had brought their feather beds with him. The escapade produced "loud disputations" between traditional and enlightened Jews in the community.[4]

Clearly interpreting his son's flight from home as an attempt to shed the restraints imposed on him by a narrow provincial life, Daniel soon thereafter permitted Jizschok to study in Breslau. It was during the move to Breslau that the young rebel changed his name to the Germanic Eduard. In Breslau Eduard first attended a free *Vorgymnasium*, or preparatory school, for Jewish youth trained in Talmud but deficient in traditional subjects. Ferdinand Lassalle, later the founder of the German Workers' Association, attended the same school for the same reason, although a few years before Eduard. Later Lassalle went to St. Matthias Gymnasium, while Lasker attended St. Elisabeth's.[5]

Running away from home and changing his name were evidence of Eduard's rebellious spirit, but even more, they indicated a desire to broaden his intellectual and personal horizons. Eduard stayed personally close to his father until the latter's death in 1852. Although unusual in his manner of departure, Eduard simply followed the practice of the many Jews from other communities who participated in a general westward migration in search of education, wealth, and, less frequently, political power.[6]

In the early 1840s the migration of the Jewish population of Posen to the west was in its first phase. In 1833 Jews had acquired the legal right to become naturalized if they fulfilled certain criteria and to move freely within the province. Migration to other Prussian provinces was also allowed, provided that state approval to do so was granted. Jews regarded the new law as progressive, and those eligible quickly applied for naturalization. Daniel Lasker received his naturalization from Prussia in 1834; thereafter he and his family were Prussian subjects. Although the father and a widowed daughter never left Jarotschin, the rest of the family moved west—to Berlin, to Mecklenbourg, to Freiburg im Breisgau, and to Galveston, Texas—as did thousands of other Jews.[7]

Eduard's choice of Breslau over Posen, the only major urban educational alternative, indicated his preference for German culture. Situated on the Oder River, which flows out of

Bohemia and on to Stettin and the Baltic, Breslau presented a strong contrast to Posen in the north. Both were centers of conquered non-German provinces, Posen of the former Grand Duchy of Posen and Breslau of Silesia. Silesia had fallen to Frederick the Great during the wars with Austria, which had begun in 1740, and had previously maintained a German connection through the Austrian Hapsburgs. Posen's exposure to German culture was less strong and less consistent. Part of Posen had become Prussian in the Polish partitions of 1772 and 1793. It was temporarily merged with the Grand Duchy of Warsaw from 1807 to 1815 and was finally transferred to Prussia in 1815. Polish Posen had only 38,277 inhabitants in 1848, but German Breslau had already reached the 100,000 mark in 1842 and was one of the fastest growing cities in Germany.[8]

In 1847 Eduard finished his gymnasium education; his record was good, though better in mathematics than in the German language. The University of Breslau was but a few short blocks from the gymnasium down the Oder Strasse, where the buildings follow the river bank.[9] Eduard soon discovered at the university and in the city in general more than sufficient nourishment for his intellectual appetite. Intellectual debate flourished in the excited atmosphere provided by the revolutions of 1848. The Springtime of Peoples was a European experience, and nowhere did revolution occur more spontaneously than in Central Europe. Coming as it did a few months after his eighteenth birthday, the new era presented Eduard with an opportunity for political as well as intellectual development.

After their early rapid successes, the revolutionaries turned their attention to the political assemblies that were then meeting to design new government structures. In Germany the focal points of revolutionary debate were Frankfurt am Main, where the National Assembly met, and Berlin, where a similar assembly for Prussia convened. Although not a political center like Frankfurt or Berlin, Breslau offered as much intellectual activity as any other major city in Germany in 1848. Eduard, though younger than most of the participants in the revolution, attended at least one rally at the university, at which Arnold Ruge spoke, wrote to the democrat Professor Christian Nees von Esenbeck, and tried to publish his own periodical entitled *Der Sozialist*.[10] All that remains of *Der Sozialist* are two letters from Professor von Esenbeck and F. Zettrach commenting on copies Lasker had mailed to them.[11] Von Esenbeck, a seventy-two-year-old botanist at the University of Breslau, was a recent convert to radical causes and headed the workers' club, which, unusually, preferred the title "socialist." His letter to Lasker in late July was complimentary, especially with respect to an article on "Nobility and Capital," but he suggested further emphasis on artisan labor.[12] Zettrach, about whom nothing is known, gave much harsher criticism; he wrote that little in the issue was either "socialist" or "scientific" and suggested it would need support from men like von Esenbeck and Julius Fröbel if it were to survive. Judging by these responses, Lasker offered his readers neither new facts nor new solutions and knew little of social theory.[13]

Sometime in late summer, Eduard despaired of making *Der Sozialist* a success and made his way to Vienna, where he participated in the October demonstrations and fought against the counter-revolution with the academic legion led by Robert Blum. In October 1848 Julius Fröbel, Moritz Hartmann, and Blum had stopped in Breslau on their way to Vienna to serve as representatives of the German National Assembly in Frankfurt and appealed to democrats and students for support. In late October the Austrian military crushed the revolution, and in early November Eduard returned home.[14] Less fortunate, Blum died before a firing squad, Fröbel was almost hanged, and Hartmann escaped to become an exile.

Eduard found it difficult to reenter the University of Breslau because of his radicalism, and he succeeded in gaining admission to study law only after the intercession of some of his former professors.[15] Von Esenbeck also encountered problems and in 1851, at age seventy-five, finally lost both his post at the university and his state pension on the improbable grounds of "concubinage"—a trumped-up charge derived from his support of women's emancipation and free love since 1845![16] Lasker's problem was much less serious, and he passed his state law exams in 1851 and 1853. Yet a young Jew's pursuit of a legal career in Prussia would be problematical at best, and a close friend persuaded Eduard that Prussia was not likely to provide the aspiring lawyer a fertile field for success.[17]

On the eve of his first state law test on May 25, 1851, Eduard reviewed his past in a pessimistic frame of mind. Seized by "complete disbelief," he doubted his abilities. But, looking ahead, he saw hope in trying to win an appointment to a state position after passing his exam. Despite occasional doubts about his talent, he looked forward to competitions in which he would be judged more on his merits than on his birth. He recognized his inadequacy in some spheres of knowledge as well as the need to digest what he already had learned. He confided in his private papers: "I cherish great expectations that the prophecy [the horoscope cast when he was seven] which made the boy proud will not have uselessly spent its healthy stimulation." He concluded that independence began with self-discipline.[18]

During these years of legal study, Lasker expressed no interest in politics and appeared to reject as a youthful indulgence the revolutionary fervor that had animated him in 1848. In 1852 Daniel Lasker died, and, frustrated in his profession, Eduard cast about for something to do. Eventually, after corresponding about the matter with his friend Wilhelm Cohn, he decided to go to London. He probably arrived there in September, and by October 20 he was already expressing dislike for the job he had taken as German commerical correspondent for two merchants, Krohn and Salomon, in Houndsditch. His duties required but a few hours each day, and his employers were ashamed to give him work so out of keeping with his talents. He gave it up eventually and tried his hand at law, but found few clients. With his younger brother Morris, Eduard joined the Freemasons on March 17, 1855. But the two brothers were not alike. Eduard could not abide business and never pursued it.[19] Morris went on to the United States, where, despite real struggles, he emerged after the Civil War as a prosperous businessman in Galveston, Texas. His son, Albert D., became a recognized genius in American advertising.

The reactionary 1850s were good years for Prussian democrats and liberals to be abroad, but Eduard enjoyed the political freedom of London as little as he did the business world. For him the "bitter bread of exile," even when eaten by choice, was a poor diet. To compound the problem Eduard found little to occupy his restless energy. At one point he turned to writing poetry. Gottfried Kinkel, whom he had met in German émigré circles, provided some friendly criticism of his work. Lasker apparently chose inner spiritual struggle as his theme, and Kinkel disclaimed any desire to criticize this subject matter: "In a transcendental night all cats are gray." What he liked best was the objective, not the visionary. Kinkel advised Eduard to concentrate on the world instead of on his own dreams. Though it might be pleasant to write a poetic diary of our personal experiences, he argued, the world would take little interest in it.[20]

Uninspired by London, business, and law, Eduard instead discovered love and perhaps rediscovered nationalism during his English sojourn. He met and fell in love with Kinkel's daughter, Johanna. Yet he never told her so in person. His national and liberal spirits were rekindled through contact with a "foreign culture and the influence of patriotic exiles" like the Kinkels.[21] He never asked Johanna to marry him, although he intended to do so. Her sudden death in 1862 left him disconsolate.

After more than two years of self-imposed exile, Eduard still had not decided what to do with his life and feared he was sinking into a lethargic malaise. Shortly before his return in 1856 he wrote his brother Max that "the last year of [my] youth, namely the twenty-sixth, must also be the last year of insecurity if my whole life is not to be lost in misdirection."[22]

Characteristically, Eduard approached even the problem of his as yet undecided future systematically. As befitted an idealist who could never be satisfied with anything as prosaic as a good job or a steady income, he planned his route to success and influence like a grand campaign. He identified "science, erudition, and observation" and, in personal character, "discretion, punctuality, and strong will" as the prerequisites for attaining professional advancement. Fantasizing about possible positions he might enjoy, he decided that the scope of action provided by a Prussian judgeship would match his abilities and goals. In any event, he recognized that he would deserve the respect of his colleagues only by mastering many fields of expertise. He never seriously considered anything but state service as an outlet for his energy.[23]

In April 1856 Lasker returned to Berlin, where he made his permanent home. He joyfully greeted a sister and close friends and was thrilled to hear German spoken again. He sensed a widespread public desire for national unity.[24] Thus the voluntary exile, the frustrated lawyer, the defeated revolutionary student, and the former *Talmud Jude* from Jarotschin returned to his fatherland. Like many in the 1850s, Lasker had chosen exile, but unlike most, he returned to Prussia while conservatism was at its peak. Others, of course, had not left voluntarily and could not return until pardoned.

The revolution had ended finally and piteously in southwest Germany in the summer of 1849. Not only did the Hohenzollern dynasty rule again in Prussia, it did so with less opposition than before the revolution. In Austria, too, the old order appeared to be in full control under the firm and intelligent leadership of Prince Schwarzenberg. And, as if to mock the liberal creed that political reform was important to commercial growth, the Prussian and German economies flourished as never before. King Frederick William IV granted his Prussian subjects a constitution carefully pruned of the pricklier thorns of 1848. Germans could vote only in a severely restricted suffrage. Lacking political leadership and subject to censorship of the public media, most citizens became politically apathetic. Less than 17 percent of the eligible voters bothered to cast a ballot in the Prussian elections of 1855.[25]

In this oppressive political atmosphere Lasker began to work in Berlin as a *Referendar*, that is, as a court lawyer who had not yet passed the exam to become an *Assessor*, or full officer of the court. He was supposed to acquire practical experience in law and could make no claim to a salary, though some remuneration might come his way. In 1858 Lasker became an *Assessor* for the city court of Berlin and spent much of his time during these years in legal work and study. The year 1858 also marked the beginning in Prussia of what was called the New Era.

Prussian political life in the 1850s largely existed as the creature of the king, Frederick William IV, and his extremely conservative cabinet. Until late in the decade Otto von Manteuffel, the prime minister, and Count Ferdinand von Westphalen, the minister of the interior, were responsible for much, if not all, of the repression that stifled political life. The ministers answered to the king, not the parliament. After Frederick William IV suffered several strokes in 1857, his younger brother William became regent in October 1858. Quiet and slow where his brother had been articulate, artistic, and alert, William surprised many by dismissing Manteuffel and Westphalen. Thus encouraged, liberals and democrats began to reorganize politically.

Elections to the Prussian Landtag in 1858 heightened the surprise: the Conservatives fell from 236 to 59 seats, and the voters returned 210 Progressives. The results stemmed from only a slight increase in the number of voters (from 16.1 percent to 22.6 percent). More significantly, a larger number of liberals now voted in the first and second classes of the electoral system. The Prussian voting system divided all voters into three classes, in which the wealthy, who paid one-third of the taxes, were placed in the upper third of the voters, the next weathiest in the second third, and the lowest taxed in the bottom third. The economic boom of the 1850s packed the first and second classes with liberal merchants and professionals, who suddenly saw an avenue to effective political power.[26]

Throughout Prussia public interest in politics grew rapidly in 1858 and 1859, and concern for foreign affairs kept pace as Italy, aided by the French, began to unify at the expense of Austria. If Italy could unify, why not Germany? Encouraged by Italian developments, liberals founded the Nationalverein (National Association) during the Italian struggle, hoping to use it as a base to direct the movement for German unification. William and his ministers reacted to the possibility that Prussia might have to help defend Austria against a powerful France by formulating plans for the reorganization and modest expansion of the army. Liberals who solidly supported unification nonetheless opposed the army reform because they felt that it would reduce citizen participation in the army. The government attempted to break the resulting deadlock in 1861 by beginning the reorganization without permanent budgetary approval from the Landtag. At this the deputies bristled and refused to grant any budget.

In the midst of this political and national reawakening, Eduard Lasker turned to politics. As for so many others, the New Era was like a breath of fresh air for the young lawyer. What might have been a successful career in law ended in 1859 or 1860. Although he continued to practice law, Lasker devoted more and more of his time and energy to politics. He first emerged in Berlin political circles as chairman of the educational committee of the Handworker Association, which sponsored public lectures for artisans. Lasker himself delivered many of them. By 1860 artisans were staunchly liberal, and Lasker's chosen field of action was much more oriented to education than to electoral activity.

Journalism offered an even wider audience, and Lasker made his presence felt through a series of articles published in the *Deutsche Jahrbücher für Politik und Literatur* (*German Yearbook for Politics and Literature*). These may not have been his first publications, but they were easily his best. Heinrich Bernhard Oppenheim, the editor and a Progressive party member, solicited the first article from Eduard in 1861 after an earlier discussion about a new journal. The monthly was an attempt to provide a more democratically national alternative to the liberal *Preussische Jahrbücher* (*Prussian Annals*). Its title, "German" rather than "Prussian," advertised its connection to the burgeoning national movement. In 1874 the Brockhaus publishing firm collected most of Lasker's articles in a single volume under the title *Zur Verfassungsgeschichte Preussens* (*Toward a Constitutional History of Prussia*). The essays constitute one of the two or three finest contemporary legal and political analyses of the Prussian state of the 1850s. The *Deutsche Jahrbücher* ceased publication in 1864, but Lasker's reputation as a talented analyst, knowledgeable lawyer, and tough-minded critic of Prussia outlasted the journal. His essays marked their author indelibly as a liberal with little revolutionary or demagogic inclination.[27]

While Lasker was establishing himself in politics as a journalist, the disagreement between the Prussian government and the Landtag became acute. The liberal deputies' refusal to approve a budget threatened the basis of monarchical rule, and William contemplated abdication. At the last moment, at the urging of Minister of War Albrecht von Roon, he decided to give his ambassador to Paris, Otto von Bismarck, a chance to solve the problem. Known as a hard-line Conservative, Bismarck did not disappoint his critics. He determined to govern without out a new budget, relying instead on the budget approved by the Landtag for the previous year. From 1862 to 1866 Prussia operated with no new budget, and criticism in the Landtag was caustic and constant. Participants dubbed the era *Konfliktszeit* (Era of Conflict), and the principle of parliamentary control of the budget replaced army reorganization as the major issue of the day. The liberal Progressive party, the largest political party, led the opposition in the

Landtag. As such, it offered a natural outlet for Lasker's political energy.[28]

By the spring of 1862 Lasker was regularly receiving notices of Progressive party meetings from Werner Siemens, an industrialist and politician, and he became politically active in the first Berlin electoral district. Simultaneously, he expanded his circle of acquaintances. He attended the salon of Oppenheim's sister, Bernhardine Friedberg, where he met the journalist Julius Rodenberg, who later edited the *Deutsche Rundschau*, a literary and political monthly that published Lasker's nonpolitical writings. Johann Jacoby, the famous East Prussian democrat, asked to meet Lasker in 1863 through another famous forty-eighter, Benedikt Waldeck. Moreover, Lasker began to engage more directly in electoral politics; on one occasion he even destroyed the popular candidacy of a lawyer named Schwarck through a cogent political speech.[29] Thus, when the Progressive Jadokus Temme resigned in 1864 from his Landtag seat in the fourth district in Berlin, Lasker was in good position to obtain the party's endorsement of his candidacy. He won the election and took his seat in the Prussian lower house. Until his death in 1884, he remained an elected member of either the Prussian Landtag or the German Reichstag, and for many years he worked in both simultaneously. In 1865 he was the youngest member of the Landtag, but he soon began to act as if he had been there for years.

In 1863 Bismarck seized on an incident involving the dynastic succession of the Duchies of Schleswig and Holstein to provide a field for Prussian action outside domestic politics. Months of complicated diplomacy resulted in war between Denmark, which claimed title to the duchies, and the Deutsche Bund (German Confederation) represented by Austria and Prussia. Winning the war presented a new problem for Prussia. By insisting on annexation of at least part of Schleswig-Holstein, Bismarck irritated Austria. Lasker campaigned for Prussian annexation of the duchies and took his seat in early 1865 during the escalating conflict between Austria and Prussia.[30]

Although the Progressives still controlled the Prussian lower house and continued to deny the government an approved budget, political attention had shifted away from the constitutional question of budget control. With one successful war completed and with another threatening, foreign affairs held center stage. Liberals like Rudolf von Bennigsen, the leader of the Nationalverein, still doubted that a Conservative like Bismarck could unify Germany, but they were increasingly mesmerized by his energetic diplomacy. In a carefully orchestrated series of moves lasting into late spring 1866, Bismarck transformed the Schleswig-Holstein affair into the much larger question of reform of the German Confederation. Sometimes his plans appeared vague and poorly defined, as when he suggested calling a German parliament without any prior agenda. At other times he was brutally clear, as when he demanded that Prussia be at least co-equal with Austria in a reformed confederation. Finally, an enraged Austria, jealous of its control over the existing confederation, began to prepare for war. During most of the spring of 1866 the threat of war was a common topic of conversation everywhere in the confederation. The conflict within Prussia was not forgotten, but it could not and did not successfully compete with Bismarck's performance.

There was no doubt where Lasker's loyalties lay: in support of national unity (with Bismarck) and of the powers of the Landtag in Prussia (against Bismarck). Like many Progressives, Lasker was unwilling to surrender on the budget issue yet did not want to sabotage possible German unity by a continued hard line on it. The dilemma of being both for and against Bismarck in the months preceding the war with Austria became a disaster in the wake of the rapid success of the Prussian troops in July 1866. Under intense pressure the Progressive party quietly fragmented. Lasker did not hesitate to join those nationally inclined Progressives who founded a new party in the fall of 1866, appropriately called the National Liberal party. As the most junior member of the Landtag, Lasker's choice took political courage: he had no way of knowing what the results might be in radical Berlin.[31]

Even the political stage changed. Bismarck's first move was to call for enactment of the reform of the confederation that he had proposed in the spring. Prussia and the states of North Germany, excluding the southern states of Bavaria, Baden, Württemberg, and Hesse-Darmstadt, agreed to form a confederation, to be called the North German Confederation, and to organize in a constitutional convention (Reichstag). Delegates to the convention were to be elected by universal suffrage, another of Bismarck's spring promises. Moreover, an assembly including delegates from both North and South Germany would meet in a *Zollparlament* (customs parliament) to discuss national economic problems. Complete unification appeared to be closer than anyone had dreamed possible a few months earlier.

Consequently, Lasker had to consider whether he would stand for the constitutional Reichstag and, if so, where. He could, of course, run in any district. But he had no home district, since Posen was largely dominated by Poles and would become more so under universal suffrage. Breslau was a possibility, but almost all his contacts were in Berlin. Unfortunately, Berlin was still largely controlled by anti-Bismarckian Progressives who did not appreciate "national" liberals like Lasker. Eventually he secured the National Liberal party nomination for the second electoral district in Berlin and campaigned against a man who proved to be a weak opponent— the Prussian minister of war, General Albrecht von Roon. The Conservatives nominated six generals for the six Berlin districts in a blatant effort to capitalize on wartime glory, but all lost ignominiously. However, this poor showing merely reflected a political blunder. After the Reichstag accepted a new constitution, Lasker had to contemplate yet another contest, this time facing a more serious contender. Since he was not likely to win against a Progressive, he accepted an invitation to stand in the second district in Meiningen in Saxon Thuringia. His combination of nationalism and liberalism, coupled with his drive and legislative record, turned Meiningen into a safe district that he never lost.

The National Liberal party became the largest and strongest political group in both Prussia and the North German Confederation, and Eduard Lasker served as one of its most active and powerful leaders. He worked long and hard at building a new and better state and left his mark on much of the legislation that created new agencies or reorganized older ones. In these domestic political labors he frequently crossed swords with Bismarck, who did not wish to move so fast or go so far. On the other hand, Lasker generally supported Bismarck's foreign policy, criticizing him only in 1869–1870 because he did nothing to add South German states to the confederation.[32]

Using a controversy with France over possible Hohenzollern succession to the Spanish throne, Bismarck goaded Louis Napoleon into war. The resulting campaign of summer and fall 1870 defeated France, pulled South Germany into the Confederation, and annexed Alsace and Lorraine as imperial territories. A triumphant Bismarck announced the creation of the Second Reich in the Hall of Mirrors at Versailles. For better or for worse, Germany stood united.

Lasker approved of practically all of Bismarck's actions. He gloried in the defeat of France and celebrated the merger with South Germany. Like Bismarck, he doubted the wisdom of the annexation of Alsace and Lorraine but supported the government's decision. While Bismarck followed the troops westward, Lasker journeyed south to persuade the anti-Prussian and anti-Bismarckian elements there to support unification with the North. He played a major role in bringing this about and to the end remained proud of his contribution to unification.

With the war over, Lasker returned, along with many others, to the task of building a new state. Most institutions initiated in the period between 1867 and 1870 continued into the Reich with only minor modifications. But the scale of activity was much broader and the substantially different societal elements to be found in the South made effective unification a difficult and continuing problem. The National Liberal party grew larger with the addition of South Germany, but many of the new members did not agree with their Prussian colleagues. Ironically, therefore, the 1870s witnessed almost constant struggle: Catholics against liberals, South against North, liberals against Progressives, and socialists against everybody. As a committed liberal, Lasker worked with his customary energy, at one time or another, against Catholics, Conservatives, Progressives, and socialists. For years Germany's largest party, supported by at least a tacit alliance with Bismarck, could do all this and succeed, and in that success Lasker also prospered politically.

Forces other than unification and regional diversity also affected the fortunes of German politics. In 1872 Lasker exposed a scandal in the booming railroad industry, an event which was closely followed by a depression in 1873. Many Germans lost their belief in the benefits of growth and turned away from an optimistic liberal belief in the value of free trade and unregulated economic expansion. Hit hard by the depression, workers organized and voted in increasing numbers for socialists rather than for Progressives or National Liberals. By 1878 the National Liberal party was in decline, and Bismarck hastened the descent by turning against the National Liberals, especially against Lasker, and by establishing new political alliances with his former enemies in the Catholic Center party. From 1879 until his death, Lasker fought a rearguard action against Conservatives, Centrists, socialists, and Bismarck. The contest was unequal, and his health failed. He died in 1884 in New York, where he had gone to see his brother Morris, to acquaint himself with the flavor of the youthful United States, and to recuperate.

Lasker's success in the Prussian Landtag and the German Reichstag stemmed largely from his tough-mindedness, knowledge, intelligence, honesty, and, above all, his indefatigable work. So conspicuously dedicated was he to his career that colleagues as well as opponents felt called upon to criticize his irritating mannerisms and stubborn self-righteousness. In the political environment of that era few men made such a commitment to public service. The experience left severe scars on Lasker's personality. Prince Hohenlohe, a contemporary Free Conservative and later chancellor from 1894 to 1900, depicted Lasker as "so serious that he is completely unassuming. He needs no money, seeks no offices, is incorruptible . . ., he turns his talent only to the satisfaction of his ambition." Karl Braun, another National Liberal, saw him as the epitome of the professional politician—a man who had no life outside the party. Braun wrote in amusement that Lasker was "a lawyer and could possess a rich practice; only he disdains it. He has neither wife nor child, neither horse nor hound, not even a cat or a canary. . . ." Nor, he continued, did Lasker enjoy wine, women, or song: "Nights he studies the printed documents . . . mornings he sits in committee, afternoons in the house, and evenings in the party caucus, where he trains the parliamentary foxes. By day he thinks of the caucus, by night he dreams of it. It is his bride . . . ." All of these peculiarities made Lasker, in Braun's judgment, impervious to corruption; but he wrote that Lasker did have one weakness: his unflagging zeal for debate and his domination of the largest party, at least in Prussia, for years.[33]

Although Lasker was capable of barbed wit, friend and foe alike criticized him for lacking a sense of humor. Bismarck joked about his puritanism; Gustav Schmoller, the noted economist, described him as "almost ascetic" in life and style. And the democratic *Frankfurter Zeitung* even wrote after his death that "Lasker was not an orator; he lacked humor, spirit and pathos; his sharp and clear logic had the power to persuade politicians, but not to excite or thrill the more or less indifferent masses."[34]

In Lasker's case, such virtues as hard work and sobriety produced hostility within his own party and at times, when he carried them to extremes, even among his own supporters. No one questioned his diligence. Many members came to meetings of the caucus unprepared to speak to issues that might be raised in the Landtag or Reichstag, but never Lasker. All reported that Lasker was consistently the best prepared member, the first to arrive and the last to leave. Ready and willing to take a stand, Lasker spoke frequently in the caucus, and many less conscientious members often relied on his homework. He served on almost every major committee formed during his career and dominated many of them. Soon this dedication led to a kind of unofficial power and Lasker wielded it in the service of truth as he saw it, which for him was synonymous with the goals of the left wing of the National Liberal party.[35]

National Liberal leaders of all types agreed that Lasker failed to employ tact in his exercise of power. In the estimation of Robert von Mohl, an older judicial theorist and noted politician, Lasker possessed all the proper political tools but lacked the quality of statesmanship: he was a good debater in a narrowly Prussian or even "Berliner" style. "His personal appearance is also flawed by a lack of dignified calm," the very calm Mohl later wrote. "He is always in rapid motion." Mohl felt that Lasker's eagerness for work and readiness to speak led him at times quickly and imprudently to become a "kind of dictator." Rudolf von Bennigsen, the titular head of the National Liberal party, recognized and depended on Lasker's ability to deliver votes on critical issues. But in 1870, when Julius von Hennig was ill, Bennigsen worried because he saw the practical Hennig as a useful counterweight to Lasker, who was always inclined to be systematic to the highest degree, in true Berliner fashion. The Württemberg journalist and National Liberal Otto Elben admired Bennigsen as the "natural" leader of the party but complained about his frequent absences and unavailability to handle party matters: "Others [clearly referring to Lasker] then determined the sense of the *Fraktion* [party caucus], and gradually a separation between right and left developed earlier than perhaps was good."[36]

Outright opponents of Lasker in the center and on the right wing of the party were blunter. Eduard Stephani agreed that Lasker and Hennig had too much power and that the former's attempt to control the caucus was "dictatorial." In his opinion, Lasker's "vanity and self-righteousness" played a major role in party difficulties. On the right, the historian Heinrich von Treitschke and his journalist friend Wilhelm Wehrenpfennig fought Lasker in the 1860s and 1870s. Treitschke commented on the *Terrorismus* of Lasker and Hennig as early as the spring of 1870. Werner Siemens, who knew Lasker from his early days in Berlin, noted that he himself could seldom speak in either the caucus or the house due to the *Parteityrannei* of Lasker and his ally Ludwig Bamberger. In 1873 Otto Bähr described to Friedrich Oetker (both were National Liberal Reichstag members) the nature of the 170-member party delegation in the Prussian Landtag: "Lasker dominated everything."[37] In working tirelessly for his goal and for his party, Lasker frequently succeeded, but he also embittered many of those he defeated.

Nevertheless, as accurate as it may be overall, this view of Lasker is not the whole truth. Lasker may have spent most of his time in political activity, but not all. Even if Bamberger felt that Lasker's taste in art and music was uncompromisingly classical, he also knew of the latter's interest in the arts.[38] Nor did Lasker always choose the classical; in Hohenlohe's presence, and to his amusement, Lasker once expressed a preference for *Plattdeutsch* (Low German or North German dialect) ballads to the great Heinrich Heine. In music he liked the violinist Joseph Joachim and the composer Anton Rubinstein. His literary favorites included Charles Dickens, Gottfried Keller, and Berthold Auerbach. In 1871 he helped to form a literary-political club that, during its short life, attracted writers like Berthold Auerbach, Karl Frenzel, Friedrich Spielhagen, Julian Schmidt, and Ernst Dohm, along with politicians like Rudolf von Bennigsen, Max von Forckenbeck, Ludwig Bamberger, and Friedrich Kapp. Close friends knew of Eduard's love for hiking in the hills of the Black Forest and in the Alps near Pontresina in Switzerland.[39]

"The North German Parliamentary Ball with Surprises." Democrats and liberals are on the left, conservatives (all military officers) are on the right, but ignored by Otto von Bismarck who has turned his back on them. Lasker is in the forefront on the left, noticeable by his diminutive stature.

Source: *Kladderadatsch*, No. 6, vol. 20, February 10, 1867, p. 24.

Cabinets-Frage- und Antwortspiel.

Nein, wenn ihr nicht wollt wie ich, dann spiele ich nicht mehr mit! Aber, um Himmels willen, wir wollen ja schon! Nur hier bleiben! Wieder mitspielen!

"Cabinet Question and Answer Game." Otto von Bismarck's threat to stop "playing" (cooperating) with the liberals in parliament over the annexation of Alsace in 1871 elicits a new panic—Lasker is portrayed as helping to keep Bismarck in the "game".

Source: *Kladderadatsch*, No. 26, vol. 24, June 4, 1871, p. 1.

Beßgehaßt und beßtgeßchüßt.

Matinée bei Herrn von Benningsen am 16. Januar.

Mein Fräulein, der Mann ist da, welcher Sie nach Hause begleiten soll. Sie können bei jetzigen Zeiten unmöglich unbeschützt über die Straße gehen.

"The best hated and the best protected." Rudolf von Bennigsen. the titular leader of the National Liberal party, tells Bismarck (in female attire) that his (her) escort home is ready (Lasker) and that it is impossible in such times to walk the streets unprotected. In January 1874 the National Liberals were near the peak of their power (notice how other parliamentary leaders look on from the other room) and Lasker, the recognized leader of its left wing, was an increasingly difficult ally for Bismarck.

Source: *Kladderadatsch*, No. 5, vol. 27, February 1, 1874, p. 20.

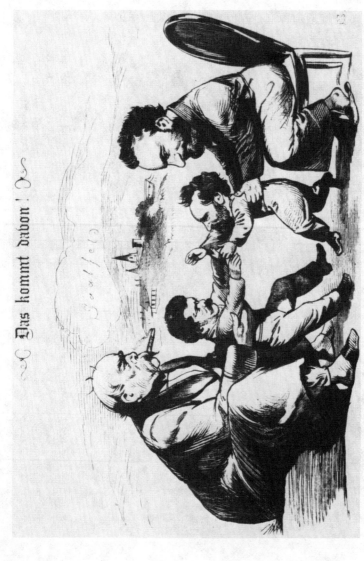

"That would be the result." If Lasker had had two sons instead of one *Mannesseele*, his romantic autobiographical novel, he could have had one of them oppose one of the Chancellor's two sons (Herbert) in the Reichstag election in Meiningen. In fact Herbert had challenged Lasker in that race, but he fared so poorly in early campaigning that he had to withdraw before the election occurred.

Source: *Kladderadatsch*, No. 32, vol. 31, July 14, 1878, p. 128.

Lasker again turned his hand to the essay form in the 1870s, but the invitation to publish stemmed directly from his rapidly rising political fame and not from any demonstrated literary talent. All of these essays were nonpolitical contributions to popular culture. "World and State Wisdom," "Word and Deed," and "Why Should One Study Language?" brought him few plaudits and much criticism. Even a friend, Arnold Ruge, told his son that Lasker should not play with philosophy because he did not understand its development. A political colleague, Johannes Miquel, wrote Lasker that he liked the article "Halbbildung" ("low-brow culture") and was sorry for its poor reception, which he attributed to the current predominance of low-brow culture.[40] But the critics were right. Where his political speeches and legal essays were factual, well-organized, and forceful, his nonpolitical essays were vague, wandering, and pedantic. Outside politics he lost the power to persuade that distinguished him in party deliberations and public assemblies.

In 1873 Lasker anonymously published a slim octavo volume entitled *Erlebnisse einer Mannes-Seele* (*Experiences of a Human Soul*). Berthold Auerbach, a close personal friend and a recognized author of real talent, wrote a brief introduction predicting a lasting place in German literature for the novel. Reviewers treated *Erlebnisse* harshly, and, despite precautions, Lasker's authorship was soon made public. Even Karl Marx chuckled over it.[41]

Erlebnisse is a novel of romantic failure. It was composed in the form of an extended memoir to a friend, to be read one year after its author's death. The literary style is heavily personal and romantic—indeed, it is vaguely reminiscent of Goethe's *Sorrows of Young Werther*. As in *Werther*, the hero suffers from discrimination because of lack of status and fortune. But where Werther's situation was unalterable, *Erlebnisse* is filled with examples of the hero's failure to carry through with his intentions.[42] And, finally, where the sensitive Werther chooses suicide, the hero of *Erlebnisse* finds an alternative in hard work and selfless devotion to political service.

Erlebnisse is very personal and largely autobiographical. The chronology is inaccurate, and some of the characters and events are fictional, but the essentials are drawn from Lasker's life and personality. The theme is the "soul" of the hero, illustrating Lasker's penchant for self-analysis, which Kinkel had already noted in 1855. What distinguishes Lasker's hero is his self-awareness. The protagonist considers each step carefully, especially those concerning his personal future, and the extreme caution he exercises in courtship is not present in his decisive attitude toward work and politics.[43]

The plot of *Erlebnisse* turns on a series of four romantic encounters, in each of which the protagonist fails to achieve his goal of marriage. More important, the novel describes the changes in the hero wrought by these successive disappointments: gradually he becomes serious and hard working, at first in order to obtain the wherewithal to marry and then, after failure, as therapy for disappointment—therapy that evolves into an alternative goal. Wounded by his experiences, the hero withdraws into himself, hiding his emotional and passionate nature from even his close friends.

In one encounter, the hero fails because the girl's parents want a more successful son-in-law. His response, though sad, is to return to "his original nature" and, quitting the "marketplace of life," remove himself from the "racecourse" of self-seeking. Success comes unlooked-for, but the hero conceals his inner self and seeks spiritual refreshment alone on long hikes in the mountains.[44]

Trying once again to win a bride, the protagonist falls in love with the daughter of a patriotic writer living in exile. The source of the initial attraction is love of fatherland, of a free and united fatherland. Through her, the hero's love of nation reawakens. But the girl dies suddenly before the two even discuss marriage. Shocked by the loss, he turns his energy to aid others in need of help.

Ironically, the hero's success, which stems from his hard work and self-renunciation, attracts the parents of his first love. They meet again, and he again contemplates marriage. But he has changed, and his ideas on freedom and public service are foreign to his intended. Forced to choose between her familial life style and his, she rejects him. Frustrated again, the protagonist seeks stability in isolation from emotional involvement and in hard work. The struggle for German unification provides timely release of his energies: "I was one of the volunteers, perhaps one of the few who, unfettered by an office, untouched by personal ambition, without a conflicting career necessitated by a normal life, became one with the fate of the country and the work was its own reward."[45]

Erlebnisse closely parallels Lasker's life. The hero's character is remarkably like his own— inner-directed, hard working, and compassionate. The description of the exiled author's daughter and household is apt and clearly based on his love for Johanna Kinkel, who had died before he had spoken of it to her. London friends later recalled his patriotism during his stay there, and, after his return to Germany, he devoted much effort to artisans' associations, which he praised as the best method of using common action to solve the problem of social distress. His description of the hero's role in German unification is direct and unabashedly autobiographical. His immediate motivation for writing *Erlebnisse* was probably a frustration that Lasker suffered in 1873 (briefly mentioned to Bamberger by Eduard's brother Max). Moreover, he was always jealous of his privacy during his public career and almost never spoke of the emotional side of his life. *Erlebnisse*, after all, was originally anonymous.[46]

In spite of the extensive parallels between *Erlebnisse* and Lasker, to what extent were the motives of the former also those of the latter? Since Eduard Lasker seldom spoke to anyone, even close relatives, of such events, he left no personal self-analysis or interpretation of his anonymous novel. *Erlebnisse* provides a clue to this side of his character when the protagonist states that "even the closest friends knew nothing about my fate and believed that I maintained myself free from temptation [to pursue monetary success] by the innocence of my nature."[47] *Erlebnisse* is important not for its literary merit but because it marks its author as acutely aware of emotions, if not always able to handle them successfully. It represents the outpouring of a passionate, not an ascetic, nature. But that aspect of his own life could be seen only in a few rapid flashes on isolated and infrequent occasions.

In February 1883 Lasker provided his own epilogue to *Erlebnisse*. His friend Ludwig Bamberger noted in his diary that Lasker seemed "lethargic," consumed by grief, unnaturally taking no interest in conversation. Bamberger invited Lasker to join him in a visit to a mutual friend, but Lasker abruptly declined. The following day Bamberger mentioned Lasker's moodiness to a group at this same friend's house and immediately observed an expression of dismay on a lady's face. Later that evening she privately told Bamberger of her relation to Lasker— how four years before he had been crazy (literally "wie verrückt") about her without showing the least sign of serious intention. Suddenly, the previous year (probably 1882) he had proposed marriage, but she rejected him. Since then he had avoided her.[48] At age fifty-three Eduard had again sought connubial bliss and again had failed—but only by accident did his close friend discover the affair.

Lasker's relation to Judaism and to the Jewish community was also an important facet of his personality and of his career. At first it was a handicap in law and later became a liability in politics. But Lasker never formally left Judaism, although he did not practice it. On the eve of his trip to the United States, he attended religious services at a synagogue in Mecklenburg only because his brother-in-law was the rabbi and the famous politician's absence would have been embarrassing. As a student Eduard attended a series of theological talks at the rabbinical seminary in Breslau but did not record his thoughts about the presentations. The Jewish community of Breslau experienced substantial religious dissension as a result of the rapid growth of the Reform movement during the same years that Lasker studied at the gymnasium and university.[49]

As early as 1865 Lasker had occasion to protest such practices as taxation of Jews to support Christian churches. In 1868 he criticized two separate ministries, Justice and Religion, for discrimination against Jews in the judiciary and in teaching.[50] As a young representative, Eduard never shrank from public identification as a Jew. More important, however, was his enunciation in spring 1867 of his basic position on Jews in German society. The issue eliciting his remarks was Jewish emancipation in 1867 from feudal and absolutist restrictions. Mecklenburg, in a fit of reactionary spite, refused to implement the policy of the new North German Confederation, and the Reichstag prepared to pass a bill specifically stating that Jews in Mecklenburg were free. Lasker took the floor unexpectedly, thanked the bill's author, Prosch, but argued that Jews wanted no special laws. If Jews were covered by the new constitution, then Mecklenburg should be simply forced to accept it. The bill died quietly, and in 1869 Mecklenburg finally had to agree with this and other aspects of the new constitution.[51]

In later debates concerning Jews, as well as in the better-known struggles over the anti-Jesuit and antisocialist laws, Lasker maintained the same position. To his logical legal mind, all special laws were violations of the universality of law. The most liberal Jewish newspaper, Ludwig Philippson's *Allgemeine Zeitung des Judentums*, sarcastically commented that elimination of special laws was good only if it included elimination of laws *against* the Jews as well. In a debate in 1873 over military service by Mennonites, Lasker stated his position with crystalline clarity: no religion, he said, was incompatible with the duties of state citizenship.[52]

The year 1873 also marked the beginning of the *Kulturkampf*, or cultural struggle against certain aspects of the Catholic church. Lasker stood solidly for separation of church and state, with the latter possessing the power to decide doubtful questions. He introduced his arguments with the comment that he usually avoided exclusively ecclesiastical issues; but he favored most of the legislation (excepting only the expulsion of the Jesuit order) because it treated all religions equally. Indeed, he cited examples from Jewish instead of Christian practice to show the rationality of the legislation. For several minutes he described failings among his own people, and in a rare reference to his childhood he remembered that community ostracism had destroyed a man financially for disobeying a religious law. He noted that Hannoverian law allowed the rabbi there to fine men for not attending divine worship. He probably intended his remarks as a tactic to show that he, a Jew, was evenhanded, but he undoubtedly meant it when he stated that one could not force another to be religious.[53]

Originally annoyed by Lasker's equity, Jewish leaders like Philippson were horrified when he criticized the Prussian law of 1847 that required Jews desiring to leave a congregation to apostatize. Lasker argued that leaving a congregation was not and should not be the same as leaving Judaism. This was a special law and an "odious privilige" for the Jews. Thus began a period in which many Jewish communities, led by Philippson and the *Allgemeine Zeitung*, organized to oppose the proposed law. They feared that it would cripple many Jewish communities by making it too easy for Jews to leave; they predicted that some would take advantage of the law to escape the communal taxes. Ironically, this position forced them to attack the most famous Jewish politician in Germany. The *Allgemeine* even questioned Lasker's qualifications to discuss Judaism, since he had been separated from it for thirty years and only recently had established contact with the highly reformed Berlin Jewish community. Actually, Lasker also had contacts with an extremely orthodox group in Frankfurt am Main led by the famous rabbi Samson Raphael Hirsch. But these relations were apparently unknown in Berlin. By June

1874 Lasker's legal acumen, once so widely praised by the *Allgemeine*, had become only "legal sophistry." The paper variously described Lasker as "crass," "vain," and "overweening."[54]

The ensuing debate occupied large segments of the German Jewish leadership for several years, but at first Lasker did not bother to reply directly to his Jewish critics. He was then at the height of his popularity and political power. However, by 1876 he rejoined the debate. In response to the accusation that he would destroy such institutions as religious schools, Lasker commented that attendance at general elementary schools would be a blessing for the Jews and the Jewish community, to which it would give new life.[55] Was he thinking of his own early yearning for a secular education? Many Jews certainly did not agree with him. The law finally passed, and some communities did experience a drop in membership; but the effect was minimal. Within a few years the bitter debate of 1873–1876 had lost its relevance for most Jews.

In the 1870s a wave of political anti-Semitism catalyzed by the depression also took aim at Lasker.[56] Regardless of Lasker's reputation in the Jewish communities or his personal beliefs, anti-Semites accused him of manipulating the National Liberal party, of protecting corruption (despite a famous speech exposing it in the railroad industry), and of exercising undue influence over such matters as banks and Bismarck.[57] Rather than add fuel to the fire, Lasker maintained public silence in the face of these and other charges. While some fellow Jews spoke out against the attacks (his friends Berthold Auerbach and Ludwig Bamberger, for example), Lasker said nothing, believing anti-Semitism to be weak. It was unsupported by the elite in society and therefore nothing to fear. "I deal with matters privately," he confided to his old friend Hermann Baerwald, "in order to prevent abuse and misrepresentation; in itself you do not need to fear publicity else I would not have dealt with them even privately." In his opinion the elections of 1881, a victory of sorts for liberals, demonstrated the accuracy of his analysis.[58]

Nor did Lasker support any form of direct intervention in the affairs of other countries in support of Jews. In the 1870s the plight of Jews in Romania became a focus of interest in many Western European states. Although many of his German Jewish friends supported protests and eventually outright intervention through the Congress of Berlin of 1878, Lasker spoke only in favor of equal treatment for all German citizens in Romania. He was not unfeeling, but he consistently avoided special interests. In 1881, when Jewish refugees from the Russian pogroms streamed westward, he joined the Alliance Israelite Universelle and the Berlin Committee for Russian Jews but never played an active role in either.[59]

By 1883 Lasker was pessimistic and exhausted. Efforts to establish a new political party had succeeded only to a limited extent. Conservatism was on the rise, and Lasker's efforts to stem the tide appeared honorable but vain. He had just experienced another romantic rejection and was extremely moody. A vacation in Nice appeared to do him some good, and Bamberger noted that he looked healthier and was more talkative, though still not his old self. His participation in parliamentary debate was as useful and as accurate as ever, but briefer now and more to the point. His voice was weak and lacked vigor. The assembly listened with anxiety as, after one embarrassingly long pause, he finished quickly. Bamberger was disturbed. At this point Eduard decided to sail to America in order to see both the United States and his brother Morris. In June, before sailing, he seemed normal to his friends but not to Bamberger, who wrote in his diary: "Dr. Zinn thinks that the brain is only enervated and not yet damaged. He [Lasker] could still get better. The condition dates from the nervous fever [1875], after which he had not recuperated long enough."[60]

In late 1883, after a long journey to London, to Galveston, Texas, and to much of the American West, Lasker returned to New York, where he intended to spend some time before leaving for home. On December 31, 1883, he gave his last public speech to an audience at Mount Sinai Hospital. His theme was philanthropy as an important aspect of the Jewish mission, which was to be the teachers of nations. Interest in works of love and benevolence was "the richest and most magnificent conception of Judaism." He even stated that charity and brotherly love were Jewish traits. The active involvement of American Jews in charitable works led him, he said, to overlook their deficiencies in the preservation of the old traditions.[61]

Was this the same Eduard Lasker who a bare six months earlier had consented to attend divine services only because of his brother-in-law's concern for his rabbinical reputation? Perhaps this speech indicated the shallowness of Lasker's Judaism, reducing it to piety, charity, and apologetics—social rather than religious phenomena.[62] These brief remarks are puzzling because they raise so many new questions about Lasker and his religious devotion. Only five days later, on the fifth of January, 1884, he died suddenly.

In common with the German press as a whole, Jewish papers gave Lasker's death wide coverage and were generally, though not uniformly, eulogistic. The conservative *Jüdische Presse* saw him as a "loving protest against the absurd lie about the materialism of Judaism." The more liberal *Israelitische Wochenschrift* called him a true son of Israel and a true Jew. His old enemy, Philippson's *Allgemeine*, praised Lasker but did not hesitate to criticize him again on several old issues, concluding on the balance that he was a great man because of his Jewish childhood—an ironic twist from the paper that in 1876 had questioned his Jewish credentials. The eulogies at the graveside, in his adopted Berlin, and in the synagogue in Jarotschin were entirely laudatory. In Jarotschin the rabbi declared that, perhaps without knowing it or even intending it, Lasker had shown the world "what a Jew is."[63]

There is real irony in these eulogies. Lasker was personally honest and sincere, but only a few Jews appreciated his secular legal emphasis on equity. His relation to Judaism showed, more than any other area, Lasker's strict and solemn adherence to legal equality within the limits imposed by politics. When his relatives praised him as a famous representative of the Jews, he responded with some heat that he had worked only for *Germans*. He based his goals on principle, chose his principles carefully, and fought for them tenaciously.

II

The Patriot

> "There is finally a German state; we live
> on secure foundations like others, and
> History knows no more 'German
> Question.' Hail to the year 1870 that,
> however much suffering it brought to indi-
> viduals, ended with the long desired great-
> ness of the beloved Fatherland."
>
> Lasker to Otto Elben
> December 29, 1870

Eduard Lasker was not only a German nationalist; he was one of the most active and fervent advocates of unification in the era of the *Reichsgründung* (founding of the empire). Lasker did not interpret nationalism as standing only for a larger state, and he paid more than lip service to the national "feelings of the people [*Volk*]," to its "good instincts," to the "brotherhood" of North and South, and to the danger from internal and external "enemies of the Reich." More than any other single issue, German unification dominated Lasker's early years in politics.

Here and in much of the following analysis it is important to note the differences between "unity" and "unification," terms that many German liberals in the 1860s used interchangeably. Unity (*Einheit*) connotes far more than just the unification (*Vereinigung*) of a new state. Abundant evidence of the distinction and its importance is scattered throughout the history of the Second Reich in the form of serious claims by many Germans that the empire, though uni-fied, had not obtained true unity. Before 1871 this distinction rarely appeared, and simple uni-fication was the usual meaning regardless of which word was used.

Although there can be no doubt that sentiments in favor of unification and nationalism derived from similar inspirations, in the context of nineteenth-century German politics they could be substantially different.[1] One could favor and support unification, as Bismark did, for reasons completely divorced from the cultural or even political content of nationalism. Nor did success in unifying Germany necessarily mean the elimination of internal hatreds and "particularist" sentiments. It is not enough to say that a given political leader was for unifica-tion: the type of unification intended and the quality of national attitude varied greatly from one to another of the German leaders of the 1860s. Almost all Germans favored some form of uni-ty and shared some sort of national feeling. They differed on the size and type of state desired and the depth of the emotion shared.

Most Germans in the 1860s were acutely aware of the weakness of the many small German states in relation to the unfriendly Great Powers, most notably France, Austria, and Russia. The political analyst August Ludwig von Rochau had earlier concluded in his *Principles of Pragmatic Politics* that "the main cause of the German problem is none other than the fragmen-tation of the institutional and national power of Germany. With united power, Germany could laugh at any threat of war or revolution. The great task is therefore—Unification." Influenced by Sir J. R. Seeley, the German constitutional historian Otto Hintze theorized that domestic freedom was inversely proportionate to external military and diplomatic pressure. Thus England was no more free in nature than the Continent, but it was geographically more secure and therefore had less need of absolutism. As Erich Brandenburg wrote in 1919: "The leading spirits would probably never have asked for change [during the era of unification] without the pressure of external danger."[2]

This is not the place to examine the consequences of Germany's response to external challenges, but it is important to note the debate that occurred in mid-century because Lasker was one of those who felt, like Rochau and Hintze, that most of Germany's domestic troubles stemmed from disunity and foreign meddling. As a result, unification became a panacea; it would provide the cure for an endless series of internal problems. Those who envisioned unification in the form of a constitutional state, as Lasker did, foresaw not one but two beneficial results from the national movement: power through unification, and more freedom through constitutional progress.[3] In late 1864 the economist Viktor Böhmert candidly expressed to Rudolf von Bennigsen his surprise at the request that the Nationalverein, of which Bennigsen was president, turn its attention to freedom: "We liberals and nationalists must have enough faith in the irresistible force of our ideas that we do not become fearful before Bismarck and company and do not begrudge them the fruits which they shake loose for us from the tree of German unity." One could see in almost all the small states, he added, how difficult it was to establish constitutional freedom without unification.[4] Little wonder, then, that such liberals worked so hard for unification.[5]

Lasker's initial involvment in the unification movement must be seen against the backdrop of liberal support for nationalism since the opening of the New Era in 1858. Few liberals opposed the use of military might in the effort to achieve unification, and many liberals shared a desire for a diplomatic offensive in pursuit of unity. But at first they had no faith in Bismarck's ability to produce results. To them, Bismarck the reactionary was not the man to mobilize German national power.

The 1859 program of the Nationalverein opened with the statement that it was motivated by "the obviously dangerous condition of Europe and Germany and the need to subordinate party politics to the great common task of German unification." The entire program was nationalistic, subordinating constitutionalism to unification. Hans V. von Unruh and other pro-unification liberals then supported Bismarck for minister of foreign affairs because they believed Prussia needed a bold policy. The Fortschrittspartei (Progressive party) also showed concern about the "insecure condition of the Fatherland's foreign relations," but felt that constitutional unification was the solution. Representative government appeared in the Progressive party program as a means for drawing together the various peoples (Stämme) of Germany. The state governments would be organized in an upper house controlled by Prussia, and the people would be unified through a lower house based on popular election. The program stated frankly that, given the present European power balance, a soundly united Germany was unthinkable without a strong central power in the hands of Prussia, based on representation from all sectors of Germany.[6]

However one describes Bismarck's political development in the 1850s and 1860s, it is clear that perceptions of him changed. Feared as an implacable and uncompromising conservative aristocrat in his early years, he gradually won respect as a competent and daring diplomat. Detested by liberals for his slavish pro-Austrian and particularistic outlook, he reversed himself on Austrian relations and became a supporter of, at the least, Prussianized German unity. Adamantly opposed to constitutions, universal suffrage, and parliaments in 1848, he became a proponent of all three in the 1860s, although his perception of their value and his willingness to manipulate them to his own advantage marked him as anything but liberal. He was a threat to liberalism because he represented a dynamic conservative alternative and, worst of all, because he could successfully use superficially liberal methods for his own ends.

By 1864 Bennigsen had come to recognize Bismarck as a danger to liberalism and wrote that the Nationalverein rejected Prussian dominance under any conditions and, still more, opposed diplomatic and military merger (*Anschluss*). Germany had not yet reached the stage where it would accept a Richelieu or Cromwell. According to Bennigsen, "A people could probably tolerate a military dictatorship in an extremity in order to secure its unity, but it could never ask for it." Two weeks later he added that there was no hope of a popular rising, whether reformist or revolutionary, to pose an alternative to the Bismarckian military-diplomatic solution. Since revolution was impossible, and since a national initiative by the Prussian government was not in sight under this or the next king, only Prussian particularism remained as the basis on which to build the confederation (*Bund*).[7]

As the limited success of the 1864 Danish war took effect in Germany, many liberals had to decide whether Bismarck's methods were really so unproductive. The liberal historian Max Duncker expressed misgivings about the liberal path to unity in spring 1865. It was fine in theory, he wrote, but the liberals had failed in 1848–1849 and had been undependable tools in 1859–1862. If Bismarck's foreign policy strengthened him politically, Duncker recognized that success for the constitutional struggle might take longer. Since Duncker held that foreign affairs deserved a special place in the life of a nation, he believed that Germans could not consider domestic problems first or they would risk losing unity. Karl Twesten, the well-known liberal politician and close friend of Lasker, wrote against the Southern view that Prussian deputies were uncritical of the Prussian government out of fear. Instead he claimed that most Prussian deputies were quiet because they were patriotic and would never agree to measures that would weaken the power and adversely affect the future of the Prussian state.[8]

Heinrich von Treitschke reflected a commonly held opinion among right-wing liberals when he wrote to Gustav Freytag in early 1865 that, if he had to choose, he would opt for Bismarck because the chancellor stood for Prussia's power and legitimate position in the North and East. Though not then an admirer of Bismarck, Treitschke felt obligated to support his foreign policy even if its success would produce another Olmütz and a "victory for all the enemies of the Fatherland." Böhmert thought that the time had come to choose between unity and freedom, and he urged the strengthening of Prussia, without whose support Germany would be helpless in the next European conflict. But he desired some assurance that freedom would follow unification.[9]

Before the Austro-Prussian war of 1866, Lasker was not entirely prepared to accept the Bismarckian solution. He criticized the theoretical separation of freedom and state power, but he agreed that one could not rely on either France or foreign events to wait until Germany was constitutionally united and secure. Schleswig-Holstein had taught him that national feeling was not yet strong enough to provide a natural solution to each crisis and that the cause of unification could expect little help from popular politics. Lasker later told the Reichstag that he had first been elected to the Prussian Landtag from one of the most radical Berlin districts after a speech calling for unlimited annexation of the Duchies of Schleswig-Holstein and Lauenburg and that more liberals than conservatives had voted for annexation in Febuarary 1865. Before 1866 Lasker saw almost no chance of war with Austria. His close friend and political ally H. B. Oppenheim disagreed but felt that Wilhelm would shrink from war and Bismarck would fall—which would be an unparalleled gain for the liberals.[10]

By July 4, 1866, the victorious war with Austria was a fact that liberals of all colorations had to live with. The question now was: How much progress would victory provide? Treitschke, much more pessimistic about liberal power than Lasker, concluded by July 30 that the "war has been begun without the service of Liberalism. This party will, therefore, according to all laws of historical logic, not dominate the near future; we must be satisfied if the present conservative government does not degenerate into a purely party rule. The position which liberalism will receive depends on the zeal with which it now proves that it wants the unity of Germany which it did not initiate." Oppenheim advised Lasker that the rest of Germany would not understand continued opposition to Bismarck, implying clearly that it would be politically dangerous to oppose such success.[11]

Lasker was ready to accept the successful Bismarckian solution to the Austrian problem, but he pleaded for national unification as the ultimate goal of the war. Since Italy had demonstrated the utility of nationalism, Germany should not let a similar opportunity slip by. Lasker could afford to be optimistic because he believed that the war's catalyzing effect on public opinion had brought about a union of the ideal and the real. "Let us vow in this great moment," he wrote in the National Zeitung, "that Europe will never be quiet until Germany is united and strong in relation to its greatness and position." French news organs already warned against Prussian aggression, Lasker wrote, but only because the goal of unification had not been made as clear as in Italy's case. No time was to be lost in convincing Europe that unification was Germany's only goal. Once united, Germany would never again be threatened.[12]

With the war still undecided, Lasker began to speak publicly in support of "freedom," which in the context of his thought at the time must be understood to mean liberal reform. He appealed to the conservatives to add "freedom" to the word "unity" on their banner. In "After the Peace" Lasker told the National Zeitung's readers on July 26 that all classes had served in the war; all had stood shoulder-to-shoulder. More important, their goal was neither victory nor expansion but unification. Moreover, Europe wanted this "healthier"—by which he meant "liberal constitutional"—unification. Prussia had stopped Austria's foreign meddling, but the German nation had aided in the struggle.[13] Considering that Prussia had in fact defeated Austria almost single-handedly—indeed, since Prussia had been forced to fight Saxons, Bavarians, and Hannoverians as well—this argument was hardly persuasive. Lasker did not at first try to establish a liberal position on unification that differed significantly from Bismarck's. As a result, his stand in the summer and fall of 1866 was largely a passive response to and a slight modification of the chancellor's initiatives.

Bismarck acted to take advantage of the Prussian military victory over Austria even before the campaign ended. Most fundamental to all later developments was his decision to establish a Prussian-dominated state in northern Germany. This action had far-reaching consequences because Bismarck remained true to his earlier promise to allow universal suffrage as the electoral mechanism of the new state's lower house. In Prussia itself Bismarck moved decisively to end the conflict over the budget by introducing a bill in the Landtag that would in effect repay the government for the withheld budgets of 1862–1866. Elections to the new Landtag, held during the height of the war, had returned a large number of conservatives and substantially fewer liberals, making passage of the Indemnity Bill that much easier for Bismarck. Concerned about the Southern states, which he was reluctant to bring into the new nation at once, the chancellor negotiated military agreements tying them to Prussia and the North German Confederation in case of war with France. Confronted by such dynamically successful action, Lasker and most liberals found it hard to be anything but passive. Like Lasker, many tried to combine domestic progress with support for Bismarck's foreign policy.

An "Announcement" to Germany, which Lasker helped to compose, explained that some liberals fully supported the government's foreign policy, which they felt to be the beginning of genuine German unification. But they urged that the separation of North and South should be only temporary. They stressed that they would strive to prevent the mistakes by which an unpopular domestic policy might threaten the success of the government's foreign policy: "In addition to armed force and the authority of weapons, Germany needs a progressive government." A policy combining progress and force was the real road to dominance for Prussia in Germany. Even though they considered themselves an opposition party, the liberals concluded their "Announcement" by emphasizing their loyalty, which *in any crisis* would always serve to subordinate party goals to national considerations.[14]

Lasker's enthusiastic support for the Indemnity Bill depended on his conviction that it was the necessary foundation for all future progress in Germany. For a variety of reasons many of the liberals who had for years denied the government a budget switched their votes in the autumn of 1866. Lasker took the position that the indemnity was not just a sanction of illegal action. He saw in the king's address to parliament and in the government's general position a willingness to end the conflict for good: this was the necessary basis for cooperation of government and people in a grand new work. Thus Lasker was unwilling to use ministerial responsibility as a *sine qua non* for the indemnity. Conditions had changed in his opinion, and who would refuse the funds necessary for such a glorious result? He stated emphatically that there was no longer any reason to continue the conflict.[15] "What is the source of all freedom?" Lasker asked. "[It] is the security of the state." England was the "happy island of legend," Lasker asserted, not because of the character of its people but because of the nation's safety from foreign invasion. Hence, in a state so insecure as Germany, the military must remain strong. Freedom from France required a strong Italy and a strong Germany, and Germans must rise to the occasion in order to prevent fulfillment of the prediction that "Eine grosse Epoche hat das Jahrhundert geboren, aber der grosse Moment findet ein kleines Geschlecht." The *Frankfurter Zeitung* correctly predicted little opposition to the Indemnity Bill, which passed 230 to 75. A major reason for its passage was the support offered by Lasker and his allies.[16]

Yet Lasker did not simply accept Bismarck's foreign policy while opposing his domestic policy. From his claim that *all* Germans had sacrificed for the war, he looked ahead to the ultimate goal of complete unity, which, he argued, depended on the fusion of force with progress. Where Treitschke accepted the final victory of conservatism, Lasker obviously hoped that the future was still ripe for liberalism to prove its value to national unity. When the delegates from the various wings of liberalism met on December 6 to coordinate policy on the next military budget, the *Frankfurter Zeitung* identified Lasker as a representative of the national wing, Leopold von Hoverbeck and Benedikt Waldeck as Progressives, Rudolf Gneist and Albert Carlowitz as members of the Left Center, and Peter Reichensperger as a delegate from the Catholics. Lasker had no second thoughts about the Austrian war and doubtless agreed entirely with Bamberger that it had been inevitable. Nor had he given up his liberal goals. The national movement was not yet complete, and he told Berthold Auerbach very movingly that it was erroneous to separate German from liberal goals.[17]

The Prussian military success in 1866, the conservative trend of the Landtag elections of July, the Indemnity Bill, and the formation of the new North German Confederation mark not the end of political liberalism in Germany but the beginning of a new epoch in its history.[18] Enjoying popular support both in the country and in the Landtag and able to draw on the wealth and strength of a larger nation, Prussia was now a respected power. The immediate problem for Lasker was the practical question of which state structure would be best for the new confederation, since it would affect both internal progress and attainment of final national unity. Subsequently, in 1867 and 1870 he worked hardest for a strong centralized state based on national representation, a solution that he thought would best answer Germany's needs.

When the first session of the Constituent Assembly of the North German Confederation met in the spring of 1867, it devoted most of its time to internal matters of constitutional structure. Lasker, however, never lost sight of the broader problem of German unity. The relation between domestic questions and national unity was the theme of his first major speech on March 11, a fervent plea for complete unification based on Prussian power. Nine years earlier, he reminded the delegates the cry had been not to lose a single German village; now no country contemplated taking *any* village. Therefore the cry should be changed: no German village that *could* be part of Germany ought to be lost. There should be no separation between North and South—and certainly no war between them. Austria, which needed no help, was not as important as South Germany. The roots of the further development of the constitution were anchored in the confederal military constitution, and the South would be secured by treaty. Lasker saw much to criticize in the draft of the constitution, but he closed as he had opened, confident in the final result.[19] Nowhere in Lasker's later public or private contributions to the debate over the constitution is there any evidence to suggest that he changed his mind.

As the deputies debated the relative merits of constitutional clauses in the spring of 1867, they were confronted with another foreign policy crisis that seemed to underline the need for a strong and stable national military force. The Luxembourg crisis offered the first concrete opportunity for Lasker and his fellow liberals to demonstrate their support for national unity and defense. The possibility of losing Luxembourg to France as Louis Napoleon's reward for his neutrality during the war with Austria caused momentary panic among such diverse liberals as Lasker, Baumgarten, Rochau, Forckenbeck, and Bennigsen. Lasker reacted by reemphasizing his support for an army budget in a statement on April 6. He claimed that he would never deny to any government the means of defense. Later he argued that the question of the South German states was a domestic German problem for which no outside help or meddling was needed. "The last foot of German earth belongs to Germany," he intoned solemnly, calling on the old—and, by 1867, somewhat ragged—doctrine of nonintervention as support. Unlike his colleagues who called for annexation, Lasker essentially supported Bismarck's solution: to remove Luxembourg from the German confederation and guarantee its independence.[20]

Written in spring 1867, shortly after the Luxembourg crisis, the inaugural program of the National Liberal party is famous for its declaration that the German state (unity of North and South) and German freedom (domestic reform) should be achieved by the same means. Many historians have used this sentence as proof of the schizophrenic nature of German liberalism, divided within itself between its longing for unification and its desire for constitutional government. More significant, however, is an understanding of what those "means" could possibly have been. There is no sound reason to accept the program's assertion that the National Liberal party could achieve both goals by using identical tactics. Nor is there any reason to believe that the same men who constantly spoke about the threat to Prussia of the European balance of power and the necessity of the war with Austria honestly knew of any means that might simultaneously unify the state and establish free political institutions. After 1866 neither Lasker nor any of his close political allies ever again seriously contemplated asking for Bismarck's resignation. They told their potential constituents: "We will never deceive ourselves about the difficulty of the task of securing liberal progress with defective constitutional weapons, in cooperation with the government which for years maintained constitutional conflict and governed without a budget." Their willingness to risk cooperation with Bismarck must be seen either as a clear example of *Realpolitik* or, in the absence of a viable alternative, as a serious self-delusion.[21]

In June 1868, barely a year after the publication of the National Liberal program, the Reichstag witnessed a spirited debate over the naval budget. The sum of money involved was small; instead, the real issue was the use of the budgetary power by the liberals to extort constitutional changes from an otherwise unwilling government. Lasker never denied that he was engaged in a struggle for power for the lower house, but he hotly denied that he would ever prevent development of the essential institutions of the state in so doing. He repeatedly stated that it was not his intention to endanger the loan for the fleet over a constitutional clause. He judged Waldeck to be wrong in his principled opposition to the fleet: the people had spoken, and one should not quarrel over constitutional rights when the existence of the fatherland was at stake! Lasker argued sophistically that violation of the principle of budgetary control was not a surrender of a popular right, since it was not yet accepted as such. In effect, he did not wish to adhere to principle if it threatened the fleet. By comparison, the principle was petty, and the laws of the confederation on indebtness should not be used as a reason to dissolve the fleet. If there were any remaining doubts about his position, Lasker dispelled them by arguing that "if a need should arise similar to the present one, and if it also concerned the establishment of the fatherland and institutions necessary to its growth, or if the pressure and security of the moment demanded it and all else was equal, I would decide in that case probably just as I will today."[22] Obviously, for Lasker unity came before freedom.

In one of his few extant election speeches from this early period, Lasker made his position perfectly clear. He told his supporters in Magdeburg on October 10, 1868, that opposition to unity came only from a few ultramontanes and particularists, along with some radicals and, more recently, the workers. What responsible person, he asked, would call for disarmament with the fresh threats on the Rhine? When Central Europe (*Mitteleuropa*) attained its final form in the peaceful dominance of the most peaceful states, then the first task would be the reduction of the army and the reallocation of state and federal revenues to peaceful purposes. Lasker was optimistic enough to sign a formal wager with H. B. Oppenheim's sister, Bernhardine Friedberg, that unity would be achieved before 1873.[23]

Once the drama of 1866–1867 was over, Lasker settled down to the daily work of a conscientious national legislator, writing new trade regulations, codifying law, and striving mightily to bend the government to his liberal wishes for the future. Never losing sight of final unity, Lasker pursued a relatively peaceful policy of unification with some faint glimmers of success until the Franco-Prussian War rudely intervened. His first move in the direction of voluntary union of the North and the South was to try to make the Prussian North more palatable to the South through progressive reform. With regard to the organization of the new provinces, Lasker went out of his way to encourage local autonomy as an inducement to merger. Prussia should proclaim to the rest of Germany and to the new provinces, he declared in the Landtag in early 1868, that entrance into Prussia and the expansion of Prussia into the rest of Germany should not and would not affect material prosperity or inhibit individual development. Recent conquests, he said, were not like the older ones, since they were *German* in nature and could allow more independent state action.[24]

From 1866 to 1871 the state structure of Germany remained confusing, and many Germans from all corners of Central Europe wondered what would evolve out of it. Prussia had not changed its name or structure, but it had annexed several smaller states, including Hannover, Hesse (Kassel), Frankfurt am Main, and Schleswig-Holstein. Thus, Prussia appeared to be an occupying power, a much larger state both in area and in population and consequently an even more dominant member of the North German Confederation. The latter possessed a Reichstag, and its very name denoted future evolution. Yet the confederation depended on its member states, largely Prussia, for its institutional structure. Furthermore, Bismarck, with a view to future development, had agreed to the creation of a national customs union [Zollverein], which had encouraged German unification economically for decades. Whether Prussia, the North German Confederation, or the Zollverein would determine Germany's future was unclear in the interwar era.

Dependent by law on monetary contributions from its member states, the confederation relied especially on Prussia, far and away the largest single unit. Lasker supported these payments, although he hoped to establish a separate tax base for the confederation. He strongly criticized those who, like the Catholic Ludwig Windthorst, wanted to keep the Prussian Landtag the most powerful of the parliamentary entities. Instead, Lasker admitted he would be happy with an organic union between the Bund and Prussia in matters concerning finances and parliament. If the constitution had to be changed to achieve such cooperation, Lasker would consent, and he interpreted the constitutional provision for raising taxes as necessarily implying the right to raise them in any way possible. To those who argued that this policy might weaken Germany by weakening Prussia, Lasker replied that the government would be stronger when its military deterrent was supported by the people and parliament rather than opposed by them. Lasker meant that a genuinely free people would also be patriotic. Then, in what appears to have been an afterthought occasioned by the military budget, Lasker asked why Bismarck had made no attempt to unite Germany by merger with willing southern states, referring specifically to Baden.[25]

The Baden affair, as it became known in late 1869 and early 1870, was Lasker's scheme to push the government into finalizing German unity by admitting the small, but liberal and willing, Baden to the confederation. In the Landtag in early November 1869 he supported peaceful expansion as an alternative to conquests involving high expenditures. He did not advocate disarmament because peace would not be assured until Italy and Germany were so securely unified as to eliminate all foreign attempts at interference. Prussian action to unify Germany would be dangerous, Lasker admitted, but friendly Baden should be accepted regardless of the risk. After the left applauded this comment, Lasker reminded the government that representatives also had national duties, which they would not leave entirely in the hands of the diplomats. At the end of the month Lasker spoke in favor of unity without war, resurrected the liberal vision of unification through constitutional means, and urged Prussia to avoid a military solution. Again evoking the concept of Prussia's destiny in Germany, he noted Bismarck's own admission of the government's unalterable commitment to unity.[26]

In February 1870 Lasker carried his message to the North German Reichstag, complaining that Bismarck had made no move to include Baden in the Bund, even though it was the most liberal and most pro-confederation of the South German states. Lasker took as his starting point the recent royal address opening the 1870 legislative session, in which Wilhelm had mentioned the ties of North and South. Lasker played down the treaties of 1866 between North and South; in his own words, all German states were united by the "natural and divine right of nationality," which, although not guaranteed by treaty, was indissoluble and inevitable and could neither be prevented nor achieved by the will of any single individual. National sentiment might be found throughout South Germany, but nowhere was it stronger than in Baden, where the only individuals lacking it were a few ultramontanes.[27]

Among the obstacles to unity was the contrast between the liberal regime in Baden and its near opposite in Prussia. Lasker professed puzzlement over the failure to include Baden, the more so since he argued that as soon as one South German state of any size entered the Bund, the southern group would dissolve as a separate entity. The entrance of Baden would signal the beginning of the voluntary unification of Germany. Intervention by France and Austria should not be feared: France was preoccupied at home in the struggle for a more liberal administration, and Austria also had many domestic problems. If these neighbors wanted to meddle in the affairs of other states, there was opportunity enough to satisfy them in Rome. In any case, fear of the consequences of foreign policy could be no obstacle, since fear should have no place in the German heart. Lasker concluded that responsibility for admitting or excluding Baden from the Bund lay with the policy of the confederal executive—in a word, with Bismarck.[28]

Response to Lasker's speech came from almost all directions. Bismarck was incensed at his meddling in foreign policy; their goals might be the same, he said, but their methods were not. Most important, Bismarck told his ambassador to Karlsruhe, Count von Flemming, that he did not want to see foreign policy at the mercy of party politics. A liberal politician from Baden, Friedrich Kiefer, appreciated Lasker's efforts and told him so, but most South German politicians seemed divided on the issue. Opposed to any discussion of Baden's entrance, Bismarck used the government press against Lasker. As Baumgarten wrote to Duncker, "one had to have the hide of an elephant not to feel the footsteps of Count Bismarck." The *Frankfurter Zeitung* showed little sympathy for Lasker and was not surprised that the government from which the National Liberals had taken orders would restrain the party's first attempt to strike out on its own. Lasker's resolution on Baden won no significant support: nothing came of it other than a lively debate in the Reichstag.[29] As the only attempt by any liberal during the *Reichsgründung* to pursue a foreign policy independent of Bismarck and to use public pressure rather than secret diplomacy to do so, Lasker's efforts to admit Baden stand as unique, though completely unsuccessful and politically poorly organized. It was a fine irony that, when war broke out in July 1870, Lasker became an ardent advocate of the Bismarckian method.

Pursuit of unification in the Reichstag became academic with the outbreak of the war against France. Unprepared, Lasker hurriedly returned to Berlin from a Swiss vacation, immediately entered the debate, and tore into August Bebel, a Social Democrat, for his opposition to the war. He enunciated his own position clearly and concisely: any nation had to defend itself, and war was necessary as the only way to punish the French, who had kept Europe in turmoil and war for a century. Victory over France, Lasker believed, would bring peace to Europe. He accused France of lust for glory, pride, and an evil will, and claimed that the French people also wanted war, as evidenced by Gambetta's motto, "Revenge for Sadowa." Lasker denied that the war involved a struggle for national expansion, but he welcomed the real opportunity that the provocation of war offered to unite true German lands into one strong state. The great majority of the people would favor and support such a goal.[30] As in 1866, Lasker assumed not only that Germany's position in the war was defensive but also that war was necessary to settle the political chaos of Central Europe. An election brochure (*Aufruf*) of the National Liberal party on August 30 reiterated most of these feelings, stating that diplomacy had denied Germany its reward (unification) for the bloodshed of the glorious battles of 1813–1815. Now rulers and people were resolved not to repeat that experience: they demanded a free, united Reich with defensible borders.[31]

The Reichstag did not meet from July 23 to December 5. With little else to do, Lasker immediately plunged into discussion of the major problems associated with the war: the question of including South Germany in a new state, the advisability of annexing conquered land, and the role of political organization and agitation in securing unity. In addition, Lasker played a significant role in determining whether the new state should be constructed by a constitutional convention or by diplomacy. Concern for these issues during wartime derived from the conviction of almost all Germans, and Lasker especially, that the war was fought to obtain unity. Defeat of France was not as important for Lasker as the results it could produce at home.[32]

From the start of the war, South Germany in general and Bavaria in particular were the most important problems. Though Bavaria took part in the war against France in fulfillment of the treaties of 1866, Bavarian leaders such as Joseph Edmund Jörg opposed the war. A defensive war against France did not necessarily mean unification with Germany under Prussian leadership, and most contemporaries believed that the prospects for Bavarian acceptance of such a German state were doubtful. Lasker's letter of August 15 to Bismarck provides insight into his scale of priorities: he would not mention the complex problem of territorial conquest, he wrote, but he cautioned that annexation was not the "German objective" of the war. The national goal was true unity, which the people desired instinctively and which the intelligent supported despite the difficulties involved. To help ensure that South Germany would join the new state, Lasker proposed a trip by Northern leaders to the South to encourage political forces for unity.[33]

Lasker was willing to use pressure from both public opinion and the South German states to sway Bavaria because he feared disunity and would not even consider the possibility of a neutral state like Bavaria existing on Germany's southern border.[34] On his trip south in the early fall with Bennigsen, Lasker made a point of personally interviewing the political and administrative leaders of the Southern states. These contacts served as the basis for his continuing interest in Southern problems and his steady, at times prolific, correspondence with many Southern politicians.[35]

Through sheer effort Lasker made himself the main political contact in the North for South Germans who favored national unity. In return it is clear from his correspondence that Lasker's view of the Southern position was shaped by the steady stream of letters he received from politicians like Julius von Hölder, Otto Elben, Heinrich Marquardsen, Friedrich Kiefer, and Marquard Barth. In a letter of August 12 describing the political situation and the goals of the war, Hölder first requested advice and direction for the National party in Württemberg. This letter may well have been the source of Lasker's initiative and the basis upon which he eventually established a liaison with Rudolf Delbrück, Bismarck's appointee as head of the central administration. On August 18 Lasker replied to Hölder that an end to the separation of North and South at the Main River was the first order of business and should take precedence over military or moral considerations. To avert the danger that the opportunity might be lost, each person and party ought to work selflessly to pressure the "government through public opinion to complete the state." Lasker told Hölder that he, naturally, did not worry about the North or about Baden and Hesse, but pressure was necessary in Württemberg and Bavaria.[36] In brief, this was Lasker's personal program for action during the war.

On the same day that he replied to Hölder, Lasker began a correspondence with Bennigsen and Forckenbeck to secure their participation in a trip to South Germany. After a flurry of letters, he told Hölder on September 6 that he, Bennigsen, Forckenbeck, and Unruh were prepared to leave, though eventually only Bennigsen made the entire trip with Lasker. The highlight of the journey was a crucial visit to Munich, the center of Southern power and of opposition to Prussia. At first infuriated by Marquard Barth, a Progressive who had provided a list of what Lasker judged to be excessive modifications of the North German constitution as the *quid pro quo* for Bavarian entrance, Lasker eventually calmed down at Bennigsen's urging, and the meeting produced an address to the king asking for unity on the basis of the North German constitution, that is, for a simple extension of the confederation. This document was obviously an attempt to find the basic conditions acceptable to the political leaders of North and South; it did not suggest any possible solution to the very real desire by Bavarians for written guarantees of Bavarian independence within the confederation. Lasker, dominated throughout this period by a strong desire for unity, did not hesitate to agree to some modifications favorable to Bavaria. During his swing through the South and later, Lasker expended most of his energy examining the interlocking questions of how much modification he could accept and how much would be necessary to sway Bavaria.[37]

From the beginning, the Lasker-Bennigsen trip drew criticism from a number of sources. The democratic *Frankfurter Zeitung* ridiculed their narrow concern for unity and called for more open diplomacy to attract the South. The South German liberal Hermann Baumgarten felt that the pair ignored the real issues, and Max Duncker agreed that the Munich meeting, which seemed to concentrate on politics and constitutionalism rather than on war, unity, and annexation, was not propitious. Baumgarten later extended his criticism by accusing Lasker of supporting Bismarck's policy of granting concessions to Bavaria. He felt that Lasker and Bennigsen had been duped by Bismarck and by the Bavarian foreign minister, Count Otto Bray. In late November Bismarck claimed that Lasker's statements about the North's willingness to grant exceptions to Bavaria had damaged the Prussian diplomatic position and had forced him to give up more than he wished. Lasker's friend Bamberger informed him of Bismarck's accusations via letter after an interview with the chancellor, who had shown Bamberger a draft of the concessions offered by Lasker, which the Bavarian diplomats had used to bolster their position. Until Lasker reassured him, Bamberger believed there was some substance to the claim.[38]

The controversy, which placed great pressure on Lasker, may have been engineered by Bismarck to blunt Northern liberal criticisms of the treaties. The accusation, so difficult for Lasker to answer, is hard to evaluate today because it depends largely on interpretation and emphasis. Almost entirely a question of constitutional structure, it is discussed more fully below in Chapter V. In any case, it is clear that Lasker later harbored an intense dislike for the Bavarian ministers who had used his draft; indeed, his unrecorded conversations with them may well have been improperly, albeit cleverly, used to extort concessions from Bismarck.

In ironic contrast to Bismarck's accusation, Lasker spent much of his time during the war working to ensure that Bavaria would enter the new German state subject to federal authority and the jurisdiction of the Reichstag. His position vis-à-vis South Germany may be found in a letter of September 15 to Otto Elben: "I have seized on the widening of the competence [of the Bund] with both hands, because any extension is a victory for unity, and the highest rights will be better secured within a single Germany than in the best intentioned small state." Bavaria was the major obstacle to the establishment of a state with uniform laws on all major issues in all areas. On November 22 Lasker told Elben that he feared that Bavaria either would not enter or would be bought with too many "shameful concessions." Hölder agreed that to buy Bavaria would be a bitter cup.[39] On a number of occasions Lasker professed complete confidence that if the other South German states joined the confederation, Bavaria could not long remain isolated.[40]

Lasker's final opportunity to express himself on the South occurred in the debate in the North German Reichstag on the acceptance of the South German treaties. Lasker drew a clear difference between Baden, Hesse, and Württemberg, all of which he trusted not to frustrate the new state, and Bavaria, which he frankly feared might do so. It was Germany's fault that a state such as Bavaria had developed alongside Prussia, he remarked, implying that in any region only one state should be strongest and that Bavaria's rise ought to have been prevented. He expressed concern over the concessions to the particularists (namely, Bavaria) but consented to accept them as the price for unity. As for the criticism that the treaties might dilute the Reichstag's legislative power, Lasker preferred his faith that the Reichstag and Bundesrat (assembly of state governments) would never be ruled by such reactionary and shameful conservatism as was the case in the lesser states. Although the treaties gave each state a measure of control that could limit the development of the confederation, he concluded that if the treaties with Baden, Württemberg, and Hesse were signed, unity would be achieved regardless of Bavaria.[41]

Several Southern politicians interpreted Lasker's speech as a blow to the treaties and were unnerved by the thought of rejection by the Reichstag. Even before the speech, Elben had written to Lasker that all of their political action in Württemberg was predicated on acceptance of the treaties and that rejection would destroy four years of party work and open the door to the French. No matter what the drawbacks, Elben argued, a united Germany was more than anyone had ever dreamed possible. On the day after the speech, Kiefer wrote Lasker from Baden to say that concessions were advisable but that "our National Liberal friends in Berlin should be agreed, after frustrated attempts at amendment, not to allow the treaty to fail in the last resort. Swallow the Bavarian pill, even if with a wry face. We will remove the shame later in the Reichstag."[42]

Lasker *had* spoken for the treaties, even if he severely criticized the Bavarian concessions. On numerous occasions he later explained his actions. He told Marquardsen that he already felt closely tied to Bavaria. Lasker was reputedly the originator of the comment that so delighted Bismarck: "The bride is repulsive, but she must still be wed." To his close Southern friend Elben, Lasker confided that he saw no insurmountable threat from the individual states and that he was happy that the German question no longer existed.[43]

Emil von Riedel, the Bavarian finance minister, protested Lasker's speech of December 5, which he also interpreted as opposition to the treaties. Lasker's blunt reply reveals his intense irritation at Bavaria. He began by denying that he had ever advised against acceptance: "The historical event was too great to be moved by petty considerations." Although the circumstances surrounding the treaties were unhealthy, Lasker had faith in the future. The military arrangements were a source of conflict that could be solved only by changes in the document, and there were humiliating exceptions in the rest of the legislation. But unity had been achieved, the rich strength of Bavaria would now be added to the rest of Germany, and the "long-separated brothers will work for the common good."[44]

On balance, Lasker adopted a logical position on the South German question. Dedicated to unity above all else, he was willing to agree to a great many particularist concessions. But he remained bitter about it. He may be excused his lack of Olympian detachment toward so emotional an issue; the only real question is whether he believed that inclusion of the South might weaken the state. The evidence shows that he did not. Even though he told von Riedel that the treaties were unhealthy, he insisted to others that they contained "healthy and centralizing elements" that would allow for growth with governmental good will and the active participation of the people. Although North Germans had gone to the very extreme limit of permissible concessions, Lasker had every confidence in the future, which would see the final and real victory of the war of unification. In 1870 Lasker thought in terms of state-oriented opposition to unity, and on this ground his prediction was correct: the Southern states were never again a threat to the German Empire.[45]

However, beneath the surface of the new state, the antiliberal and anti-Prussian Catholic Center party had begun to grow, as Lasker knew and feared it would. In Bavaria the "Patriots," as the Catholic political wing termed itself, exerted considerable pressure in opposition to the treaties. Lasker advised his Bavarian colleague Marquardsen that the moderate wing of the Catholic party should be wooed. On October 18 Hölder informed Lasker of the rising ultramontane activity in Württemberg. Bennigsen told his wife in late January that the Reichstag session would end within two weeks in order to prevent the government or the Catholics from stealing a march on the liberals in the coming campaign. More disturbing was Bamberger's request for Lasker's help in defusing the Catholic sentiment that threatened his election in Mainz. Bamberger carefully pointed out that it was a question not merely of his election but of the entire anticlerical movement. Indeed, he had been obliged to move to a new district in order to escape the ultramontane voting power that would have made his defeat certain. Still optimistic in 1871, Lasker referred to the results of the elections of that year as solidly national.[46]

The nationalism found in the successful efforts by Lasker and his liberal allies to unite North and South must be considered largely in terms of centralization and power. The public played no role other than in the rhetoric of men like Lasker or in the front lines. More significant to Lasker's nationalism was the annexation of Alsace and Lorraine. Early in the war Lasker had taken the stand that annexation was not the goal of the war, but he did not directly oppose it. Historically, Lasker was right: annexation was a secondary goal of the war, overshadowed by the South German negotiations. Yet the necessity of working with men in the South like Hölder who wanted annexation badly led Lasker to have second thoughts about it. Hölder told Lasker frankly that nationalism meant little in the face of the French threat; until Alsace and Lorraine became German again, they should be held by the military and ruled by Germany.[47]

Forckenbeck posed the problem for liberals with admirable clarity in a letter to Lasker on August 20. He could accept annexation, he wrote, if justified as the necessary price for unity with the South, as a crucial element in military security, or as insurance for an enduring peace. But with no rationale for it readily apparent, Forckenbeck opposed annexation, though "only the Progressives agree with me." He was not nearly as optimistic as Lasker about the future of a state with new lands and a defective constitution. Bennigsen appeared more concerned about what would be done with the territories than about whether to do anything at all. By August 28 Lasker had made his decision. If the award of Alsace and Lorraine to South Germany meant achievement of a general confederation, he told Kiefer, then the price was not too high. Since this did not prove to be a genuine possibility, Lasker still had to face the simpler question of annexation to the Reich. Although he admitted that he did not know how to determine the borders of Germany, he explained to Forckenbeck on November 10 that he felt that no purely French area could be taken without serious reasons.[48]

To be sure, Lasker did not ardently support annexation, but neither did he fervently oppose it. Nor was his an unusual stand among North German liberals. More isolated was the rabidly pro-annexation policy of Lasker's close friend H. B. Oppenheim. In "The Price of Victory" Oppenheim used nearly all the arguments in the annexationist armory. Germany conquered to establish law, not for the joy of the hunt, as in France! If Germany had lost, France would have taken the four million Germans of the left bank. Alsace-Lorraine had no real national life; who ruled the provinces mattered little to the inhabitants there. Furthermore, they did not know how to rule themselves; the people were, in essence, no different from those in the eastern provinces, Silesia, or Holstein. Finally, since it had been conquered for Germany, not for Prussia, Alsace-Lorraine would have to be annexed to secure an era of peace. "The price of victory is twofold," Oppenheim wrote, "the security of the frontier and domestic unity." Lasker supported annexation, but not on the terms of the South Germans or of men like Oppenheim.[49] For him, the primary goal remained, as always, unification. Alsace-Lorraine was merely the price.

After annexation occurred, Lasker successfully opposed any involvement by the Reichstag in Alsace-Lorraine until its inhabitants had elected representatives. Legislation on that area's problems, he believed, should be based on knowledge of local needs and desires if Alsace-Lorraine was to form an integral part of the Reich and remain loyal to the state. For the same reason, Lasker advocated the construction of an imperial railroad through the territories; it was in the national interest to bind these new provinces to the older ones, and he disclaimed any strategic considerations. But he could not tolerate the hostile attitude of most of the representatives elected to the Reichstag from the formerly French lands. When the Alsatian deputies voted, which was infrequently, they usually joined the opposition.[50]

As 1870 drew to a close, Lasker saluted the passing year, which had been so full of meaning for Germany, at last united in a single state. For Lasker, the euphoria of German unification lasted through most of the 1870s, thinning as the decade waned but never entirely evaporating. Nevertheless, the heroic age was over. The new battlefields became the Reichstag, the Bundesrat, and the federal ministries. Generals Roon and Moltke remained for a time, though possessing much less significance and power under the new institutions. It almost seemed for a while that Bismarck, too, the indispensable diplomatic genius, was doomed to suffer a gradual weakening of his grasp on the government. Yet Bismarck's personal position vis-à-vis the king and the bureaucracy had never been stronger and his personal prestige never higher than in the era immediately following the formal creation of the Second Reich. The question facing the liberals was whether, having played only a supporting role in the final act of unification, they would be strong enough to exact genuine cooperation from the government.

In the decades after 1871 unification became a historical fact, replaced by issues concerning the defense of the Reich. Since most legislation in the peaceful 1870s concerned domestic matters, legislators like Lasker devoted little time and less energy to diplomatic problems.[51] The development of these domestic issues is largely a separate story and will be treated as such in later chapters. But the drama of unification was not quite over, and some note should be made of the most significant problems stemming directly from unity and of Lasker's reaction to them.

In the area of foreign affairs, Lasker gave the government wholehearted support. Owing to the government's reluctance to discuss foreign policy in the Reichstag, to the passivity of parliament, and also to a genuine dearth of diplomatic problems, no major debates over foreign policy held public attention in the decade following unification. Lasker once criticized the government for not giving the Reichstag more facts on diplomatic developments, but in the same speech he declared: "You may treat German policy from whichever standpoint you will, but you always come back to the fact that all the parties have the fullest trust in the foreign policy of the Reichskanzler [imperial chancellor], and that alone provides us with complete reassurance." He even defended Moltke against the implication by Jörg that the general was either afraid of or hostile to France. Rather, according to Lasker, Moltke pursued the path of peace. Lasker seldom discussed foreign affairs in his correspondence, almost entirely ignoring what for his counterparts in France and England was daily sustenance.[52] Nonetheless, nationalism and foreign policy considerations may be seen obliquely in his stand on legislation relating to such issues as the military security of the state.

Superficially, Lasker's record on control of military expenditure appears in direct and even violent opposition to the government. This circumstance can be attributed to the dual nature of military legislation after 1871. Lasker never had the luxury of making separate decisions on measures for the defense of the Reich, as was the case with regard to parliamentary control of the fiscal affairs of the state. Consequently, he opposed the military budgets in 1871 and 1881 with negative votes and in 1874 with strong criticism, though at no time did he reject the principle of imperial defense or a strong army and navy. It was this principled opposition on constitutional issues that the government press later used to label Lasker as unpatriotic.

After 1871 Lasker took a number of public opportunities to clarify his attitude toward national unity and the importance of the Reich. Had he wished to renounce or dilute his role in unification, he could easily have done so. Instead, he used these occasions to reiterate his support for the Reich and his confidence in the future. As a candidate for the Reichstag from Frankfurt am Main in late December 1873, Lasker faced the difficult task of selling himself to voters who were not favorably disposed to Prussia and who did not agree that unification was a good thing. Much of his Frankfurt speech was devoted to apologetics about his past defense of nationalism, whereby he sought to characterize his previous actions as both necessary and good. The speech was not successful as an attempt to win support among the residents of Frankfurt: Lasker lost the race. Yet it is significant because it presents a relatively straightforward defense of his support for Bismarck's policies in a city notoriously anti-Bismarckian. Lasker reaffirmed Germany's obligation to take what belonged to it and to end the old *Zerrissenheit* (disunion). He explained that it would have been unequaled stupidity to have rejected the treaties with the South because of some minor flaws. He also defended the annexation of Alsace-Lorraine as important in winning sympathy for the Reich in the South. He even told his audience seriously that Prussia had ceased to be a military state and that the Reich controlled defense. Decentralization was the road to future development, he told his anti-Prussian and anti-centralization listeners. Germany was conscious of the limited effectiveness of its national work, but the only solutions were new institutions and active participation by all the people.[53]

On January 18, 1877, Lasker delivered an address to the Society for the Public Good in Leipzig entitled "The Future of the German Empire." In it he warned that there were real threats to the state from within, most importantly from the Center party. Solid Prussia could not be shaken even by the united action of all four opposition parties, but the empire could not withstand such an attack. Still, Lasker remained optimistic about the Reich. The state was not as immature as it seemed because the bases for unity had been there, waiting expression for a thousand years.[54] Taken by itself, the Leipzig speech might well be seen as a temporary indulgence in patriotic rhetoric, but it was consistent with Lasker's record since 1865.

After their break with Bismarck in 1879–1880 over the antisocialist laws and the protective tariffs, Lasker and his allies were harshly criticized by the government press and government spokesmen as antinational, a charge that clearly rankled men who had long worked hard for unity. Lasker finally spoke publicly to this issue on January 25, 1882, in defense of the liberal record in the task of unification. In a debate over the political freedom of officials, Bismarck had accused the liberals of building legends about the constitutional monarchy. Lasker replied that the imperial chancellor had built legends of his own, the first of which was the myth that the German people, especially the liberals, had opposed unification and that only Bismarck's efforts had produced success. In fact, the liberals, frustrated by the king at Olmütz, had not opposed a strong foreign policy in the Era of Conflict. Lasker himself had been elected to the Landtag from a radical Berlin district even though he was a nationalist. Liberals had voted for the annexation of Schleswig-Holstein in February 1865, and many had also voted for the indemnity and the new constitution of 1867. In 1870 the liberal populace had forced the Southern ministers to go to war and later to join the Reich. As for love of the king, Lasker stated emotionally that he came from an area, Posen, where the inhabitants enjoyed few privileges but uniformly expressed true personal loyalty to the king. The person who should be under attack, the person who tried to separate king and people, was Bismarck.[55]

Unbeknown to almost all of his public, Eduard Lasker was president of the German section of a London-based body called the International Arbitration and Peace Association. At first glance this simple fact would seem to reveal the man as an idealistic and peaceful advocate of friendship among nations. Indeed, it seems to show him as a critic of Bismarckian power diplomacy. In reality, though, nothing could be further from the truth. In his acceptance of the position as president, Lasker wrote, in English, that differences between nations were unavoidable and that they should be settled, "if possible, amicably, and by force when necessary."

Developing this idea, Lasker continued that two new forces were helping to prevent war: the consolidation of states and the growth of popular political power. The second seemed to need no explanation, but he substantiated the first by arguing that the present area of danger was Eastern Europe, where states were still in flux, just as a few years earlier it had been Italy and Germany. The two recently united countries, now forces for peace in Central Europe, exemplified good reasons for the association to *encourage* national consolidation. Lasker concluded: "I do not in the slightest degree apprehend that strenuously to cooperate in the attainment of so high and ideal a purpose can have the tendency of blinding men to those stern necessities of actuality within which human life is providentially placed."[56] Obviously, Lasker's brand of peace in the early 1880s was still that of 1864, 1866, and 1870. He never conceived of major conflicts between consolidated states, implying that they were forces for peace simply because they were unified!

Whether campaigning in Frankfurt or speaking in parliament, Lasker consistently expressed the same priorities: belief in the necessity of unification, in the inevitability of the wars with Austria and France, and in the predominant value of unity as fashioned in 1871. The success of his national policy must be judged in conjunction with German domestic development, since he intended unity to produce a more liberal state as well as a stronger one.

III

The Rise of the National Liberal Party

"Liberalism must become capable of governing."

Hermann Baumgarten
October 1866

It is impossible to discuss Eduard Lasker's political ideas, goals, and actions without some reference to the party within which he labored. More than most of his colleagues, he was a professional politician, and party structure meant considerably more to him than to the hordes of *Honoratioren* (notables) who traditionally entered politics. Recent analyses of political party behavior persuasively argue that conditions of party organization, composition, and voting record influence the voting pattern of the individual, if only in subtle ways.[1] To understand fully Lasker's political record, then, one should view it within the context of the party structures that determined his daily *modus operandi* and presented him with the programmatic parameters within which his own ideas took shape.

Unfortunately, the historian of nineteenth-century Germany possesses few aids in this task. There are almost no monographs on party activity, few analyses of party structure and organization,[2] only a very few dependable biographies of political leaders,[3] and almost no separate treatments of the National Liberal party.[4] It is to be hoped that these lapses in the scholarly literature will soon be remedied. Until then, the present discussion must serve to place Eduard Lasker in proper perspective by analyzing his and his fellow National Liberals' social characteristics and voting record.

Tables 3.1, 3.2, and 3.3 show the National Liberals as the largest single party in the Reichstag in the 1870s, although even at its height it lacked a simple majority by at least forty-five seats. The Prussian Landtag exhibited a similar distribution of seats. These figures cannot be interpreted to mean National Liberal dominance over the Reichstag, the Landtag, or the administration. At its peak, the National Liberal party could engineer majorities on a variety of legislative actions, but it could not secure genuine cooperation with Bismarck either politically or administratively. Although Bismarck at times cooperated with the National Liberals, he remained above a working partnership. Appointed by king and emperor, he ignored the claims to power of any of the large parties. The National Liberals were never really unified, and their popular support among the voting electorate was much weaker than is commonly assumed. In a political system that featured so many different parties, it was difficult to mobilize serious opposition to Bismarck's power. The success enjoyed by the National Liberals in the 1870s was built on a weak base.

The multiparty system of the first years of the Second Reich reacted sensitively to small variations in the popular vote. A comparison of popular vote (Table 3.2) to Reichstag size (Table 3.1) shows that parties could increase their popular support but lose substantially in what were three-, four-, and even five-cornered elections. One of the best examples is the 1877 election in which the Center party lost 95,000 votes and gained two seats while the National Liberals gained 52,000 votes and lost twenty-five seats. In terms of percentage of popular

Table 3.1

Number of Seats Held by Major Parties in the Reichstag, 1867–1881

Party	1867 I[a]	1867 II[b]	1871	1874	1877	1878	1881
Liberal Imperial			30				
Conservative	59	64	54	21	40	59	50
German Imperial	39	34	38	33	38	56	27
Liberal Union							47
Center			58	91	93	93	98
Polish	13	11	14	14	14	14	18
National Liberal	80	78	120	152	127	98	45
(% of total)	(26.9)	(26.2)	(31.4)	(38.2)	(31.9)	(24.6)	(11.3)
Progressive	19	29	45	49	35	26	59
Social Democratic		3	1	9	12	9	12
Other	61	54	12	21	33	34	35
Independent	26	24	10	7	5	8	6
Totals	297	297	382[c]	397[d]	397	397	397

Sources: Data for 1867 and 1867–1870 are from Fritz Sprecht and Paul Schwabe, *Die Reichstagswahlen von 1867 bis 1907. Eine Statistik der Reichstagswahlen nebst den Programmen der Parteien und einem Verzeichnisse der gewahlten Abgeordneten* (Berlin, 1908), p. 322. Data for 1871 and after are from Max Schwarz, *MdR. Biographisches Handbuch der Reichstage* (Hannover, 1967), pp. 820–21.

[a]Elections to Constituent Reichstag.

[b]Elections to first regular legislative session.

[c]This figure includes the deputies from the newly unified Second Reich but not those from the imperial lands of Alsace and Lorraine.

[d]Beginning in 1874, deputies from Alsace and Lorraine sat in the Reichstag.

votes cast, the National Liberal party reached its peak in 1871, when it received 29 percent of the total. In each succeeding Reichstag election its share of the total slipped, eventually falling to a low of 12 percent in 1881 after the secession of the left wing led by Lasker. This erosion of the National Liberal popular vote occurred during an era of generally increasing voter participation. Barely 50 percent of eligible voters cast ballots in 1871 as compared with 63 percent in 1878, a figure that dipped temporarily to 56 percent in 1881.[5] Ominously for the National Liberals, the most notable increases in the popular vote were posted by their political enemies, the Center and Social Democratic parties, while the less hostile Conservatives and Progressives showed smaller increases.

Nor was the National Liberal party a cohesive unit in this period. Internal unity, though always important to a political party, is much more vital in a multiparty political framework. As the largest party in the Reichstag, the National Liberals had the best opportunity for success against an executive who possessed full veto powers, but only if the party possessed strong internal cohesion. However, at the time of its founding in 1866–1867, the very concept of

Table 3.2

Popular Vote (in thousands) for Major Parties in Reichstag Elections, 1871–1881

Party	1871	1874	1877	1878	1881
Liberal Imperial	274	98			
Conservative	536	353	523	742	812
German Imperial	348	391	424	790	382
Liberal Union					450
Center	718	1,439	1,344	1,316	1,177
Polish	176	208	216	216	200
National Liberal	1,128	1,394	1,446	1,296	614
(% of votes cast)	(29.0)	(26.8)	(26.7)	(22.4)	(12.0)
Progressive	349	458	402	358	646
Social Democratic	107	352	493	437	312
No. of Eligible Voters	7,656	8,523	8,943	9,124	9,090
Total votes cast	3,888	5,190	5,401	5,761	5,097
(as % of eligible voters)	(50.7)	(60.8)	(60.3)	(63.1)	(56.1)

Source: Schwarz, *MdR*, pp. 804–5.

"party" was vague, and the first German parties were formed through the coalescence of generally like-thinking groups of parliamentarians and active citizens.

The first mechanism of the emerging parties was the "election committee" formed by interested citizens, usually drawn from the economic or intellectual elite. Local and national election committees developed throughout the later 1850s and the early 1860s, providing slates of candidates and general programs to which, it was ho;,ed, all could somehow adhere.[6] Because candidates could run in any district they chose, and because of the large number of run-offs resulting from a multiparty system, personal prestige and reputation played an important role in electoral success. Though many deputies were forced to campaign vigorously, most of the leaders of the National Liberal party either came from "safe" districts or were popular enough to win on their own without much party organization.[7] Only when pressure from both right and left grew at the end of the decade of the 1870s did the National Liberals pay more attention to organization and tactics.[8]

Within the elected assembly the need for organization became apparent as early as 1848, and by 1867 all major *Fraktionen* (factions) had begun to construct some form of parliamentary organization. The National Liberal members of the Reichstag met frequently, almost daily at times, to discuss party goals with respect to particular pieces of legislation or to arrange the speaking order of party representatives on the floor of the chamber on crucial issues. Unfortunately, no record exists of the votes in the party caucuses, and no minutes were kept. The National Liberal *Fraktion* had an Executive Committee whose main purpose was to organize these discussions and votes in order to produce uniformity in voting. Differences of opinion, it insisted, could be worked out in the caucus rather than in the harsh light of public observation. Moreover, policy decisions arrived at through caucus by party leaders usually became

Table 3.3

Number of Seats Held by Major Parties in the Prussian Landtag,
1866–1882

Party	1866	1867	1870	1873	1876	1879	1882
Conservative	119	125	114	30	41	110	122
Free Conservative	17	48	41	35	35	51	57
National Liberal	34	99	123	174	169	85	66
(% of votes cast)	(9.6)	(22.9)	(28.4)	(40.2)	(39.1)	(19.6)	(15.2)
Liberal Union						19	
Center	15		58	88	89	97	99
Old Liberal Center	24	15	11	3			
Left Center	53	35					
Progressive	61	48	49	68	63	38	53
Social Democratic							
Polish	21	17	19	18	15	19	18
Independent	8	45	17	16	21	14	18
Totals	352	432	432	432	432	432	432

Source: Ernst R. Huber, ed., *Dokumente zur Deutschen Verfassungsgeschichte* (Stuttgart),
1968), 2: 535.

Note: The National Liberal party appeared during the 1866 session, as the result of secession
from other parties.

the policy of lower levels of party activity. Consequently, the Executive Committee was the
strongest, most organized, and most influential force in the National Liberal party.[9] The membership lists of the National Liberal Executive are available for the period from 1870 to 1881
and are essential for a study of the actions and composition of party leadership.

Table 3.4 shows the size of the National Liberal Executive Committee for each legislative
session from 1871 to 1878. Though almost exclusively a parliamentary institution, its stands
on legislation were of critical importance to party members at all levels. With one exception,
the editor Friedrich Zabel, these men were experienced and successful politicians who had campaigned for office at least once and normally several times. The Executive was not, then, entirely out of touch with grass-roots opinion in Germany even if its members spent most of their
time in Berlin.

Whereas membership on the Executive Committee was an honor and a power conferred by
election from the party caucus, membership in the caucus, the *Fraktion*, was substantially
different. In the early period, entrance into the National Liberal *Fraktion* was usually achieved
by signing the program of the party or even by a simple declaration of agreement with its main
goals. The *Fraktion* met formally before important votes or discussions; if two-thirds of the
members were present, the rule was that no one should vote against its decisions in the
Reichstag. Disagreement could be expressed only through absence or abstention. The rule
seems to have been observed, if unanimous or near unanimous votes on bitterly debated issues
such as the 1874 military bill and on the second antisocialist bill of 1878 are any indication.

Table 3.4

National Liberal Reichstag Executive Committee, 1871–1878

Legislative Session	Total NL Reichstag Membership	Number on NL Exec. Comm.	Exec. Comm. Members not in RT	Exec. Comm. as % of Total *Fraktion*
	(1)	(2)	(3)	(4)
1871	120	14	2	9.8
1874	152	16	0	10.6
1877	127	21	1	16.6
1878	98	9	0	9.0

Note: Friedrich Zabel and Heinrich Bernhard Oppenheim were not elected Reichstag members in 1871, and Oppenheim was not reelected in 1877, but both still served on the Executive Committee. Zabel was editor of the party organ, the *National Zeitung*, until his death in 1874, and Oppenheim was a close personal friend of the most powerful Executive members. They are not included in the percentages in this table.

Following the internal struggles of 1878–1879, the caucus decided to draw up a new membership list "in which each should record himself by signature, in order to determine who reckoned himself still a member." Lasker later wrote that *Fraktion* meetings exhibited greater antagonism between members than was evident in the Reichstag but that such differences were reconciled by agreement on major goals and by compromise.[10]

One factor that tended to divide the party internally was the diversity of its members' backgrounds. Like any party, the National Liberal party was a composite of the occupational, social, educational, and regional backgrounds of its members. In addition to its utility in explaining the party's vote on individual issues, this information also fleshes out the bare bones of party description and is important in understanding internal splits. Such information, admittedly incomplete, has been assembled in Appendixes A and B.

German parliamentary analysts have always been impressed by the high percentage of officials—municipal, state, and national—in the National Liberal party.[11] Taken as a discrete occupational group, they lead the next significant categories of businessmen, landowners, lawyers, and professionals. Moreover, as the information in Appendix A shows, the proportion of officials in the Executive Committee was even higher. Yet the statistics may be biased and may not adequately reflect occupational diversity; more complete data on the Executive Committee show that many officials, especially in the higher ranks, were also landowners or professionals. What is true for the leaders may not also hold for the rank and file, but if many officials were also landowners or professionals, then it casts serious doubt on the characterization of the party as dominated by officials.[12] In any case, the National Liberal Executive Committee boasted few businessmen, despite their second-place ranking among occupational categories within the party.[13]

The religious coloration of the party was generally Protestant; 7 percent of the members were Catholic, and only 1 percent were Jewish.[14] However, all four Jews in the Reichstag delegation also served on the party Executive Committee. When the party split in 1879–1880, two

Catholics and two Jews, including Lasker, led the secession.

In an era of newly achieved unification, regional origin played a major role in party composition. The most glaring regional conflicts involved Prussia and South Germany. Thirty-eight (32 percent) of the National Liberal Reichstag members were elected from South German districts in 1871, but only one of them was elected to the Executive Committee: Ludwig Bamberger from the ninth Hessian district near Mainz. More significant, perhaps, only twenty-eight candidates came from Prussian electoral districts, but six were chosen for the fourteen-member Executive.[15] In 1871 the National Liberal party was "national," but its Executive Committee was Prussian. Between 1871 and 1881, eighteen of thirty elected Executive Committee members came from Prussian districts, and seventeen served simultaneously in the Prussian Landtag during much of that time. Only five of the thirty were South Germans.

In almost all cases, the men elected to the National Liberal party were well educated, as were most Reichstag deputies in the era before Social Democratic electoral successes could exert a leveling influence. Most party members (59 percent) had studied law, though few actively practiced it. Law was a common educational preparation for politics, but fewer members of the Conservative party (20 percent) possessed legal training than did members of other parties.[16] The National Liberal Executive Committee boasted seven editors, eleven lawyers, two professors, and a physician.

In addition to the formal organization of the Executive Committee, two informal, but still identifiable, groups existed within the National Liberal party: the Liberale Gruppe (Liberal Group) and the Liberale Vereinigung (Liberal Union).[17] After a very vague early existence, both groups came to be defined in terms of their eventual secession; but they had constituted recognizable elements within the party for years prior to the final break. Friedrich von Schauss and Joseph Volk, both South Germans, led twelve other deputies in secession to form the Liberal Group in July 1879.[18] The Liberal Union, originally comprising nineteen National Liberals led by several luminaries from the Executive Committee, including Lasker, broke away in September 1880. About all that the two groups had in common was their decision to leave the party. Whereas the Liberal Group supported Bismarck, the Liberal Union was anti-Bismarck on several key issues. They also differed in social composition, with many more businessmen belonging to the Liberal Union.[19] By comparison with the party, the Liberal Union was underrepresented in the category of national officials.

Only three members of the Liberal group were elected from Prussian districts; four came from Bavaria and two from Württemberg. None had previously belonged to the party Executive Committee or the Prussian Landtag. The Liberal Union, by contrast, exhibited political and geographical strength from the start: seven of the original nineteen had been members of the Executive Committee at least twice and elected to the Reichstag three times. Two of them, Forckenbeck and Stauffenberg, had been officers of the Reichstag off and on since 1870. Eighteen of the forty-five Liberal Union members elected in 1881 had also served in the Prussian Landtag. In that year twenty-six members came from Prussian districts and twenty-two from within the pre–1866 Prussian borders; only eight Liberal Unionists were elected from South Germany. Neither secessionist group drew any members from Hannover, where the power of Bennigsen and Miquel kept the National Liberals faithful. Both groups exhibited similar religious affilations, although the Liberal Group had no Jewish members and far more Catholics, including the group's two leaders, Schauss and Volk. The Liberal Union was much the more active in the Reichstag.[20] Finally, and most significantly, in 1881 the Liberal Group elected only a single candidate, while the Liberal Union won in at least forty-five districts.

Information on social composition also helps to evaluate party strengths and weaknesses in pursuit of essential goals as the National Liberal party defined them. Unlike Lasker's goals, which remained reasonably consistent throughout his career, the party's goals were always a shifting composite of views reached by the resolution of competing forces. We might gain a clearer picture of the National Liberal goals if we had consistently accurate descriptions of its caucuses. Unfortunately, we have only a few tantalizing glimpses from diaries such as that kept by the Württemberg politician Julius von Hölder. Instead it is necessary to evaluate the National Liberal party in terms of how it supported legislation in the Reichstag and how it stated its policies in printed programs.

Legislative success for any left of center party in the era of German unification involved two distinct struggles: first, with Otto von Bismarck, who seemed to have become ensconced as a virtually permanent chancellor; and second, with the system itself, which gave the Prussian king real independence from parliament in his role as federal executive. Bismarck's intelligence, enormous success, and extreme popularity made opposition to him difficult at best. The system could not be altered by the Reichstag alone, no matter how unified the parties in it might be. As a result, the continually frustrated opposition parties gradually divided into some factions that were unwilling to bend on any issue and others that would make concessions in order to obtain at least part of their program. The system encouraged the development of a politics of compromise, which became firmly established in Germany by the end of the 1870s.[21]

Basic to Germany's politics of compromise was the concern for power rather than ideals. One of the best exemplars of this thinking in the mid-nineteenth century was August Ludwig von Rochau, originator of the word *Realpolitik*, who argued in 1853 that practical politics dealt only with power—all else was speculation.[22] Ludwig Bamberger, himself no mean practitioner of the art of compromise, agreed with August Bebel that a head of state was prone to compromise by nature, but he insisted that politicians also lived by principles, if only very broad ones. The key, he correctly noted, was to distinguish between a healthy and an unhealthy compromise.[23] These men saw compromise as a tactic by which one accepted the immediately obtainable without giving up hope of someday securing the perfect solution. Such choices must be judged not at the time of the compromise but at some point in the future when one can reasonably expect to see either some fruits of the bargain or its failure.

In this light the question becomes: Did the National Liberals compromise the goal of parliamentary control over the administration, which had been the binding force in the Progressive party during the four-year struggle over the budget in the Era of Conflict? After the conclusion of the successful war with Austria, the Prussian Landtag, including the core of the later National Liberal party, voted to indemnify the government for the budget increases denied since 1862. Within the year, the National Liberals accepted the constitution of the North German Confederation without ministerial responsibility, a new budget clause, and daily pay for Reichstag members, and they approved a three-year military bill that effectively frustrated the principle of annual budget review and approval. Yet, even though they did not achieve their goals, the liberals gave up nothing in 1866–1867, and they retained control over new taxes as in 1862. The new Reichstag still possessed a negative power—assuming that members could assemble the required votes—to prevent the government from engaging in costly new programs. Denied positive direction of the state, they still had the means to harass the administration, as they had done in the Era of Conflict. Even so, most National Liberals felt they could obtain more by cooperation.

A desire to work with the new state permeated the National Liberal leadership. The Hannoverian Johannes Miquel is best known for his comment that politics no longer could ask what was the ideal but what was the possible. For Miquel, as he had earlier stated, the possible meant working with the government. In October 1866 the South German liberal Hermann Baumgarten wrote: "Liberalism must become capable of governing." Heinrich von Treitschke, the noted historian, advised essentially the same principle in a December 1866 article devoted to evaluating the liberals' strengths and weaknesses. In the first days of the constituent Reichstag in March 1867, the normally cautious Rudolf von Bennigsen felt that the new National Liberal party would have "influence," and he hoped that the Reichstag would secure sufficient power to extract concessions from the administration. Perhaps the lengthiest analysis of what the liberals' relationship to the government should be came from Karl Twesten, a formerly strong anti-Bismarckian who now argued that the National Liberals must cooperate *because* of their weakness. Bamberger later stated publicly that cooperation with the government was necessary to make even small gains. The democratic *Frankfurter Zeitung* dubbed the National Liberal party the "cooperators," taking a dim view of the twenty-four points of its June 1867 program. The program promised a lot, the paper observed, for a party that admitted it would take what it could get.[24]

As the National Liberal program stated, the party would solidly support the foreign policy of the new state but would go its own way on domestic issues.[25] The period between the Prussian victory over Austria in 1866 and the war with France in 1870 was practically devoid of important diplomatic initiatives. Lasker's open criticism of Bismarck and of the government during the Baden affair in late 1869 and early 1870 was an exception. Little criticism of the government's foreign policy was heard because there was little to criticize.

Domestic policy was another matter. The Reichstag devoted itself to reform of the penal code, and liberals and progressives began to push for legislation to correct what they considered to be the mistakes or omissions of the 1867 constitution, although with little significant success. During these years, Lasker and the National Liberal Party forced the resignations of a number of government ministers in Prussia and the confederation, but they failed to secure reform on financial issues and on the death penalty. Since ministerial responsibility to parliament and the payment of Reichstag deputies (the *Diäten*) already had been defeated by the administration in the 1867 constitutional assembly, it is doubtful that men like Lasker would have continued to cooperate with Bismarck indefinitely. From the beginning, there were negotiations to include one or more National Liberals in the cabinet, but none was acceptable to Bismarck.[26] Examples of the party's discontent may be seen in the speeches of men like Lasker, in the growing irritation between the right and left wings of the party, and in statements hostile to the government by many left-wing liberals. Forckenbeck wrote to Lasker in April 1868 complaining of Bismarck's reluctance to give up any real power, though he still hoped that the chancellor might relinquish some control in the future. Bamberger denied that Bismarck wanted to destroy parliament, but he admitted that when it came to giving in, Bismarck did not like to compromise. Lasker felt that the government would cooperate only when compelled to and would give way only on insignificant matters.[27]

War with France and the establishment of the Second Reich wrought a change in National Liberal politics as profound as that of 1866. No explicit bargain was concluded between Bismarck and the National Liberal party. Yet the party's support on the South German problem during the war, on the Alsatian annexation, and on the war itself was more than tacit acceptance of the administration's leadership. After the war the National Liberals openly operated as a pro-government party; indeed, National Liberal votes secured the administration's legislative program in sessions of the Reichstag and Landtag from 1871 to 1877. The military bills of 1871 and 1874, the *Kulturkampf*, and the sweeping reform of the penal code were all carried on a solid foundation of National Liberal votes. Internally, however, the party was increasingly torn by the tension of continuing struggle over how far it should go in accommodating Bismarck.

The year 1874 marked both the apogee of National Liberal legislative power and the beginning of its demise. Lasker had shown his willingness to compromise on sensitive issues. He had even approved Bismarck's use of a special, secret fund, although he well knew that it would be applied in a blatantly political fashion, in order not to poison the spirit of cooperation with the government. But the debate over the new military budget, which called for Reichstag approval only once every seven years, was so bitter that it caused a serious split in the party. Treitschke, a National Liberal himself, attacked the opponents of Bismarck's military bill in the pages of the prestigious *Preussische Jahrbücher*, which he edited. Lujo Brentano, another member of the National Liberal party, reported that Lasker believed Treitschke had acted with support from Bismarck and that Lasker's "and almost all opinion is agreed that now a [new] *Kulturkampf* begins against us."[28]

Bismarck certainly displayed hostility toward the left wing of the National Liberal party from at least 1874 on. At one point in early 1875 he described Lasker as "the real illness of the state." Talk of reorganizing the National Liberal party began to circulate. H. B. Oppenheim mentioned it to Lasker in November 1875, and even Miquel agreed on the need for reorganization; but Oppenheim predicted that if Bismarck withdrew support from the National Liberals, few would oppose him, including Miquel. Poschinger reported on December 18, 1875, that Bismarck wanted no new majority and repudiated any desire to break with the National Liberals, but he would like to see its right wing and the Free Conservatives strengthened. In July 1876 Oppenheim suggested forming a new, smaller party, one more disciplined and more "able to govern."[29]

Just prior to the crisis of 1878 the pleasures of cooperation with Bismarck had worn very thin indeed. Well before Bismarck's turn toward protection in 1879, Rudolf von Delbrück, sensing the government's changed attitude on tariff matters, resigned as president of the Reichskanzlei (Imperial Chancery) in 1876 in opposition. Bismarck attempted to secure Bennigsen's services as a minister but ended the overtures when asked to accept the more liberal politicians Stauffenberg and Forckenbeck as well. The party's failure to place members in the cabinet was critical, but Bennigsen appears to have been sincere in not attributing the breakdown of the ministerial negotiations to Lasker, as some suggested. On the other hand, in a famous off-the-cuff remark, Bismarck accused Lasker of "spitting in Bennigsen's soup." Later, when Bismarck needed to replace Otto von Camphausen, he again rejected Bennigsen as a man tainted by association with Lasker. From 1874 on, Bismarck used every opportunity to try to purge the National Liberal party of its "Lasker wing." Despite Lasker's power and ability, there was never any serious possibility that he would gain a ministership. In 1879 Lasker questioned Bismarck's willingness to accept the National Liberals in his cabinet, arguing that if the chancellor could not agree with Bennigsen, he could agree with no one.[30]

When the break came between the administration and the National Liberal party, it was Bismarck's doing rather than that of the National Liberals. The occasion was the second anti-socialist measure of 1878. The National Liberal party was internally divided on the proposed statute to outlaw the Social Democrats, but only a small percentage of its members was willing to turn against the government and Bismarck. A revealing insight into the party's attitude toward cooperation with the government may be found in a memorandum to Bismarck dated September 16, 1878, from Prince Hohenlohe, who had no vested interest in the National Liberal party and whose analysis is telling. He reported to the chancellor that, although unhappy with the administration, the National Liberal party was not a real party of opposition: "The rational elements of this party see, in a conflict between the German middle class and the imperial government, especially with respect to South Germany, a danger for the empire. They will, therefore, not call for a conflict." Hohenlohe further related that a witness had heard Lasker argue for the need to avoid such a conflict and, in a meeting of party leaders, discuss whether he would not be wiser to remain in the wings for the near future, since he knew that "his appearance easily irritates your Excellency." Hohenlohe doubted the firmness of such a "good intention," but he advised Bismarck to accept the law as amended because "I think that, in light of the anxious German middle class, any law against the socialists is better than none. For any law brings the cooperating middle class into opposition to the Social Democrats, widening the gap between the two. But if these people are in danger, they will later agree to anything."[31]

The next blow against the party was the powerful support that the government gave to protective tariffs in the winter and spring of 1879, just months after the National Liberal party's unanimous support for the antisocialist bill. It was then that Lasker and his allies began seriously to discuss dividing the party into those who would oppose and those who would support the government. Within the year, the split occurred.[32]

The most obvious, and perhaps the only, alternative to cooperation with Bismark's administration was alliance with the other political parties in the Second Reich. Yet in the entire history of the pre–1914 empire liberal parties never successfully cooperated with other opposition parties. In the period 1867–1884 the National Liberals joined only two coalitions: with the small group of Free Conservatives (Deutsche Reichspartei) in the 1870s, and with the Progressives in 1884. In the first case, the coalition was formed to support the government; in the second, the result was a merger into a single party that had no power and eventually in 1892 split over another military bill into factions reminiscent of the pre-merger days.

National Liberals avoided cooperation with the Social Democrats and with the Conservatives. The former were too radical, the latter too reactionary. Furthermore, it would have been unthinkable to work openly with the Poles or Danes, who were in any case too weak to be very useful. Since almost all National Liberals believed in the *Kulturkampf* against the Catholic church, the chances of serious cooperation with the Center party were virtually nonexistent. The Progressives on the left and the Free Conservatives on the right were closer ideologically and cooperated with the National Liberals at various points, but any serious tie meant irritation of the opposite wing of the party and was consequently avoided until 1884, by which time it was too late.

Historians often cite the unwillingness of the National Liberal party to deal with the masses as a major reason for liberal political failure under Bismarck. Some have argued that the liberals were too removed from the real world, that they wished to fight for their goals only with ideas and moral weapons. Hans-Georg Schroth, for example, scathingly wrote: "Liberalism was consequently willing to discuss anything. It debated political matters, it debated even the workers' question, because it could not control either in any genuine sense." Political problems appeared to Prussian and German liberals as primarily moral or legal issues: they defended convictions instead of seeking power. More important, the liberal parties did not understand the mass parties; they would not and could not adapt to mass politics. According to Eugene N. Anderson, the competition from the Center and the Social Democrats excited only "feeble attempts to escape their dilemma."[33]

Underlying the National Liberal failure to secure genuine cooperation with Bismarck and the government was its inability to demonstrate political unity in the Reichstag. At the peak of its power in 1874, the party controlled 152 of 397 seats in the Reichstag. Nor did the party ever have enough allies among the other political parties to make up the difference between a plurality and a majority. Like Lasker, most National Liberals found it difficult to work with the representatives of rival ideologies, including the Democrats. Since Bismarck represented power as well as conservatism, National Liberal leaders reckoned on forcing him to recognize the necessity of cooperation with the largest party in the Reichstag. For a time in the early 1870s Bismarck cooperated, but when he cut his ties to the National Liberal party, it became rapidly apparent that the latter was helpless. By contrast, Bismarck proved willing and able to compromise with nearly any other significant party.[34]

Within this general system, Lasker's actions placed him consistently in the left wing of the party. He led the attacks on the Catholics and on the seven-year military budget while standing solidly in support of free trade, a modern constitution, and a progressive legal system. As we will see in the next chapter, he did this because law was fundamental to Lasker's political outlook.

IV

The Role of Law

"It would be much more significant for the Peoples'
Representatives to strive after the good law than to
possess it."

Eduard Lasker
January 29, 1867

In the modern world law acts as one of the most important of the forces binding society together. Yet it was a progressive concept of law that was a force for change in the stifling environment of absolute government that dominated much of Germany in the early nineteenth century. In the view of a growing number of lawyers, judges, and professors of jurisprudence the development of statutory law and legal institutions had lagged behind the evolution of much of the rest of society both in Germany and in Europe. Changes in specific laws, in legal codes, in judicial organization, and even in lawmaking came to be seen by liberals both as intrinsically good and as necessary to create a better, more rational society. In the hands of liberals, law became a political weapon whose use was frustrated by the conservative orientation of most German rulers. Thus, temporarily, men who would normally not have been revolutionaries frequently became radical when confronted by inflexible and unthinking governments.[1]

Inspired by the revolutions of 1848, liberal legal reformers appeared all over Germany. It was no accident that such a large number of lawyers, judges, and law professors played an active and productive role in 1848. The centers of their attention were the representative assemblies that sprouted so rapidly in the spring and summer of that year, because they provided a new forum for securing legal change. Overnight parliaments became dynamic forces for legal reform that was progressive without being revolutionary. When the revolutions failed, the parliamentary bodies lived on. Despite alterations in the electoral laws, government interference, and a strictly censored press, these assemblies continued to perform their duties as legislatures. After the liberal advances of the New Era, provoked in part by the change of dynasts in Prussia in 1858, all of these assemblies achieved a significance that far exceeded their limited role in the reactionary early 1850s. As a lawyer and as an elected member of the Prussian Landtag from 1865 on, Eduard Lasker exerted a powerful influence on law in a wide variety of ways.

Contemporaries like Heinrich von Sybel and modern historians like Leonard Krieger agree that, whatever else he might have been, Eduard Lasker was an advocate of the *Rechtsstaat*. Modern texts define this term as belief in a state in which law, rather than arbitrary administrative action, describes and defines most public processes. In a *Rechtsstaat* the bureaucracy functions to carry out the directives of the state in a manner strictly conformable to law. This concept did not develop in a vacuum: its intent was to make law serve as a corrective to absolutism. However, once the absolute state was forced to share its power with society, lawmakers began to think beyond simple limitation of the state. The *Rechtsstaat* came to mean, in a more general sense, faith in the efficacy of law in ordering society. With their attention diverted from the threat of absolutism, believers in the *Rechtsstaat* found less and less common ground in their attempts to apply law to society. Many who had been willing to use law as a defense of civil rights were not so eager to use it as a tool to change the state. Lasker entered public life in a world in which legal action meant both anti-absolutism and progress.[2]

Between 1861 and 1864 Lasker wrote several articles for the *Deutsche Jahrbücher* in which he attacked the absolutist Prussian state, pointing out that the underlying weakness of the system was its dependence on a small number of individuals: "The health of the state organism ought not depend on the possibility of a good ministry." The only sure and lasting cure for such insecurity was legislative action by the people's representatives; specific, precise laws, in Lasker's view, should replace fickle and outmoded ministries. Along with many of his contemporaries, Lasker wanted Prussian life to be regulated according to a system in which the worst evil was to break the law. He described the contrast between the Prussian government and the Progressives accurately in 1863 when he stated that the people wanted the law to rule but the king wanted the executive to rule. Reform of the law was not possible because society lacked certain judicial and political organs. Lasker predicted that the Prussian people's greatest achievement would be to establish those institutions and then to change the law.[3]

The vision that sustained Lasker during the 1860s and 1870s was one of a state in which law rationally ordered and accurately reflected the needs of society. He contributed tremendous support for reform and codification of German law. To Lasker law was both one of the essential elements of national unity and the expression of his fundamental concept of man. The most simple law was self-preservation, Lasker wrote, but even though man exhibited many characteristics of the animal, he had the capacity for compassion, which modifies the right of the stronger: "The goal of culture is to establish a condition in which one can safely secure his goods and enjoy them without one part of his nature serving as the price for the other." Struggle was necessary to humanity, Lasker admitted, but it was not necessarily endless. The great task of culture was to secure peace, and the best means of doing so was through law. Not incurably optimistic, Lasker realized that progress did not come without some setbacks. In the case of Prussia and Germany, Lasker observed that previous neglect had created a situation so near to revolution in so many areas that reconstruction could not occur all at once.[4]

Lasker did not treat law simply as a weapon to be used to secure and defend individual freedom, as is often charged of nineteenth-century liberals, nor did he deal with freedom in an abstract fashion. He was a practical man, an organized and precise Berliner (at least by adoption), and he had little use for theory without a sound grounding in reality. "All who enroll in a societal order must be obedient," he stated, "but the inclinations and motives for obedience differ." One kind of man, he theorized, obeyed when he saw no alternative because he lacked power; the other obeyed only when convinced of a law's necessity. He believed that since 1815 open discussion had liberated Germany from rulers who enforced obedience without regard for the people's feelings. Laws demanded obedience, but in an open society discussion would ensure that only acceptable laws would be enforced. No one, Lasker told a campaign audience in Camburg in 1878, expected all forty million inhabitants of a state to agree on all issues, but they must agree to resolve their differences by lawful means.[5]

Legal theory or jurisprudence as such played little role in Lasker's career, except in reference to a specific case or as support for a particular piece of legislation. A well-educated, practical sort of lawyer, Lasker made his greatest contribution to the German legal system as a legislator concerned with the best wording of uninspiring statutes on such topics as the trade code. Analysis of his theoretical attitude to law therefore depends on a close examination of his legislative action.

In discussing the generation of European liberals prior to 1848, John Stuart Mill commented: "Those who admit any limit to what a government may do, except in the case of such governments as they think ought not to exist, stand out as brilliant exceptions among the political thinkers of the Continent." In this sense Lasker was willing to give the state power to do anything that the people, through their elected representatives, would accept as law and that the executive could enforce. By contrast, Heinrich von Treitschke contended in his essay "Freedom": "There are personal rights so noble and inviolable that the state should never suppress them." It would be inaccurate to conclude that Lasker valued fundamental rights less than did the more conservative Treitschke. Although Lasker did not insist that the constitution of 1867 contain a bill of rights, he placed great emphasis on such principles. He believed that the correct legislative process would eventually produce the right laws. It is vital in understanding Lasker to realize that he assigned the highest value to process, both judicial and legislative.[6]

In the early years of his legislative career Lasker emphasized uniformity of law at all levels. He relentlessly pursued the most insignificant examples of what he termed "juristic anarchy," at first in the Prussian Landtag and later in the German Reichstag. There were, of course, literally thousands of cases of legal conflict or simply of difference in a country composed of more than thirty sovereign states. In some cases judges were poorly trained and not fully cognizant of the law. In other cases established legal principles were not followed because the courts involved either had never heard of the principle or did not care. In many cases the law was simply so complex that few jurists knew or cared to learn its intricacies. Lasker soon made a name for himself as a legislator who knew the law and insisted on its consistency and uniformity.[7]

It was natural for Lasker, concerned as he was about legal uniformity, to attack the chaotic manner in which laws were collected and made available to the judiciary and the public. He charged that the law codes were presented in half-written, half-verbal form and were never summarized. Because of government inaction, they existed much as they had in the eighteenth century. The establishment of the North German Confederation in 1867 provided the impetus for reform of the legal system as well as for codification of laws. Lasker understood unification to include such reforms as rationalization of the legal system. He constantly urged reform and codification of the law so as to provide the new state with a uniform set of laws that, he hoped, would pacify the states annexed and attract Southern states still not included. Indeed, the movement for unity would be strengthened, he argued just after the Austrian war, if Prussia's legal system could be made more attractive to the rest of Germany. He repeated this argument on the eve of the French war, pointing out that enemies of unity agitated against merger on the grounds that the South German legal systems would be harmed by contact with the comparatively primitive and absolutist Prussian law. These anti-Prussian polemics could be defused by reform.[8]

Since he firmly believed that all citizens must be subject to a uniform law within Prussia, Lasker naturally extended this principle to all newly annexed territories. Early in the debates of the North German Constituent Assembly in March 1867, he reasoned that common citizenship meant that "the question whether penal law must be common [to all member states] is, in my opinion, already decided in the clause which we have already accepted [relating to] common citizenship. Since any citizen of any state [within the confederation] is thereby a citizen of all member states, it is necessary for him to know the laws of his land."[9] In 1867, knowing the laws of the land meant that the common man would have to be aware of the very different legal systems of twenty-two states, a clearly unreasonable requirement, Lasker submitted. The logical solution was to codify the laws of the member states under the authority of the confederation and thus to create a land united by a "common speech, trade and spiritual life." Lasker saw no contradiction between such characteristics and law because he held that common legal belief was a fundamental element of the concept of nationality. Nor did Lasker want a loose confederation in which each state could develop its own laws on matters of common concern.[10] With some modification, the North German Confederation accepted this argument, and the transition to a unified legal code began with the constitution of 1867.

The first legislative period of the North German Reichstag, 1867–1870, divides into two segments based on amount, type, and importance of legislation. The first two years were dominated by political clashes between the administration and parliament over the balance of government power. After the failure of the attempt to secure a responsible ministry in the spring of 1869, the Reichstag turned to more mundane affairs. Of the sixty-one roll-call votes taken in 1869–1870, fully twenty-five dealt with aspects of the penal code and eight with the trade code. Thus legal codification was clearly a large part of the Reichstag's work in 1869–1870.

The most immediate conflict involving the legal system was over the type of code to be adopted. Lasker boldly voiced his opposition to simple extension of the Prussian system. The occasion of his speech was a debate over the wisdom of creating a supreme court to resolve problems between states concerning commercial law. Lasker supported a supreme or federal court in 1869 and again in 1870, even wishing to locate it in Leipzig rather than Berlin. If there was any doubt as to his motive for the choice of Leipzig, he made it clear that he wanted a federal rather than a Prussian law code. To those who worried about checks on the court, Lasker stated unequivocally that it would be better to establish federal controls than to accept Prussian law, which non-Prussians could not understand. In reference to earlier problems in Prussia, Lasker noted: "I would be least desirous of accepting a Prussian law, root and branch. We have already made a bad trial of that—let us not repeat the experiment." In 1870 he stated that it was common knowledge that the Prussian minister of justice appointed judges primarily on the basis of their political viewpoint. A supreme court would help to establish a truly unified law in practice as well as in theory. Indeed, Lasker regarded the commercial supreme court as a training ground for cadres of judges who could later act for the confederation in all phases of law.[11]

Uniformity of laws within the state meant, to Lasker's way of legislative thinking, not just agreement on a basically similar code but also the power of a central institution to change that code when necessary. The only national institution capable of performing this function was the Reichstag. In 1870 and 1871 legal codification became one of his minimum prerequisites for merger of North and South, despite his concern over Prussian legal backwardness. As late as March 1870 Lasker denounced Prussian reluctance to implement liberal reform as a primary reason for the Southern agitation against *Anschluss*. Southern states, he claimed, had enjoyed a wholesome legal development in the first half of the nineteenth century, and they feared that union with Prussia would prevent further progress. After the war he argued for jurisdiction by the Bund rather than by separate states as the basis for further reform of the civil law.[12]

Lasker regarded this movement for codification and reform of the law as the opening of a new era of jurisprudence. As he stated before the Reichstag in 1869, the entire legal code would have to be revised. Omissions in the code, such as laws regulating prison conditions, would have to be added in the future, and reform bills that were defeated would have to be re-written and resubmitted. But in 1870 Lasker was not willing to defend principle to the end; he refused, for example, to vote against the penal code just because it did not abolish the death penalty. He saw the new code as a step forward and a harbinger of improvements to come. Thus he opposed radical changes that might endanger passage and explained that he and his friends were trying not to establish a totally new law code but to codify and rationalize the existing one. The *Justizgesetz* (judicial code) of 1872 is commonly regarded as the first step toward codification, but that direction had already been decided in 1870. However, the battle over substantial changes in the code was just beginning. Although codification was finally completed in 1896, the years after 1872 brought little serious liberal reform.[13]

On a somewhat more sophisticated plane, legal uniformity meant application of law to all citizens equally. Variation between the legal rights of soldiers and those of civilians irritated Lasker, and he spoke on the subject numerous times, especially in the debates on the penal code of 1872. Beyond the differences between civil and military law, he was concerned about whether the "spirit" of the civil penal code existed in the military penal code and about inequities in the application of the law to officers and enlisted men. He produced stories and facts to demonstrate that officers were privileged over both civilians and enlisted men. In cases in which a citizen went to prison, an officer was only put under house arrest, and a private got bread and water in isolation. Nor could Lasker accept the practice of allowing a convicted officer to remain in the service at his old rank. Although Lasker obtained no significant victories in this area, his efforts reveal his strong desire for complete uniformity.[14]

In 1875 the imperial chancellor wished to make foreigners responsible before German courts in Germany and, in cases of crimes against Germans committed within foreign states, responsible to the consulate courts abroad. Lasker argued that such a law would produce a situation in which a foreigner would not be punished for an action in Germany against one of his own countrymen but might be punished by German courts if the crime was against a German citizen and was illegal by German standards. Lasker was only calling for reciprocity—uniformity on an international scale—but since the issue involved Polish workers' problems, Bismarck accused Lasker of lacking in patriotism. Denying the accusation, Lasker explained that uniformity of the law was a higher consideration.[15]

With regard to judicial structure, Lasker opposed the creation of separate and special enclaves within the legal system, which violated the principle of a consistent federal law code. To give special powers or rights to commercial courts would fragment legal practice. The same was true, Lasker stated in early 1878, of special courts for political crimes. A year later, after considerable and heated debate over the antisocialist laws, Lasker reiterated that it was "not advisable to subject individual cases to special penal laws and to evade the general rule of the penal code."[16]

The three most important special laws that Lasker attacked related to the Jesuits, the Jews, and the socialists. In 1872, as part of the *Kulturkampf*, the administration introduced a bill to expel the Jesuit order from Germany. In most respects Lasker supported the laws against the Catholic church, known collectively as the May Laws in Prussia; he felt the Catholic church was hostile to progress and to German unification. But he regarded the bill to outlaw the Jesuit order as a special law because it punished a whole group of German citizens without regard for the actions of individual members. Judging by the similarity of reasoning, Lasker may well have been influenced by a letter he received from a colleague, the aging Karl Biedermann, the week before he spoke on the bill. A Saxon historian, editor, and politician, Biedermann argued that the anti-Jesuit bill was a special law in the worst sense, and he pointedly asked what the liberals would have said if earlier there had been a law against the members of the Nationalverein. He confided to Lasker that he would vote against it, even though most of his constituents favored it. He did not care if it split the party, though he was upset and sick over the pressure involved in making the choice. Possessing a stronger stomach, Lasker also voted against the law in full awareness that he was swimming against the current and had almost no hope of success. For him, it was a matter of legal principle.[17]

The religious laws directed at the Catholic church led to Lasker's involvement with the Jewish communities of Prussia, who enjoyed state support in the form of a special law of 1847. Lasker attacked the special laws for the Jews, though himself Jewish, because he thought that all religions should be treated equally under law. Furthermore, this law for the Jews gave secular judges power to decide religious questions that should be outside their jurisdiction. Despite bitter attacks on Eduard Lasker by his fellow Jews, the Prussian Landtag passed legislation in 1876 essentially making Jews subject to the same laws as Christians. Again Lasker stuck to his principle, this time in the face of religious rather than political pressure.[18]

Only a few years later, when the Social Democrats found themselves in a position similar to that of the Jesuits earlier, Lasker again faced a difficult choice. After Max Hödel's attempted assassination of Kaiser Wilhelm I on May 11, 1878, Bismarck blamed the Social Democrats. The political problems generated by this act will be discussed later, but the bill Bismarck quickly introduced to the Reichstag to suppress Social Democracy was a special law—and Lasker fought it. He did not fight because he favored violence or Social Democratic rhetoric; nor did he oppose legal methods to prevent or suppress violence or illegality. He fought it because it was not good law.

Lasker told his colleagues that such a special law had never been submitted to any parliament in a constitutional state. He criticized the law on the grounds that it would be impossible to enforce, or, at least, impossible to enforce fairly. The law failed to define who was a Social Democrat, and it was even vague on what activities were punishable. Moreover, Lasker charged, the draft of the law did not differentiate between Social Democratic goals and methods. Many Social Democrats were innocent of any illegality and should not be judged on the basis of membership in a group. He ridiculed the law's supporters for not even defining the goals of the group they condemned. By contrast, the anti-Jesuit law was at least clearly defined and rigidly written. After bitter debate, Lasker's opposition to the bill triumphed, 251 to 57. Again, Lasker had adhered to principle, this time under enormous pressure from the government, the conservatives, and the right wing of his own party.[19]

Lasker's problems with the antisocialist law were not to be resolved so quickly and successfully. A second attempt on the Kaiser's life on June 27 allowed Bismarck to dissolve the Reichstag and call new elections in an obvious move to change the ideological composition of the National Liberal party and the party alignment in the Reichstag. His intention was clearly to resubmit the antisocialist bill. Bismarck's son Herbert ran against Lasker in Thuringia but was ignominiously forced to withdraw when faced with certain defeat.[20] In his campaign Lasker ridiculed guilt by association and argued that only actions should be subject to prosecution. However, the *Frankfurter Zeitung* detected wavering in the National Liberal opposition to the bill as early as June 27 and in Lasker on August 17, 1878. The paper's reading of the *Berliner Autographische Correspondenz*, controlled by Lasker, seemed to show Lasker ready for a tactical retreat to a compromise. This change of mind was probably inspired by the election results; amid the general bad news for the National Liberals, Franz von Stauffenberg was defeated in Bavaria. On September 12 the *Frankfurter Zeitung* reviewed the lead article in the *Berliner Autographische Correspondenz*, which deemed the antisocialist law a special preventive law and the basis for a police state. But the article also asked whether it might be possible to find a suitable legal mode of expression for it. The *Frankfurter Zeitung* assumed that a logical mind would answer in the negative.[21]

The second clash over the antisocialist law occurred when Bismarck introduced a bill similar to the first in the new fall session. The decline in National Liberal power from 127 to 98 seats in the Reichstag had weakened Lasker's position. Moreover, the second assassination attempt came so soon after the debate on the first bill that it undoubtedly caused many representatives to have second thoughts. The new attempt, coupled with intense propaganda pressure from the government press, changed the public mood to support some kind of repressive legislation. At this point Lasker changed his strategy. Whereas he had earlier condemned the law, he now tried to improve it. On October 11 he spoke in opposition to the inclusion of a prohibition against workers' cooperatives on the grounds that they were not Social Democratic organizations, were apolitical, and were beneficial to Germany through their economic activity. He attacked the bill for specifying supervision by the bureaucracy, especially by the police, and advocated action through the courts as in all other criminal cases. He also repeated his call for prosecution of individual acts, asking rhetorically whether the Reichstag really wished to exclude the Social Democrats from the general law code. But he seems to have known that the answer to his question was "yes."[22]

Lasker also objected to the law's prohibition of public election meetings by the Social Democrats on the grounds that such regulations were completely outside the normal purview of the law. Nor did Lasker have any faith in the ability of the police to determine fairly which meetings should be disbanded. Again Lasker tried to convince the Reichstag that it should differentiate between acts that were legal and harmless and those that were illegal and dangerous.

In the final debate on October 18, he admitted the right of the state to internal self-defense. Although he castigated Bismarck for having created a change in the public mood since May, Lasker capitulated to the obvious demand for a bill and spent much of October working to produce a clear expression of the law. He wished it well understood that transgressions against the state, not Social Democracy itself, were to be punished, but he failed to secure, as he admitted himself, any written guarantees against misinterpretation. Because he had little faith in the government, he asked for and obtained a time limit for the law of two and one-half years; by then, he thought, the danger would be over, and the law could be allowed to lapse. In his concluding speech, he pessimistically reviewed the possibility of the Reichstag seizing the initiative against the administration. Yet he was obviously more afraid of the public's response to the inability of the government and representatives to solve a recognized problem: "So, gentlemen, we must choose one of two evils." Lasker and all ninety-four of his National Liberal colleagues voted for the antisocialist law, and it passed easily, 221 to 149.[23]

Under great pressure Lasker had violated his personal principle of opposition to special laws, and he later told his close relatives that this one vote was the only action in his political career that he clearly regretted. As early as September 1879, he recognized that fair enforcement and reasonable interpretation had not been secured. His unsuccessful opposition to renewal of the law in 1880 was noted by the *Frankfurter Zeitung*, which sarcastically compared it with his 1878 arguments for the bill.[24] The law lapsed in 1890 under quite different circumstances, and it did not work any great effect on German law in general. By the time of Lasker's death, the principle of uniformity in law was fairly well established, despite the antisocialist law. Politically, however, that law seriously affected both the Social Democrats and the National Liberals—and, of course, Eduard Lasker.

Next to legal consistency on Lasker's scale of values stood equitable, intelligent, and independent enforcement of the law by courts and by the bureaucracy. Such enforcement involved the legal system, which was neither unified nor responsible to the legislature. As a member of the Reichstag, Lasker had some power, primarily through passage of legislation, to affect the bureaucracy, but not enough to effect real changes in bureaucratic action. This impotence was a major obstacle to improvement of law enforcement, since many of the basic inequities derived from administrative action. In nineteenth-century Germany, interpretation of law in a formal sense depended largely on the judiciary, assisted by the police and the executive, who together exercised considerable power. As one of his first public acts, Lasker analyzed and criticized the role of law in the Prussian state. His basic complaint was that a hostile legal process, poor judicial action, and biased police enforcement left citizens vulnerable in the enjoyment of their essential rights.[25]

The judicial structure of Prussia had never inspired Lasker's respect. In 1866 his attack on Minister of Justice Graf zur Lippe had really been directed at the judicial system. Especially concerned by the poor preparation of judges, Lasker sarcastically doubted whether there were in all Prussia enough qualified men to fill the 3,843 judicial positions. Moreover, in his opinion, the universities were too theoretical in their training of future jurists. Many young jurists were not personally at fault for their lack of legal knowledge, since they had been co-opted directly into the judicial system from the university without any practical legal experience. The result, Lasker felt, was that too many appointees were poorly informed and lacked independence of judgment.[26]

More significant than lack of sufficient preparation was the tendency of crucial parts of the judicial system to act in a prejudicial manner. In 1866 and 1868 in Prussia, and again in 1874 in Germany, Lasker criticized the legal system for its bias in favor of the prosecution. Trials began with a written summary of an investigation by the prosecutor, which served as the background for the judge's decision, rendered after listening to verbal discussion by both defense and prosecution. According to Lasker, the ultimate decision about the fate of the accused was most often definitively decided at the written level; the verbal process was simply a melodrama. The problem stemmed, he claimed, from an incomplete adoption of the French system of investigatory prosecution: "We have adopted from France the process of prosecution by the state's attorney, but we have simultaneously retained the state monopoly of prosecution. Therefore, while the two parties in the case should appear before the court, private persons are entirely excluded from the right to prosecute." In 1868 he was more damning:

> The complaint arises, not simply in the lower stages but throughout the system, that the prosecution is far better established than the defense, so that one can accurately say that our criminal process is essentially a prosecuting institution. A much higher position is granted to the prosecutor than to the defense; proof of innocence is generally treated with suspicion or reluctance. It has even become normal to emphasize on the first stage of the examination only proof of guilt, and to leave exoneration entirely to the later verbal discussion.

Unlike England, Prussia had no tradition of the "sacred principle of evidence"; rather, justice depended on the outlook of the individual judge. The prosecutor alone had the right of appeal. If he lost in the lower court where one judge ruled, he could try for a three-to-two verdict in a court of second instance or for a four-to-three ruling in a high tribunal.[27]

In his discussion of the procedural practice of the imperial legal system in 1874, Lasker provided a descriptive analysis that nicely supplements his critique of 1868. Prussian legal problems had become German legal problems. Again he complained that the investigatory stage was dominated by the prosecutor, to whom the examining judge deferred; the verbal discussion before the trial judge was not begun until the state's case was so well prepared as to be unshakable. Throughout, Lasker commented, the accused was kept in the dark and could understandably see himself as nonessential to the proceedings. The defendant was not a fully participating member of the process because he had no knowledge of the case the prosecution was building (in the judge's quarters or the police department), but the state often stationed a third person in the jail to report on the discussions between the accused and his counsel. Lasker had no use for this aspect of the civil law, and he accused the state of favoring a system that tried to catch as many defendants as possible by using any legal devices whatsoever.[28]

In many ways Lasker felt that abuses by the police were at least as detrimental to the system as the failings of the judiciary. The problem was made more frustrating because the legislature could exert only indirect control over the police. The tone of many of Lasker's later criticisms of the police may be found in his article, "Police Power and Legal Protection in Prussia," which appeared in Oppenheim's *Deutsche Jahrbücher* in 1861 just before the outbreak of the Conflict Era. The law of May 11, 1842, contained the program of a police state, Lasker began, because it made the securing of a judicial hearing so difficult for the citizen: "Only those who could show that a privileged or contractual right had been infringed by a police regulation could find a path to the judge; appeal on the ground of the general law, on the basis of personal rights, or on the basis of property opened no doors to the judge." Lasker furnished numerous examples of police abuse, most stemming from the 1850s but still prevalent in the early 1860s. The law of January 17, 1845, he argued bitterly, ought to provide for freedom to choose one's occupation, "but who will provide me with the legally guaranteed right to carry on an occupation if the police refuse it or take it away?" In England the police only carried out the law, Lasker noted in 1868, but in Prussia the police so pervaded society that both private and public law had to yield to police power. And this abuse continued because the highest echelons of the state supported the police and protected them.[29]

Lasker not only criticized the absolutist state of the Manteuffel and Puttkamer eras of the 1850s; he also consistently attacked what he considered to be the undue and overweening power of the police in Prussia and Germany. In January 1870 he took to task Rudolf von Gneist, one of the greatest legal historians of his day, and coincidentally also a National Liberal and a former member of the opposition to Bismarck in the *Konfliktszeit*. After peevishly observing that Gneist was not the only font of knowledge about English law, Lasker commented that he could not believe that Gneist had really said that freedom under self-government began with the right of the police to enforce laws without judicial review. The *habeas corpus* laws and the principle of immediate trial by a judge in England proved the contrary. Whereas the police in Prussia could hold a suspect for four-week periods renewed at will, in England such an abuse of individual freedom on mere suspicion of wrongdoing was not possible. Not long after his encounter with Gneist, Lasker spoke directly to the Conservatives in the Reichstag, accusing them of permitting any evil against citizens' rights in order to save their "holy bureaucracy." The Conservatives and their allies responded with laughter, but Lasker continued: "You believe that if you have a powerful police behind you, you have saved the state; that is the agency with which you wish to rule (the right wing laughed and the left applauded) while we wish to have free citizens."[30]

Specifically, Lasker criticized the use of police power by the government: "Wherever one looks the government is ready to act as a police agency. Even where one cannot imagine police activity to be involved, an office which never before carried the title 'police,' appears ready to act as such. Under these conditions all our laws are superfluous." Though the administration claimed that the *Landrat* (district magistrate) was only an instrument of the government, Lasker argued that since 1850 the *Landrat* regarded himself as an independent police official and that the people, including factory owners and landowners, believed he could do anything. Lasker was under no illusions as to whom the *Landräte* owed their allegiance: they had little understanding of the true meaning of their function and less loyalty to parliament and the law than to the state administration. Nor was this police power simply directed against Catholics, as the Centrist Hermann von Malinckrodt claimed. Rather, it was part of the general history of "our" police state.[31]

Although optimistic about the success of codification of the law and confident about the future of Germany and liberalism, Lasker never really moderated his suspicion of the police. Time and again he emphasized his distrust of the police, and he fought any new extension of police powers to political areas such as control of the press. In the uproar over the antisocialist law in 1878, Lasker uncharacteristically voted for a bill that depended for its fair enforcement on the police. Soon recognizing his error, he expended a great deal of effort, unsuccessfully, in protesting application of the law. In 1882, after seventeen years of legislative action (twenty-one as a public figure) against the police, Lasker told the Reichstag that the police had returned to the arrogant and politically tendentious style of the 1850s, to wit, to the Manteuffel era. The German police, he said, were acting in the "Prussian style."[32]

Lasker not only criticized the incestuous relationship between the state and the police; he also charged that the judiciary was influenced by the state through the Ministry of Justice. Count Leopold Lippe, who had been minister of justice during the Era of Conflict, was one of the first ministers to leave after the end of the struggle. Indeed, Lasker contributed forcefully to his downfall through bitter attacks on the floor of the Prussian house. Lasker had no use for the man who had invented the *Lückentheorie* (the "gap" theory by which Bismarck had justified his rule for four years without an approved budget), issued the repressive press decrees of June 1, 1863, refused to pay members of parliament who were also government officials, prosecuted a representative for a speech in the Landtag after a similar case had been thrown out by the high tribunal, and advised the government to sell railroad assets without parliamentary approval. Moreover, Lasker charged, Lippe had misused his power over some four thousand judges and seven thousand lower judicial officials by issuing an election circular urging them to work and vote against the opposition. Lasker further accused Lippe of manipulating salaries, positions, and advancements in favor of pro-government men. In November 1866 he called for Lippe's resignation, which occurred within the year.[33]

In early 1868 Lippe's successor, Gerhard A. W. Leonhardt, was welcomed into his ministership by another speech from Lasker on the subject of state pressure on the judiciary. Lasker's message to Leonhardt was that the state should cease its political interference in judicial administration. He specifically attacked the government's practice of moving judges with liberal sympathies from the criminal to the civil court or from the capital to the provinces. It was especially offensive that such transfers most often occurred following cases involving the political use of the press.[34]

But Lasker could do little more than talk about the need for an independent judiciary, since neither the Landtag nor the Reichstag possessed any significant power over the government. Reform depended upon the good will of the government—ultimately, on Bismarck. Though varying between hostility and neutrality to the liberals, the Iron Chancellor never gave up control of the central administration. Lasker complained as early as 1867 that state examinations for judges did not assure accurate administration of the law. With little success, he tried to secure statutory guarantees that law would be reviewed by the courts, but the weakness of his attempt is apparent in his comments on the projected new imperial Ministry of Justice in 1876: "I hope that for the important offices appropriate appointments will be made, because, basically, that will decide whether the administration of justice of the Reich will be truly independent and not remain what it is presently—an annex of the Prussian Ministry of State." Despite his hopes, the first two ministers of justice were Prussian, and each had advanced to the Reich post from its Prussian equivalent. The imperial Ministry of Justice opened in 1877; in 1878 the state, by Lasker's own description, began the return to reaction.[35]

Control of the police proved equally difficult for Lasker and the left in a constitutional system lacking ministerial responsibility to parliament. On a number of separate occasions Lasker spoke against bills that either allowed for increased police power or were vague enough to permit it. Usually he tried to replace police supervision of laws with judicial review; in any case, he always tried to prevent any increase in the already immense power of the police. Nevertheless, Lasker introduced no legislation to curb police power directly at any time in this period. If the police acted more moderately in the early 1870s, it was not because of legislative action.[36]

Denied a frontal attack on abuses in the "holy bureaucracy," Lasker attempted to undermine the flexibility enjoyed by lower-level bureaucrats, whether judges or policemen, in interpreting the law. The Prussian press refrained from editorial comment, lasker claimed in 1869, because no one was sure how paragraphs 101 and 102 of the penal code, relating to the press, would apply—or, more aptly, be applied by someone unsure of the law. Lasker felt very strongly that unclear and ambiguous laws compounded the built-in problems of hostile state prosecution and biased law enforcement. A partial answer to this problem was to phrase the laws in such a way as to leave little or no doubt in the mind of either policeman or judge as to its meaning. He generally followed this principle carefully, as in 1876, when he demanded that instructions on sentencing be written into the penal code so as to eliminate inequities stemming from differing interpretations.[37]

By 1875 Lasker had recognized that clarity was not enough. As he explained: "A law can almost never be so clear and precise in itself for all cases, that one is generally certain that each man knows the correct legal solution. . . ."[38] In 1876, when the government submitted the draft penal code for the Reich to the Reichstag, Lasker criticized parts of it bitterly, but he distinguished between the system of punishment, which was still archaic, and the improved definitions and descriptions, which he termed the greatest service of the code. However, it still left too much room for subjective interpretation. Lasker argued that in absolutist states a written bill of rights was a necessity because the limits and goals of law were not well enough known and had to be spelled out. Of course, Lasker had not supported such a clause in 1867, and in 1876 there was no going back. His only possible solution was improved wording of existing laws.[39]

At first Lasker conceived of a steady improvement in the judiciary through unification and centralized supervision carried out by higher appellate courts. The main task of such institutions would be to ensure that the lower courts, on whom the burden of work fell, accurately interpreted the law. No law, Lasker believed, should be written in such a way that would allow the judge to act as lawmaker. The law should be clear in itself so that the lawmaker need have no further concern with it. Jealous of the lawmaking ability of parliament, Lasker consistently fought any extension of this function to a judiciary appointed by the government. Even in divorce cases, Lasker opposed allowing a judge to decide on the basis of his own opinion. But his attempt to write exact laws was frustrated by the government's political use of its power to appoint. Lasker complained in 1876 that most influential positions went to conservatives: [political appointments] "appear to me to be the tacit reward by which the minister has reconciled himself for the aid which he gave us for healthy liberal laws." The last hope, according to Lasker, was the high governmental court; but despite the requirement that at least half of the court's members be qualified judges, almost all were ministerial advisers. Since many served simultaneously in the Justice Ministry, Lasker questioned their independence.[40] The situation degenerated further in the Puttkamer era of the 1880s.

Defense against absolutism was not Lasker's only legal objective. On a number of occasions he advocated other reforms of the law with varying degrees of success. More important to the historian than the numerous individual cases is Lasker's attitude that the need for changes in the law came from a changing society. He argued for new laws on commerce because the old were hindering rather than encouraging the flow of credit. Since society now needed credit, the laws should be changed. The same conscious effort to change the structure of the legal system to reflect the needs of society more precisely may also be found in Lasker's legislative action on all substantive problems. In no case should theory outweigh social necessity. For this reason Lasker was willing to go much further than many of his contemporaries in changing the law.[41]

Reason and humanitarianism, according to Lasker, should accompany adjustment to the changing needs of society. In most cases he used reason and compassion as arguments in support of laws that were essentially practical. Harsh prison conditions were inhumane; they were also hated by the people and caused bad publicity in the rest of Europe. Laws that were vague or biased were also hard to enforce. Discriminatory laws, such as those against Jesuits or socialists, were inequitable; they were also dangerous because they caused more hate than they prevented. Lasker supported few causes on entirely rational or moral grounds or for solely humanitarian ends. Yet, though oriented primarily to the practical side of life, Lasker was also committed to a rational approach to law and legislation, commenting in 1868 that "if one separated the *Rechtsleben* from scientific development, the genuine, true source of law would dry up." He understood science, in its broadest sense, as implying rationality.[42]

One of the few major issues superficially humanitarian in content that Lasker supported was abolition of the death penalty in the North German penal code (see Table 4.1). Yet even here Lasker thought in practical terms. He reasoned that the safety of the state did not depend on hanging, that the pardons currently granted in four-fifths of the cases did not endanger order, and that abolition would be a strong point in favor of unity with South Germany. He also appealed to morality, attacking the death penalty as a solution that eliminated all chance of personal reform and redemption. He used Jewish law (a rare occurrence for Lasker) as an underpinning to his argument, maintaining that even in the Old Testament the application of the death penalty had been severely modified. And he questioned, but did not oppose, the right of a state to take the life of a person. Realizing that public opinion was not behind him, he nevertheless believed that educated people agreed with him, and he urged his colleagues to take the lead rather than wait until the whole country was behind them. In the end Lasker accepted a new penal code that did not abolish the death penalty because he did not feel that one part of an entire code ought to be more important than the whole.[43]

Two groups of bills voted upon in the North German Reichstag and in the German Reichstag provide an excellent basis for analyzing Lasker's use of the law to promote political progress. In the 1867–1870 session the issue was political agitation and the application of legal sanctions against instigators. On the first three bills (see Table 4.2), numbers 69–71, dealing with the wording of the laws, Lasker opted for clarity and precision. But he could not agree to Bill No. 72, which would have made it permissible to advocate illegal actions publicly. He also opposed eliminating the six-week minimum sentence for agitation among the military. Moreover, he opposed Bill No. 74, which would have curtailed the government's right to monitor agitators. His opposition to Bill No. 75, to punish those who verbally denigrated the state, the last in this series, is not a contradiction; Lasker probably considered such a loosely written law to be of dubious legality. Taken as a whole, this series of votes shows Lasker to be concerned with clear wording of laws but fully in favor of punishing those who would use illegal activities to oppose the state. On all votes the National Liberal party and its Executive Committee were in general harmony, though the absentee rate was quite high, indicating possible latent disagreement. Only one Executive Committee member, Wilhelm Wehrenpfennig, a right-leaning member, broke ranks. Lasker always voted with the majority of the party and agreed with the Reichstag in only two cases.

In the 1874–1877 session of the German Reichstag, Lasker voted on a series of important bills affecting the legal status of the press. His record, partly shown in Table 4.3, indicates that he accepted the principle that the press should be legally liable for any articles that it financed that encouraged illegal actions. However, he wanted a jury trial, a limit to the number of those responsible, and protection of the publisher's right to withhold knowledge

Table 4.1

Reichstag Roll-Call Votes on Bills Relating to the Death Penalty,
1870

| | | Number Voting | | | | | | | | |
| | | In the Reichstag | | In the NL Party | | In the NL Exec. Comm. | | | | |
Bill Id	Content (Date)	Yes	No	Yes	No	Yes	No	Abs.[a]	RvB[b]	EL[c]
	(1)	(2)	(3)	(4)	(5)	(6)	(7)	(8)	(9)	(10)
62	Abolition (March 1, 1870)	118	81	2	51	2	9	5	N	Y
65	Abolition only in cases of treason (March 16, 1870)	104	99	54	2	12	0	4	Y	Y
92	To include the death penalty (May 23, 1870)	127	119	22	44	3	12	1	N	N
93	Murder of king-princes punishable by death (May 24, 1870)	128	107	21	41	4	10	2	N	Y

Source: All roll-call votes are taken from the *Generalregister zu den stenographischen Berichten über die Verhandlung und die amtlichen Drucksachen des constituirenden Reichstages des norddeutschen Bundes, des deutschen Zollparlaments und des deutschen Reichstages vom Jahre 1867 bis einschliesslich der am 24. Mai 1895 geschlossen III. Session 1894–95* (Berlin, 1896).
Note: The "Bill Id" was assigned by the *Generalregister* to all bills in chronological sequence.
[a]Abs. = absent
[b]RvB = Rudolf von Bennigsen
[c]EL = Eduard Lasker

about an author. Lasker voted to limit the chancellor's power to control distribution of condemned foreign publications in Germany. The bill mandating a jury trial in press cases passed easily, but it revealed the old right-left split in the National Liberal party (77 to 54). Though not visible in the laws themselves, all of these discussions of agitation and the press concerned the political role of the German Social Democratic party in some way.

Lasker's position on legislation directly relating to agitation, free speech, and the press was not radical, though it was solidly liberal. He argued that openness in society was good in the long run and that free discussion of any topic would eventually work to the benefit of society. He obviously drew a line between discussion of alternatives and any form of active

Table 4.2

Reichstag Roll-Call Votes on Bills Relating to Agitation,
1870

		Number Voting								
		In the Reichstag		In the NL Party		In the NL Exec. Comm.				
Bill Id	Content (Date)	Yes	No	Yes	No	Yes	No	Abs.[a]	RvB[b]	EL[c]
	(1)	(2)	(3)	(4)	(5)	(6)	(7)	(8)	(9)	(10)
69	Better wording (March 19, 1870)	88	109	41	12	12	0	4	Y	Y
70	Better wording (March 19, 1870)	110	86	52	1	12	0	4	Y	Y
71	Better wording (March 19, 1870)	87	109	43	8	10	1	5	Y	Y
72	To punish agitators (March 19, 1870)	110	78	0	49	0	12	4	N	N
73	To eliminate 6 week minimum sentence (March 21, 1870)	94	89	1	46	0	9	7	Abs.[a]	N
74	To abolish police surveillance of agitators (March 21, 1870)	82	94	2	38	0	8	8	Abs.[a]	N
75	To punish those who make the state despicable (March 23, 1870)	111	88	10	39	0	11	5	Abs.[a]	N

Source: Roll-call votes are taken from the *Generalregister*. See source to Table 4.1.
Note: The "Bill Id" was assigned by the *Generalregister* to bills in chronological sequence.
[a]Abs.= absent
[b]RvB = Rudolf von Bennigsen
[c]EL = Eduard Lasker

revolution.[44]

To Lasker, the fundamental aspects of the legal system that he had helped to formulate for Germany were its uniformity and its increased emphasis on the courts rather than on administrative officials. Very much disturbed by the antagonisms aroused, most bitterly on the left, by the passage of the legal code of 1876, Lasker tried to justify his actions to the public in a leng-

Table 4.3

Reichstag Roll-Call Votes on Bills Relating to Press Offenses,
1874–1876

		Number Voting								
		In the Reichstag		In the NL Party		In the NL Exec. Comm.				
Bill Id	Content (Date)	Yes	No	Yes	No	Yes	No	Abs.[a]	RvB[b]	EL[c]
	(1)	(2)	(3)	(4)	(5)	(6)	(7)	(8)	(9)	(10)
180	To prohibit financing of illegal acts (March 19, 1874)	162	159	108	12	17	2	5	Y	Y
181	To prohibit financing of illegal acts (March 19, 1874)	158	148	109	7	19	0	5	Y	Y
184	Control of the foreign press (March 24, 1874)	156	162	13	108	3	16	5	Abs.[a]	Y
202	Jury trial in press cases (November 22, 1876)	212	105	77	54	18	4	2	Y	Y
206	Freedom from testimony for publishers (November 28, 1876)	238	50	105	16	21	0	3	Y	Y
209	State laws on press to stand (December 19, 1876)	198	146	131	3	23	0	1	Y	Y
210	Press offenses illegal only in areas where published (December 20, 1876)	195	124	1	133	0	23	1	N	N
211	Repeat of 206 (December 20, 1876)	186	120	3	126	1	22	1	N	N

Source: Roll-call votes are taken from the *Generalregister*. See source to Table 4.1.
Note: The "Bill Id" was assigned by the *Generalregister* to bills in chronological sequence.
[a]Abs. = absent
[b]RvB = Rudolf von Bennigsen
[c]EL = Eduard Lasker

thy brochure entitled *The Struggle over the Judicial Code*. He recognized the drawbacks of the new code, including the smaller number of judges, the failure to regulate the state's attorneys better, the immunity of officials from prosecution, and the continued power of the prosecution. Yet, although it might take years, men would eventually realize that the successes were greater than the deficiencies. Lasker especially valued the increased independence of the judiciary, the use of a jury in press offenses, the establishment of a supreme court to review lower court procedures, the limitation of press responsibility, and the elimination of prejudicial summation in jury trials. In 1876 Lasker valued the new code as a step in the right direction. He seems to have felt, as he did on other issues, that the direction would not substantially change.[45]

Based on his own explanation of his position on legislation, Lasker stood in the mainstream of the German civil law tradition. Though he differed with men like F. K. von Savigny and even Gneist, Lasker supported only those reforms in the legal structure that promised to eliminate the worst vestiges of the eighteenth-century absolutist state. He knew much of the English common law tradition but emphasized the importance of the written law as a protection against capricious interpretation. For him, the key to an effective judicial system was the intelligence of the lawgiver and the competence of the law interpreter in *knowing* the law. Lasker represents the tendency among nineteenth-century German lawmakers to reform the law without severely changing the system or seriously limiting the power of the state over the judiciary. Under such conditions, any significant future progress of the legal system in Germany depended on the progress of the state.[46]

V

The Power of the Constitution

> "Lawmaking activity begins with the discussions of
> the lower house."
>
> Eduard Lasker, 1862

> "We, the Reichstag deputies, are the living source of
> law . . . ."
>
> Eduard Lasker, 1869

No other area of state and national history provides so convenient a basis for cross-national comparison as does constitutional analysis. It is possible to date accurately the emergence of constitutional ideas and programs, pre-representative governmental forms, and, finally, acceptance of some form of constitution. According to traditional wisdom, constitutions are a Western European product, originating in England and moving eastward in the course of the eighteenth and nineteenth centuries.[1] Germany experienced the problems of modern constitutional development beginning in the early nineteenth century—relatively late by contrast to the rest of Europe.[2]

The major battles of constitutional history were over by 1715 in England, 1787 in the United States, and 1815 in France. By these dates the essence of Western constitutionalism—substantial direct control over government through some form of popular representation—had been established. However, severe struggles over the extent of control and the degree of representation continued throughout the nineteenth century. The Napoleonic wars had exposed German politicians, statesmen, and intellecuals to French constitutional ideas. After 1815, constitutionalism made its appearance in Germany despite the energetic resistance of almost all governments. The early stages of German constitutional development owed a great deal to the Western European experience.

In retrospect, the year 1848 can be identified as the point of emergence for constitutionalism in Prussia. Both the constitution written by the revolution and that decreed by the king in 1849 permitted substantial control over monarchical government by a parliament. Much of South Germany had received constitutions during the Napoleonic occupation and retained them afterward; especially after 1830, some North German states either wrote constitutions or reformed older ones. Prussia's significance for German consitutional development stems from its position as the largest and most powerful German state outside Austria and from the model its constitution provided for the constitutions of the North German Confederation and the Second Reich.

The remnants of the constitutional forces of 1848 were too weak to defend themselves successfully in the Prussian assembly in Berlin. From 1850 to 1858 they did nothing but protest feebly against the Manteuffel regime. The liberals' second major attempt to exercise substantial control over the government began in 1861 with the issue of army reform and relied on the budget clause of the decreed constitution of 1850 rather than on the barricades of 1848. By 1865 the contest had become a waiting game: the Prussian Landtag waited to see how long Bismarck could govern without a new budget and higher taxes, and the king waited to see if Bismarck could secure either without loss of state power. Bismarck may have toyed with alternative solutions, but his opponents seem to have had no viable alternative to waiting; they rejected revolution and would not even consider refusal to pay taxes in protest against an "illegal" budget. The military victory at Königgrätz in July 1866 effectively ended the second attempt at parliamentary control of the Prussian state.

It is important to recognize the difference between constitutional rights and their exercise. Nineteenth-century Germany displayed many gaps between constitutional theory and practice. In evaluating German constitutionalism, one must distinguish between a right and the ability to implement it; for example, in budgetary matters the legal basis to deny the government a budget existed, although few German assemblies ever managed to do so. The *Königsberg Hartungsche Zeitung* recognized this gap between theory and practice in 1862: "Parliamentary government is not a legal question but a question of power and, as such, the product of development. No letter of the law can bring it about; only a series of legal battles, of surmounted illusions and disillusions, of long experience can do so."[3]

There was no unified third attempt to control the Prussian government through a test of power. But after the war with Austria the liberal opposition initiated a number of constitutional changes that sought to establish greater parliamentary control over the government. In this third, inglorious epoch Eduard Lasker, one of the most powerful proponents of change, played an important role in political attempts at parliamentary dominance.

Lasker was not a political theorist or academician, but as a liberal politician active during an era in which absolutism began to lose its grip on Prussia, he was greatly concerned with the structure of the state. Most of the changes made in these years were conceived in the heat of political struggle and guided, sometimes erratically, to completion by men like Lasker. Lasker's views on what a constitution could and should do were unsystematic and biased in favor of those changes that could most profoundly move society in a liberal direction. This concern was natural for a young lawyer who matured during the reactionary 1850s and entered political life after 1858, but it makes analysis of his constitutional ideas very difficult. Nevertheless, the development of Lasker's thought can be traced in four major areas: the purpose of the constitution, the structure of the state, the power of the legislature relative to that of the executive, and the role of local self-government.

The Constitution

Few writings of German politicians of the 1860s provide the historian with a better insight into the opposition to absolutism than the essays by Lasker that appeared in the *Deutsche Jahrbücher* between 1861 and 1864. In one essay after another Lasker dissected and criticized the Prussian constitution of 1850 and its administration by the state. Pinpointing the major shortcoming of the constitution as its weak protection for civil liberties, he commented that the document had obviously been written by reluctant hands, since "limits are established for the state power, but are left undefined." It offered no security against invasion of privacy, no way to preserve constitutional rights, and no control over the government, since ministerial responsibility was only a vague theory. The Prussian Constitution might appear modern to the shallow-minded, Lasker sarcastically wrote, but the probing statesman would recognize the appearance of modernity as illusory.[4]

Yet the constitution was not wholly useless, and Lasker believed it could have become far more than an illusion. Lasker noted that Prussia's first parliamentary epoch actually began with the regency of 1858 "in the sense that the results depended on the disposition of parliament and the relation of the government to parliament." The key was the king. Lasker recognized his importance and power as established by the 1850 constitution, but he carefully pointed out that, although monarchy made the person of the king inviolable, the constitution gave responsibility to the ministers. Under absolutism the king had exercised sole decision-making power over the definition of citizenship, or so Lasker thought, but the constitution abolished this arbitrary choice. Even at the height of the conflict in Prussia, Lasker was convinced that the existing constitution made all acts subject to law and therefore not absolutist. Even those powers of the king that were not regulated by law depended upon the structure as a whole: "A governmental act that does not respect the laws lacks legality. For that reason each government act is subject to the responsibility of the minister (Article 44)."[5] Within the government, however, the king's ministers operated almost completely without oversight, as Lasker demonstrated at great length in his articles on the judiciary and the police. Although irritated at the absolutist actions of the Prussian state in the 1850s, Lasker then (and later) felt that the constitution could be made to work with relatively simple modifications.[6]

In this respect, Lasker's sentiments were shared by almost all liberals and democrats. They hated Bismarck before 1866 because he violated the Prussian Constitution. One of Lasker's reasons for accepting the decreed constitution of 1850 was that it reflected what he perceived to be the needs of society, as he believed every constitution should. Unlike F. K. von Savigny, Lasker thought that the Prussian Constitution was historically sound because it had replaced outmoded absolutism with representation and open discussion. In his opening speech in the North German Reichstag Lasker emphasized that constitutions must of necessity conform to the needs of the people—to their cultural, educational, and national life. In the 1871 debate over Alsace-Lorraine, he protested that legal and constitutional regulations should not be drafted until after the Reichstag determined the needs and the desires of the people. In "Cosmpolitan and National Wisdom" Lasker criticized the adaptation of foreign constitutions without knowledge of the basic facts about Germany, explaining that there was "an interaction between the rule of reason and the form of state conditions." His posthumously published attempt at a political memoir is an essay in Prussian history that underlines his lifelong belief in the linear historical development of Germany. In short, Lasker believed that constitutions should derive from the country's needs and that the Prussian-German document did so.[7]

There is no doubt that Lasker conceived of the constitution as a mechanism that would help to solve Germany's problems by reconciling the people of the various regions and different classes through common representation. He melodramatically proclaimed the "Word" to be the most powerful weapon, "for only the convincing or persuasive Word destroys isolation, builds powerful organizations, and trains a real corps of leaders." Lasker argued that lack of opportunity for free discussion had caused many of the revolutions since 1789 and certainly underlay the movements of 1846–1848 in Germany. Despite setbacks in almost all other areas, the great triumph of 1848 was the right to free discussion guaranteed by the Prussian Constitution. Although powerful special interests, especially landowners, threatened to curtail open discussion, Lasker argued that the masses were potentially more powerful but must be persuaded to support change. He believed that the proper arena for open discussion was parliament, which had been given unlimited lawmaking power by the constitution. With the concurrence of the king and the upper house, admittedly not always an easy matter, the lower house could pass any law. As such, parliament was a process available to all and thus the best way to resolve political conflict.[8]

His acceptance of the constitutions of 1850 and 1867 did not mean that Lasker ceased all efforts to improve them, only that parliamentarianism was his chosen method for changing the constitution or the state structure. Though recognizing the serious drawbacks of the system, he still felt that the parliamentary process was the best way of securing results. Since the form the state would take was the most pressing and far-reaching question in the early period, it ought to be treated first.

The State

There is no doubt that Lasker favored a centralized state. He worked for it from the first, calling in 1866 for a "responsible" government instead of control by a loose confederation based on treaties. Eventually he accepted a compromise that has been very important for modern German history: a combination of centralism (the Reichstag and the chancellorship) and confederation (the Bundesrat). He emphatically rejected union based on military treaties as too dangerous in its tendency towards absolutism. And he accepted the proposed *Bundesstaat* (centralized confederacy) because it allowed for national and liberal expression in the Reichstag. Overemphasis on states' rights in a confederation without a Reichstag could lead, Lasker told the North German Reichstag in 1868, to civil war, as it had in North America. He essentially agreed with Treitschke, who argued that in a *Staatenbund* (confederation) the states rather than the citizens were the constituent elements. After he accepted the constitution of 1867, Lasker lost no opportunity to add power to the central state and to withhold it from the Bundesrat. A nation possessing one law, one language, and one moral code should not, in Lasker's opinion, live under the disunity of a confederation, as in Switzerland or the United States.[9]

On innumerable occasions Lasker supported centralization. He worked for a separate income for the Reich, helped to solidify the Reich's taxing power, and opposed whenever possible the Reich's dependence on monetary contributions from the member states in the form of mixed prorated quotas. The army was a Reich matter, Lasker stated in 1872, and not at all a concern of the individual states. He fervently supported the right of the Reichstag to legislate in all areas for the whole Reich, modified only by specific constitutional provision. If a local state law conflicted with a Reich law, the latter, according to Lasker, must prevail. He warned that the country would be thrown into anarchy if each individual state retained power of review over Reich laws. And because he feared the pro-Catholic attitudes of states like Bavaria, he supported Reich control over education.[10]

If there is no question about Lasker's desire for a strong, centralized state, his attitude toward individual states, such as Prussia and Bavaria, is not always clear. At first glance, his record on the relation of Prussia to Germany appears to be contradictory—at times criticizing Prussia as too absolutist, at other times praising it as the salvation of Germany. Notwithstanding these apparent variations, there is an underlying consistency in Lasker's political record. He desired and defended Prussia's dominant role in the Bundesrat, where it possessed enough votes to veto any constitutional amendment and where an anti-Prussian veto would depend on an improbable coalition of all non-Prussian delegates. As early as 1867 Lasker expressed concern over this clause as a source of potential weakness if the South joined the opposition already present in the North German Confederation. When South German membership in the confederation appeared imminent in 1870, Lasker argued that Prussian approval should be required for all constitutional changes. He wrote a Southern friend only days later that, although the fourteen-vote veto in the Bundesrat was a weakness, it had some justification, and he did not believe that it would prevent the development of the Reich in the near future. Should the South or the small states form a coalition to oppose necessary legislation in the Bundesrat, it would be necessary for Prussia to use the power of the Reichstag "in order to reform these dangerous aspects." Hence, Lasker's willingness to grant Prussia a privileged position in the Bundesrat stemmed more from distrust of the South, desire for basic centralization, and faith in future Reichstag reform than from trust in Prussia.[11]

Prussian dominance in almost any other area of domestic affairs frightened Lasker. He desired a new, independent parliament for both the North German Confederation and the empire. His fear of Prussia may well have been a reason, unvoiced, for his eventual, reluctant support for universal male suffrage both in the confederation and in the Reich. On judicial matters Lasker often tried to use the confederation or the empire to secure progressive laws that were difficult to obtain in Prussia. He told the Reichstag in 1869: "We . . . made no secret in previous years that the drawbacks and the [unfavorable] conditions in Prussia induced us to introduce legislation [here] applicable to the whole confederation." Lasker warned the Reichstag that the opponents of free speech in Prussia wished that the same restrictions existed in the confederation. In the spring of 1870 he criticized Bismarck's control of the foreign policy of Prussia and of the confederation, and in 1872 he spoke against locating imperial ministers in Berlin, hoping that ministerial control of the budget would not develop as it had in Prussia. On still other occasions Lasker refused to give Prussia special legal consideration, arguing that to do so would infringe upon the competence and equality of the confederation.[12]

South Germany was a different problem entirely, partly because of its anti-Prussian, Catholic, and rural character, and partly because of the circumstances of its union with the North German Confederation during the war with France. Lasker's record of strong support for the merger of North and South is marred only by Bismarck's accusation that his willingness to concede too much in private conversations with Bavarian leaders forced the chancellor to grant more autonomy to Bavaria than he had desired. In letters to Bamberger, which he asked not to be published, Lasker denied that he had in any way given up meaningful advantages, and he accepted full responsibility for his conversations in the South. He reminded Bamberger that he had changed his mind on some points, including his original opposition to separation of finances in the military budget. Bamberger admitted that Lasker appeared innocent, although Bismarck's irritation at Lasker and Lasker's irritation at the Bavarian leaders for using his conversations to gain advantages was very real.[13]

In fact, Lasker's stand on the conditions of South German admission to the Reich is consistent with his stand on the structure of the German state. However the Bavarian negotiators used them, Lasker's talks, letters, and working drafts of constitutional modifications affecting the South all reveal a strong desire to avoid any exceptions on fundamental issues such as centralized finance, a unified legal system, and imperial military control. Lasker wrote to his colleagues Max von Forckenbeck and Rudolf von Bennigsen on October 6 that, according to confederation law, he could not accept the Bavarian demand for the independent administration of the army in Bavaria. He made no comment on the Bavarian desire to retain an independent legal system but seemed to agree with Rudolf von Delbrück that control of the post, the telegraph, and the beer tax were not of basic importance. On the twenty-third of October he reported to Delbrück his fear of Bavaria's desire for independence on the military budget. The next day Lasker felt compelled to inform Bennigsen that he could not, as Bennigsen had, allow Bavaria an absolute veto on the extent of Reich jurisdiction. He reported to Delbrück again that merger with one or all of the South German states would not necessitate major alterations in the North German Confederation, although some changes would be unavoidable. The important point, according to Lasker, was to extend the confederation to both parts of Germany, waiting until after acceptance to push for reform. But changes were not to be made at the expense of the unity of the Reich on a sound constitutional basis: "Where this danger threatens, the legitimate desire to realize the goal now must yield."[14]

The draft memorandum that Lasker forwarded to Delbrück listed and commented on all the major points at issue, although apparently not in any order of priority. The competence of the confederation as it existed, Lasker claimed, must not be altered in any particulars, as for example over the legal system. If Bavaria would not accept equal treatment, then "two classes of confederation would be constructed." Lasker wished Bavaria to recognize clearly that it was entering a confederaton in which Prussia retained its veto power. To allow a second veto would cripple the confederation; Prussia, on the other hand, presented no threat because its power was the same as the confederation's. Prussia was not an exception, Lasker argued; rather, it was the basis of the state. Legislatively, the Reichstag would simply add the South German districts that composed the Zollparlament. Lasker wanted an executive in the form of a federal chancellory competent to enforce Reich laws everywhere in Germany, although judicial review would be vested in a supreme court. Establishment of new institutions, such as the court, were not to be excluded from the jurisdiction of the Reichstag. Finally, Lasker's draft emphasized that individual state financial administration was not permissible, since it would split the confederation: "Common financial needs and revenues constitute the focus of any state's essence." Lasker undoubtedly shared the fear of his friend and colleague Eduard Simson that if Bavaria had its way, the Reich would become a second Austria.[15]

When the South German Julius von Hölder later raised the question of the degree to which the National Liberal party in the South could campaign for centralization, Lasker recognized the problem. His reply is a candid and fairly complete summary of his basic goals:

> We will not encroach upon the fruitful activity of individual federal states or ever seek to impose on the Reich anything unnecessary out of a narrow desire for centralization, but we will strive for everything the Reich needs to give it the full power of a federal state, and, where necessary, [we will] add correctives to the constitution in this sense. Above all, we wish to construct, besides common laws, common organizations and institutions which will give these laws reality and authority in all areas of the Reich. For example: [we wish] a well-organized imperial ministry, a court which will defend the higher authority of the imperial laws over the state laws, and similar institutions.[16]

In the end Lasker voted for the treaties with Bavaria and Württemberg, even though they contained decentralizing tendencies. The North German Reichstag voted 195 to 32 for acceptance, with the National Liberals contributing 60 of their 62 votes for approval, including a unanimous vote by the party Executive Committee. Lasker explained to Gustav Freytag that his vote was intended to establish the Reich on a constitutional footing that could later be improved. But he was not happy with the Bavarian treaties and expressed his irritation in numerous private letters. Yet when it came to the final question of approval or rejection of a new Reich, Lasker later stated publicly in the Reichstag in 1873 that there had been only one answer:

> Does anyone in the hall today regret our decision? I recognize that the union with Bavaria retards our domestic development in many ways, not only as Representative

Richter thinks in the resubmittal of bills and in the energetic opposition which this
necessitates; no, the entrance of Bavaria—as anyone who has experienced the preli-
minaries knows—must be an obstacle to the progress of the Reich. But it was necessary to accept even this humiliation in order to make the Reich complete.[17]

In fact, the treaties with South Germany that established the Second Reich modified the form
of the Bund only in regard to the Bundesrat, where the conservative and decentralizing forces
received some support and where Prussian dominance slipped a trifle. To be sure, the admission to the new state of millions of Catholic South Germans represented a sizable demographic
and political change, but it was hardly an immediate threat to the Reich, and it did not change
the form of the state. Economically, the entry of the South introduced a new element that
eventually favored protective tariffs, but these interests remained ineffective until supported by
Bismarck, the Northern manufacturing interests, and the East Elbian landowners in the economic crisis of the 1870s. The constitution of 1870–1871 differed from that of 1867 in only one
other respect—the complete lack of any constitutional convention.

Histories of the *Reichsgründung* are quick to point out Bismarck's hostility in 1870 to any
discussion of the treaties or constitutional changes by representatives elected from all over
Germany. Yet most fail to note that liberals like Lasker agreed wholeheartedly with Bismarck.
It is startling to read Lasker's arguments against a popular assembly, knowing his fervent support for the representative principle and his record of hard work in the 1867 constituent
Reichstag. His first specific mention of the problem appears in a letter to Delbrück on
September 24, 1870, in which he states: "Practically there follows, among other things, no
wish for a new constitutional Reichstag, but rather simply for an extension of the Bund and the
acceptance of logical modifications to the present constitutional procedures. It would be very
complicated if the flood gates of desire were opened before the Bund secured and constitutionally established itself." The rest of the letter reiterates in greater detail his belief that, as in the
petition to the king of Bavaria, the nationalists wanted only an extension of the Bund that
would preserve its centralized nature and retain the power of Prussia.[18]

The question of whether to hold a new constitutional convention became a political problem
when the Central Committee of the Progressive party publicly proposed it. Lasker immediately
objected to any convention and even managed partially to convince Hermann Schulze-Delitzsch
of the dangers and complexity of such an assembly. He wanted to prevent the honorable
members of the Progressive party from once again causing failure by adopting an unsupportable
position. He related the news of the Progressive declaration to Marquard Barth in Munich,
adding that few Progressives endorsed it and predicting its failure: "We do not believe that a
public controversy is necessary, especially since the present conditions warn against any unne-
cessary political struggle." To Simson on October 2, Lasker mentioned some parliamentary difficulties to avoid because there should be no struggle between allies on questions of form. His
concern was "how to negotiate without appearing to dictate." He explained the situation to
Forckenbeck and Bennigsen in a letter four days later, mentioning his talk with Schulze-
Delitzsch and concluding: "Neither side desires a controversy, and I give no great weight to the
declaration." In November, German political attention turned to the North German Reichstag,
where the decision would be made.[19]

Lasker wanted no serious discussion of a constitutional convention in the Reichstag, since it
might open a Pandora's box of argumentation and perhaps cause the failure of the treaties. In
late September Lasker wrote to Barth of his hope that no *party* interest would interfere with the
great national work. The best defense against any opposition, he noted, was to hold fast to the
existing constitution of the North German Confederation and look for reforms only within this

context. He told Delbrück that he hoped no structural change would occur now and that any such change should be left to the next regular Reichstag. Until peace was made, no one wanted long, drawn-out parliamentary debates. Lasker expressed the wish that the debates on acceptance of the treaties with the South would proceed as quickly as possible. The result was a short session and easy approval with little substantive discussion.[20]

What Lasker secured through his support of Bismarck's diplomatic action vis-à-vis the South was not only a larger territorial basis for the old 1867 constitution but also a new distribution of internal political forces. His later problems in trying to change the structure of the German state stemmed not only from the constitution but also from this new political base. In this respect the strength of the representative element within the governmental structure was of crucial importance.

The Legislature

It is impossible to point to a constitution created after 1789 that does not include a representative body of some type, and it is probably fair to say that the parliament was the soul of the German constitution. Lasker certainly thought so: he spent a disproportionally large amount of his political efforts attempting to produce the right balance of force between the legislative and executive branches. Parliament's importance for Lasker stemmed from its duty to make laws. "Lawmaking activity begins with the discussions of the lower house," he wrote in 1862. Legislative law was better than decreed law because it was more permanent and possessed a closer, more genuine relation to society. Moreover, a strong parliament would present no threat to the central power. "We are," he solemnly told his colleagues, "the living source of law; we will be called upon to interpret life." In the Germany of 1867 and especially of 1871, Lasker saw parliament as a unifying element in contrast to the particularistic Bundesrat.[21]

The lawmaker in such a parliament would be important, and Lasker laid great emphasis on his character, representative duties, and independence. In the Era of Conflict, he admitted, intelligence and discernment had not always been necessary or desirable qualities in a legislator; he needed to know little more than which side to support, and often he understood almost nothing about politics. But the new constitution for the North German Confederation made that style of politics obsolete. After 1867 Lasker urged that representatives be chosen for their foresight and intelligence and for their willingness to oppose the will of the people when necessary. He later fervently criticized Catholics, workers, and Jews for claiming representation only or primarily by certain legislators or parties. Lasker consistently and emphatically argued that every member of parliament represented *all* the people, although in making the laws or acting on policy each should vote his own mind. In the fight over the abolition of the death penalty, Lasker asked the representatives to have the leadership and courage to vote against the will of the people. He did not agree with the extreme position espoused by Georg Freiherr von Vincke, who claimed that a representative should avoid any overt contact with voters. But he felt that a representative had a duty to vote his conscience in the Reichstag while remaining faithful to the true interests of the people. He showed on numerous occasions that he was conscious of public opinion on crucial issues, and he campaigned vigorously, when forced to, in his own electoral districts. He would have agreed completely with Heinrich von Treitschke's 1861 Kantian formulation of a code for the good legislator: "What you do in order to purify, mature, and liberate yourself, do also for your people!"[22]

For a truly representative and independent parliament to emerge, several changes in the electoral system of 1866 had to occur. Among the first problems Lasker faced was whether to support universal or limited suffrage. He hesitated to accept the direct, equal, and secret ballot in the mid–1860s. Yet, although he may have been a late convert to the cause of universal suffrage, he soon became a staunch proponent of it within the Reich—but not in Prussia, and especially not on the local level. As his liberal friend Hans Viktor von Unruh noted in his diary of 1867, no one really expected the success of this radical step, and all were concerned about the future results of giving decision-making power to the propertyless and uneducated masses. The program issued by the National Liberal party in Berlin in June 1867 declared its support for universal suffrage. But the party was unaware of the possibility of the reform's perversion in a society controlled by a hostile bureaucracy and denied freedom of the press, assembly, and association. On the eve of the first election to the North German Reichstag on Febuary 11, 1867, Lasker confided to his friend Berthold Auerbach that the next day would show whether the first results of the expanded suffrage would really mean the true emancipation of the people. He was satisfied, though not exuberant, about its effect; on later occasions he referred to universal suffrage as an agency of political education.[23]

Yet Lasker never thought that universal suffrage was applicable to all situations. Although he eventually worked for its extension to Prussia, he opposed its introduction to local elections in the *Kreisordnungen* (county ordinances) of 1872. He contended that it was not good sense to allow those who paid no taxes to decide how other people's money should be spent. For Lasker the problem resided not in voting regulations but in the willingness of the local community, and especially the landowners, to work selflessly for the common good. He attacked the Center party's support of universal suffrage as motivated solely by the thought of the easy votes they might obtain. In turn, the *Frankfurter Zeitung* ridiculed Lasker's "platonic" attachment to universal suffrage, charging that he had forgotten his own past as an oppositionist and that it was unfair to fear parties with "destructive" tendencies. In 1876 Lasker criticized the Prussian *Dreiklassensystem* (three-class electoral system) on the state level but defended its use in the *Gemeinde*. The head of the Social Democrats, August Bebel, castigated Lasker as the leader of the liberal opposition to universal suffrage in the community and asked how he could have won in Frankfurt am Main without the three-class voting system. The *Frankfurter Zeitung* often took Lasker to task for his divided, conflicting positions on universal suffrage. On August 22, 1877, it noted the discrepancy between Lasker's position on suffrage in Reich and *Gemeinde*, suggesting in a telling argument that Lasker feared that the increasingly leftist and anti-National Liberal tendency of the Berlin voters would spread to the industrial Rhineland and that socialists might profit from a system of universal suffrage. Although Lasker never admitted it, the *Frankfurter Zeitung* may well have been correct: Lasker feared the political force of the Social Democrats in the 1870s. Nor was Lasker alone in his fears. His close political ally Bamberger deplored the unthinking acceptance of universal suffrage. On the other hand, right-wing liberals on the staff of the *Preussische Jahrbücher* regarded any trust in the masses as a "charming illusion" nourished by liberals like Lasker.[24]

Aware that equitable representation did not stem solely from the right to vote, Lasker worked hard for a bill establishing electoral districts with approximately equal numbers of voters. In the 1869 debate Lasker did not attempt to achieve perfect equality in the districts—a discrepancy of ten thousand did not trouble him—but he described a 400 percent variation as a "class electoral system" that could be criticized on the same grounds as the three-class system. Though not completely happy with the final bill, Lasker voted for it along with all other National Liberals (fifty-two), and it passed narrowly by 95 to 88. Lasker was less successful in opposing the section of the bill that denied soldiers the right to vote. Here the National Liberal party split, thirty-two joining Lasker in opposition and seventeen supporting the bill and helping it to pass, 114 to 75.[25]

A more subtle obstacle to equal representation was the financial burden imposed by election to the Reichstag. Payment of representatives' expenses would be a misfortune, Theodore Bernhardi had declared in 1865, because it would bring the wrong type of people into parliament—those who would not belong and would not work except for the tempting daily pay of three talers. Many like-minded individuals also feared the political hostility of aspiring "new people." At first Lasker energetically supported the *Diäten* (per diem remuneration), although he refused to sacrifice the constitution of 1867 because such a clause was not included in the final draft. By the mid–1870s Lasker admitted that he no longer even spoke on the subject because there was nothing new to be said—he simply voted for it. He might have added, "and watched it fail." Between 1867 and 1881, fifteen roll-call votes were taken on the *Diäten*, the largest number of votes on any single bill during this period. Supporters of the *Diäten* won on eleven of those occasions (with the National Liberals contributing their affirmative votes fourteen times), only to see the bill fail in the Bundesrat. Comparison of the votes by house and party may be found in Table 5.1.[26]

The voting record reveals one of the most clear-cut differences between Lasker and Bennigsen, the titular leader of the National Liberal party. Although in favor of the *Diäten* in the first vote on it in the Constituent Assembly, Bennigsen absented himself on all votes in the first regular Reichstag session and voted either to table it or to oppose it from then on. With the exception of the first vote, Lasker and Bennigsen opposed each other on all subsequent votes.

Whether directly, in the North German Confederation and the Reich, or indirectly, in Prussia, the final basis of representation was the people, and Lasker showed real concern for them. Lasker constantly, freely, and loosely used the term *Volk*. In his opinion the *Volk* were a more secure base for the state than absolutism; the *Volk* carried the burdens of the war with Austria; the *Volk* wanted only unity in 1870; the *Volk* were liberal—always the *Volk*. Lasker's use of the word indicates that he meant only the people in general and not any specific segment or class; nor did he connect a specific set of cultural values or prejudices to the *Volk*. Despite his repeated praise for the *Volk*, Lasker did not regard himself as their servant. Though prepared to work hard for the common man in a variety of ways, he believed firmly that he had been elected to exercise *his* good judgment and to apply *his* powers of rational analysis to German problems.[27]

If he often worked for the people, there were other occasions when his support was missing. Throughout his public life, Lasker mistrusted the ability of the people to make discerning choices. For a man who said he regretted only one major decision in his life (approval of the second antisocialist law), this attitude may smack of egoism, but it is indicative of his values. Lasker placed great weight on accuracy and intelligence and was not at all sure that the *Volk* possessed either. In 1866 he noted that those who were ignorant of the Prussian past were astonished at the calm with which the people accepted the *Lückentheorie*, the gap theory by which Bismarck governed without an approved budget—the first step to "anarchy and the end of constitutionalism." Lasker had no use for the unofficial Assembly of German Representatives of 1866, he told H. B. Oppenheim, and felt it tactically unwise to hold such a meeting unless supported by unanimous public opinion. Schleswig-Holstein, he continued, had taught him that a sense of unity was still lacking among the people; it was shameful, but German unity could expect no adequate support from the masses. This last regret was exactly in line with what the even more pessimistic Karl Twesten and Julius von Hennig felt in the mid–1860s.[28] Lasker and his political allies desired mass support, but only when it agreed with their policies.

Table 5.1

Reichstag Roll-Call Votes on Bills Relating to the *Diäten*, 1867–1881

Bill Id	Content (Date)	In the Reichstag		In the NL Party		In the NL Exec. Comm.			RvB[b]	EL[c]
		Yes	No	Yes	No	Yes	No	Abs.[a]		
	(1)	(2)	(3)	(4)	(5)	(6)	(7)	(8)	(9)	(10)
9	For *Diäten* (March 30, 1867)	136	130	63	12	10	1	1	Y	Y
13	Against *Diäten* (April 15, 1867)	178	90	37	31	7	5	0	Y	N
29	For *Diäten* (April 2, 1868)	92	97	40	8	7	2	5	A	Y
31	For *Diäten* (April 18, 1868)	100	104	44	7	7	2	5	A	Y
43	For *Diäten* (May 5, 1869)	109	94	47	6	9	1	6	A	Y
45	For *Diäten* (May 12, 1869)	100	110	43	9	8	1	7	A	Y
125	To table *Diäten* (April 20, 1871)	117	208	20	89	3	17	3	Y	N
126	To table *Diäten* (April 20, 1871)	152	175	43	67	5	15	3	Y	N
127	For *Diäten* (April 20, 1871)	185	138	74	32	17	4	2	N	Y
129	For *Diäten* (April 25, 1871)	186	128	74	32	16	3	4	N	Y
157	For *Diäten* (March 26, 1873)	114	91	48	22	10	4	11	N	Y
159	For *Diäten* (April 30, 1873)	145	85	54	18	14	3	8	N	Y
171	For *Diäten* (Febuary 12, 1874)	229	79	89	37	17	4	4	N	Y
192	For *Diäten* (January 9, 1875)	158	67	65	36	15	5	4	N	Y
197	For *Diäten* (November 30, 1875)	179	58	66	31	13	3	7	N	Y

Source: Roll-call votes are taken from the *Generalregister*. See Table 4.1. The "Bill Id" was assigned by the *Generalregister* to bills in chronological sequence.
[a] Abs. = absent
[b] RvB = Rudolf von Bennigsen
[c] EL = Eduard Lasker

In the controversy over the bill to abolish capital punishment, Lasker commented that, unlike the intelligentsia, the "great masses" had not concerned themselves with the bill. He proclaimed his willingness to accept the decision of the uneducated but obviously did not like the rejection of educated, "scientific" opinion. One of the strongest props of the bureaucracy, it seemed to Lasker, was the political immaturity of citizens who automatically accepted any official's word. The assassination attempts of 1878 exposed the double edge of relying on the *Volk* on some issues. Lasker realized that popular reaction was emotional and widespread. In his speech on the second antisocialist bill, Lasker devoted substantial time to popular pressures, criticizing Bismarck for using and encouraging these forces for his own ends. After the second assassination attempt, Lasker charged, Bismarck, "who knows the people as no one else," knew it was time to appeal to the masses. In later election speeches Lasker admitted that the people were afraid of violence, but he warned that their fear was being manipulated by the greatest tactician of all time to achieve his ends. Lasker never regained his old optimism about the future of liberalism, and he cautioned against any new conflicts that could not be clearly understood and supported by the people. Tariff issues were too complex to be a base for real opposition, since most people could not understand them. In *Fünfzehn Jahre*, Lasker wrote that the masses did not comprehend the fine points of the antisocialist crisis, which made campaigning difficult. As early as 1875, the *Frankfurter Zeitung* had also recognized this problem, sarcastically writing that the *Volk* did not understand subtle differences and would choose a Bismarck over a Lasker any day.[29]

On the other hand, Lasker had little use for the Junker nobility and large landowners, and he had no ties to big business. If he favored any class, it was the middle class—understood in a very loose sense. He worked hard for the artisans because they came closest to his ideal of self-help and independent action. His natural habitat was parliament and his private study, supplemented from time to time with intelligent conversation, close friends, and an occasional excursion into the mountains. Lasker was sincerely embarrassed by all the sudden attention produced by his speech on corruption in 1873. It made him immensely popular, but he was no tribune of the people and did not care to be one.[30] Lasker's lukewarm support for universal suffrage and his approval of the three-class voting system in *Kreis* and *Gemeinde* should be seen in the light of his highly ambivalent feelings toward the German *Volk*.

The strength of parliament in Prussia and Germany depended on a number of secondary procedural privileges and powers. Lasker especially desired parliamentary control over internal affairs, such as the daily agenda, roll-call voting, and speaking order. He opposed giving the government any right to determine the validity of election results, pushed strongly for written rules regulating house activity (*Geschäftsordnungen*), argued against a long legislative term, and successfully blocked any formal meeting of the Reichstag on French soil during wartime. He disliked the power of the *Herrenhaus* (House of Lords) in Prussia and opposed allowing it any initiative in financial affairs, but he saw little chance to reform it. He greeted Simson's appointment to the upper house in 1872 as an opening toward reform, though nothing ever came of it.[31] However, none of these issues was controversial or as important as the question of the immunity of Reichstag and Landtag members from criminal prosecution.

The Prussian Constitution of 1850, as well as the constitutions of 1867 in the North German Confederation and of 1871 in the Reich, provided for partial immunity of elected members of the lower house but did not guarantee complete freedom from arrest and prosecution. A member caught committing a crime could be arrested and prosecuted by the government so long as it was not expressly forbidden to do so by parliament (article 31). In no case could a member be prosecuted for his vote or his comments in the house (article 30).

Free speech was never seriously questioned in the Reichstag, but Lasker, Twesten, and others had established this principle between 1866 and 1869 only on the basis of court action. The immunity bills (see Table 5.2) presented in the 1867 session and again in 1874 attempted to forbid any arrest of a member of the Reichstag during a legislative session. Lasker supported the 1868 bill vigorously but was strangely silent in 1875. Neither bill succeeded, but whereas Lasker and his National Liberal colleagues favored the legislation nearly unanimously in 1867, only a very few supported it in 1875. Lasker was absent on the final vote; among the leaders of the party, only Forckenbeck voted for the bill, which failed by fifteen votes. Like the *Diäten*, immunity from prosecution seemed to be too risky to the pro-government National Liberals in the mid–1870s. Lasker did successfully oppose a government-sponsored bill to impose curbs on agitation in the Reichstag in 1879, and he verbally defended the Social Democrats against hostile police. But these were holding actions in contrast to his frontal assault on the government during the early days of the North German Confederation.[32]

Parliament possessed few powers strong enough to bend the government to its will in either Prussia or the North German Confederation in the 1860s and 1870s. For all of Lasker's praise of the efficacy of open discussion, he too realized that neither the Prussian nor the later German government would be swayed by discussion unsupported by a more concrete force. The only weapon parliament could wield was that of budgetary control. This tactic, of course, had been attempted between 1862 and 1866 with a notable lack of success. Because budget control was both a weapon to be used against the government and the necessary foundation of the new state's strength, liberals like Lasker were torn in conflicting directions.

The North German Reichstag secured control over the budget in 1867. The constitution stated that the entire budget must be approved prior to each fiscal year. Although the constitution did not specifically forbid a repetition of the Prussian government's action in ruling without a budget in 1862–1866, one can understand the liberal prediction that the government would, as the king himself stated, never again resort to that method. On the other hand, no provision of the constitution prevented a multiyear duration for parts of the budget, particularly of the large military expenditures. The greatest obstacle to approval of the constitution became the controversy over whether the military budget should be open-ended—that is, approved until passage of new legislation—or whether it must be approved for a strictly determined period. In 1867, when Lasker and seventy-four of the seventy-seven National Liberals present accepted the three-year military bill as a compromise, Lasker knew the risk he was taking (see Table 5.3). Not wishing to repeat the mistakes made in Prussia, Lasker wanted the right of yearly control over the budget recognized as a basic power of parliament. He correctly gauged the future role of the military budget: "As the military clauses compose the foundation of the draft [of the constitution] and in the future will always remain the root of the North German Constitution, so the military budget is also the foundation of the right of control of the budget; and if you entirely exclude the military budget from us, you have thereby reduced the right of budget approval almost to the level of illusion." He equated the proposed system of automatically escalating increases (military expenses were to be calculated on a fixed per capita basis) with dictatorship, which could be borne only temporarily. Hence, he reluctantly accepted a fixed sum for a fixed time period.[33]

A few days later Lasker again spoke on the question of the budget, this time criticizing Finance Minister August Freiherr von der Heydt for commenting that, if a future parliament rejected a budget, he would ignore the vote. Such an act, Lasker insisted, would represent a return to absolutism and make a mockery of budgetary control. The National Liberal party recognized parliament's incomplete budgetary power, and its June program listed fulfillment of the budgetary power as the most important task of the next Reichstag. But the National

Table 5.2

Reichstag Roll-Call Votes on Bills Relating to Parliamentary Immunity,
1868–1875

		Number Voting								
		In the Reichstag		In the NL Party		In the NL Exec. Comm.				
Bill Id	Content (Date)	Yes	No	Yes	No	Yes	No	Abs.[a]	RvB[b]	EL[c]
	(1)	(2)	(3)	(4)	(5)	(6)	(7)	(8)	(9)	(10)
30	Immunity (April 3, 1868)	119	65	56	0	13	0	1	Y	Y
35	Immunity (March 16, 1869)	140	51	51	0	13	0	4	Y	Y
199	Curbs on *Reichstag* agitation (December 9, 1875)	127	142	5	96	1	11	11[d]	Abs.[a]	Abs.[a]

Source: Roll-call votes are taken from the *Generalregister*. See Table 4.1. The "Bill Id" was assigned by the *Generalregister* to bills in chronological sequence.

[a]Abs. = absent
[b]RvB = Rudolf von Bennigsen
[c]EL = Eduard Lasker
[d]Includes four declared abstentions, which were very rare.

Liberals never achieved this plank during Lasker's political career. Instead, budgetary messages to the Reichstag based on multiyear military clauses were the rule, causing bitter debates. Military expenditures per se were not at issue, at least not within the National Liberal party, but the evasion of annual approval by the Reichstag was a real concern.[34]

As in other aspects of parliamentary life after 1867, Lasker found himself fighting another holding action against multiyear military budgets. In the fall of 1867 he unsuccessfully opposed the inclusion of a clause allowing for the "necessary strengthening" of the army, which, although not acted upon, was obviously an attempt to emplace a means of evading Reichstag approval. The Reichstag defeated it, 165 to 81, but the National Liberals suffered a major split, 45 to 24. The importance of budgetary approval resided in its power as a lever: the government's real need for money was one of the few sources of parliamentary power. In 1871, with another three-year military budget at issue, Lasker renewed his arguments of 1867 to claim that the administration wanted to be free of the Reichstag, and he warned that too many years without parliamentary control of the budget amounted to absolutism. The bill, passed over Lasker's negative vote, again seriously split the National Liberals. The 1874 debate became agony for Lasker and the National Liberals because of the government's proposal, as in 1867, for an open-ended military budget, the *Aeternat*. In the end both sides compromised on a *Septennat* (seven-year military budget).[35]

Table 5.3

Final Reichstag Roll-Call Votes on Military Budget Bills,
1867–1880

		Number Voting								
Bill Id	Content (Date)	In the Reichstag Yes	No	In the NL Party Yes	No	In the NL Exec. Comm. Yes	No	Abs.[a]	RvB[b]	EL[c]
(1)		(2)	(3)	(4)	(5)	(6)	(7)	(8)	(9)	(10)
16	3-year budget (April 16, 1867)	202	80	75	2	12	0	0	Y	Y
147	3-year budget (December 1, 1871)	152	128	53	43	11	10	2	Y	N
188	7-year budget (April 20, 1874)	214	123	140	0	22	0	2	Y	Y
243	7-year budget (April 16, 1880)	186	128	65	5	13	3	4	Y[d]	N

Source: Roll-call votes are taken from the *Generalregister*. See Table 4.1.
Note: The "Bill Id" was assigned by the *Generalregister* to bills in chronological sequence.
[a]Abs. = absent
[b]RvB = Rudolf von Bennigsen
[c]EL = Eduard Lasker
[d]Lasker had seceded from the National Liberal party by this time.

The 1874 military bill was first and foremost a constitutional issue so far as Lasker was concerned, because it revealed the military administration's desire for immunity from parliamentary control and criticism. He had no major complaint about the size of the budget request or its use by the army, and he foresaw no future obstacle to easy passage of even greater requests during emergencies. The only question was whether the administration would share power with parliament. However, politics also played a role, since rejection of the military bill could well mean the fragmentation of the National Liberal party and loss of governmental support and cooperation in other areas. The party supported the compromise unanimously in the Reichstag, 140 to 0, obscuring the very real internal divisiveness. Lasker voted for the bill out of fear for the party, but only after bitter opposition in the party caucus. In 1880 he opposed renewal of the *Septennat* on the same grounds, but it too passed. Avoidance of the *Aeternat* is perhaps grounds for terming his policy partially successful, but, though not a rout, the *Septennat* was a disheartening retreat from earlier principles and hopes.[36]

A final struggle against the government's desire to evade annual budgetary approval occurred in 1881, when the government tried to alter the constitution to allow for the calling of Reichstag sessions every second year. On this question liberals opposed the Iron Chancellor with rare success. Lasker identified the proposal as a symptom of the desire to reduce the power of parliament rather than as an innocuous attempt to improve the organization of legislative action. If the Reichstag did not meet yearly, he told his colleagues, it was as good as finished. The opposition amended the administration bill to order the convening of parliament in October every year, which represented a mild setback to the king's prerogative to call and dismiss the lower house. The opposition amendment carried narrowly, 147 to 132, with even the rump of the National Liberal party, after the secession of the Liberal Group and Liberal Union, voting for it 47 to 1. Compared with the *Septennat*, the victory was modest at best.[37]

There were also subtler, less significant ways for the government to escape parliamentary supervision in money matters. Lasker made a solid part of his early political reputation by calling his fellow legislators' attention to the government's practice of buying, building, or operating properties such as railroads and then selling them. Prussia had become deeply involved in the ownership of railroads, and Lasker argued that any income from such ventures must be included in its annual budget. Although the total sums were not great in the 1860s, Lasker opposed state ownership because of the vast potential for future evasion of Landtag supervision. In 1866 he felt that most of this income had been funneled into the war. Fully conscious of the large role played by the state in Prussian financial life, he argued that even the leasing of railroads required permission from the lower house. He raised the same question on issues involving artillery factories, debts, confiscation of monies (from the king of Hannover after the 1866 war), and emergency war funds. Never the cause of a major confrontation with the government, these incidents nonetheless gave Lasker a reputation as the watchdog of the Reichstag.[38]

The government's failure to report income from the operation or sale of state property was only one facet of the serious difficulty that both the Reichstag and the Landtag experienced in obtaining reliable and complete data from state ministries to use as the basis of legislative commission investigations and their own deliberations. In 1868 Lasker ascribed the financial problems to the state accountants, who, he claimed, possessed the only real knowledge of Prussia's finances. What could an isolated representative do, he demanded, if a department head bemoaned the lack of money and asked for more? "Yes, gentlemen," he stated, "self-government is not merely a question of politics, but a question of finances." Lasker maintained that parliamentary power signified little without the factual basis necessary to reach reasonable and persuasive conclusions. But the government disliked discussion, especially hostile and probing analysis of its budgetary requests. This attitude elicited a bitter response from Lasker in the autumn of 1869. Incensed by a comment that deputies should not speak without factual knowledge, he criticized the government for making no effort to cooperate in providing that information. If, Lasker added, correct accounting was the only issue, there was perhaps no need for elected representatives. For his part, he said he would speak whether he had adequate figures or not and for as long as he thought necessary.[39]

In 1871 Lasker returned to his prewar concern with finances and government accounting procedures. The budget message for fiscal 1872 especially irritated him. The government presented it, according to Lasker, without adequate substantiation but practically demanded approval. In the spring Lasker pushed a government bill to establish a general accounting office, which was to be technical and nonpartisan. Yet, how much help would it be, he wondered, if the government could still deny the Reichstag necessary data. He claimed that the government's proposal would merely allow the general accounting office decisive control over *which* errors to publish. Lasker suggested that the accounting office be a review office jointly controlled by parliament and the administration. But the government's view prevailed on February 21 by a vote of 310 to 43—and Lasker voted for the government's draft. The situation did not improve, however. The government remained jealous of its control of information, and Lasker and the liberals spent much of their time in later years impotently criticizing its activity.[40]

The struggle in Germany to achieve the other pillar of constitutionalism, ministerial responsibility, has a rather limited history. No direct attempts were made to secure a ministry responsible to the parliament in Prussia after 1866, and only two were made in the North German Confederation. Both of these efforts took the form of bills stating simply that the ministers were responsible to the house; there were no attempts to exercise power over the ministers through budgetary control. At first Lasker opposed any type of ministerial responsibility that did not allow for meaningful control by the Reichstag. The key questions were: Who should be responsible and how. Countersignature by the federal chancellor would be an empty formality, Lasker argued, if it was necessary for all orders of king, army, and government. No one could possibly know what he was signing in such a large number of cases. True responsibility could be exercised only by an expert. After a pithy description of the wide range of powers to be given to the federal chancellor, Lasker concluded that the executive was not properly decentralized. He was probably serious, and he certainly understated the case: of all the changes in the North German Constitution, almost none affected the position of the executive. Bismarck would compromise the rights of the upper house, the army, and even the king, but only on dire necessity would he dilute his own power.[41]

In a speech delivered on March 27, 1867, Lasker recognized the imbalance in the powers of the executive and legislature. The executive was so strong that Lasker feared it might expand into the relative vacuum left by the weak legislature. The cure, he thought, was ministerial responsibility, which would give parliament a nonbudgetary weapon, and he attempted to amend the constitutional draft to allow the king of Prussia, as president, to name responsible ministers. Defeated by a standing vote, he then tried to apply responsibility to the federal chancellor, Otto von Bismarck. Since an attempt by a Progressive, Carl Ausfeld, to include a responsible ministry in the constitution had failed just the day before, Lasker had to choose whether or not to agree to the chancellor's "moral" responsibility to the constitution, which his colleague Bennigsen had proposed. He ultimately did so only in order to obtain a constitution, as he explained to the Landtag on May 8, 1867, when he advocated Prussian approval.[42]

Lasker's desire for a constitution was so strong that he was willing to accept one with built-in obstacles. Where he and Twesten had fought the king and the upper house in Prussia, they now also had to struggle against a series of other governments in the Bundesrat; none of them was very favorable to liberals, and each answered only to its subjects in an indirect fashion. During early discussions in the spring of 1867, and after approval of the South German treaties in December 1870, Lasker recognized the problem that the confederation posed to reform of the constitution. By the time of the second direct attempt to secure ministerial responsibility in 1869, the National Liberal party had been won over to Lasker's viewpoint, as Table 5.4 shows. Had Bennigsen and his followers decided to vote "yes" in 1867 along with men like Lasker, Forckenbeck, Hennig, and Hugo Fries, their leverage would have been greater, because the constitution was not yet adopted. In 1869 the bill for ministerial responsibility carried, but it was never approved by the Bundesrat. There was no third attempt in Lasker's lifetime.[43]

After his acceptance of the North German Constitution, Lasker's strategy changed: he argued less against the office of federal chancellor and more in favor of the creation of responsible ministries. The reason—the presence of the popular and successful Count von Bismarck—was obvious to all. In 1868 Lasker agreed that the thought of the Iron Chancellor's resignation was horrifying, but he added slyly that perhaps Bismarck might return as chancellor without his present ministers. Since Bismarck was not willing to give up power, even in the form of his ap-

Table 5.4

Reichstag Roll-Call Votes on Bills Relating to Ministerial Responsibility,
1867–1869

Bill Id	Content (Date)	Number Voting								
		In the Reichstag		In the NL Party		In the NL Exec. Comm.			RvB[b]	EL[c]
		Yes	No	Yes	No	Yes	No	Abs.[a]		
	(1)	(2)	(3)	(4)	(5)	(6)	(7)	(8)	(9)	(10)
4	Ministerial responsibility (March 26, 1867)	86	177	25	48	4	8	0	N	Y
39	Ministerial responsibility (April 16, 1869)	111	100	57	2	14	0	2	Y	Y

Source: Roll-call votes are taken from the *Generalregister*. See Table 4.1.
Note: The "Bill Id" was assigned by the *Generalregister* to bills in chronological sequence.
[a]Abs. = absent
[b]RvB = Rudolf von Bennigsen
[c]EL = Eduard Lasker

pointees, Lasker turned his attention to a bill proposed by Johannes von Miquel designed to give the Reichstag the power to indict government officials. This power was necessary, Lasker explained, because "one minister will never voluntarily prosecute another, especially not on the basis of responsibility." The bill passed 131 to 114—the National Liberal party was nearly unanimous in its support, 67 to 1—but it failed in the Bundesrat. Table 5.5 shows that similar attempts to weaken the executive short of ministerial responsibility produced similar results.[44]

The theme of Lasker's 1869 speech in favor of ministerial responsibility illustrates the problem of weakening any office dear to Bismarck. Lasker argued that no other European state was run by only one responsible minister. Even in England, the key to government was the unity of ministers behind the prime minister. The bill was, Lasker carefully explained, not an attack upon Bismarck but a means of giving him more flexibility in delegating authority on factual matters, thereby relieving him of some of the drearier burdens of office. Nor did he wish to saddle Bismarck with obstinate ministers; he merely wanted responsible officials united behind the head of the ministry. To hear Lasker speak, the proposal was innocuous enough, but Bismarck would have none of it, claiming that the federal chancellorship was perfectly suitable and lacked only the right titles. Lasker had perceptively commented in his speech that ministerial responsibility had nothing to do with particularism, unity, or foreign affairs but essentially concerned whether or not one man should run a major state: "That is the difference, and we must establish this difference clearly."[45]

Lasker continued to voice his support for government by responsible ministers throughout the 1870s but acted seriously in support of it only in the spring of 1877. It is highly probable that his renewed vocal support was linked to the National Liberal attempt to persuade Bismarck to accept a leader or leaders of their party as government ministers. Lasker now emphasized the need for a closer relationship between the administration and the legislature. Cooperation was particularly needed on financial matters because individual party members did not possess enough factual knowledge to be able to introduce such legislation themselves, although their votes were necessary for passage. Bismarck's reply, three days later, was a noncommittal reiteration of his old stand that the *Reichskanzleramt* (chancellor's office) was sufficient to act on financial matters as an executive institution. Lasker retorted that "for a ministry this head [the chancellorship] is too big, and the other limbs [the ministers] are too small." Otto von Bismarck seriously considered inviting one or more National Liberals—but never Lasker—into his cabinet. Lasker wrote to Stauffenberg on October 9, 1877, that Bismarck "finally appears to share the view that parliament and the administration can no longer remain so completely separated as in the past." The National Liberals asked for three portfolios—for Bennigsen, Stauffenberg, and Forckenbeck—but, although Bismarck may have agreed in talks with Bennigsen at Varzin, he never finally made the offer. He demurred instead that Lasker was responsible for wanting too many ministers, though Bennigsen's correspondence does not substantiate this claim. In any case, the political scene soon changed with the government's desire for protective tariffs, the assassination attempts on the Kaiser, and the end of the *Kulturkampf.*[46]

Before we leave the question of ministerial responsibility, it should be noted that Lasker and those in favor of checks upon the government were not wholly powerless. E. R. Huber is certainly correct in stating that they could have acted against the government within the means provided in the constitution had they controlled enough votes in the Reichstag. Sufficient votes for a concerted effort to bring about legal change never materialized, but the liberals did bring pressure to bear on the administration, even forcing Bismarck to rid himself of ministers in a number of cases. Lasker helped to eliminate Graf zur Lippe and von der Heydt, and he personally destroyed Privy Councillor Hermann Wagener in 1873. Although this was power of a sort, it was insignificant in contrast to the immense resources Bismarck could tap. Huber is technically correct on purely legal grounds, but the political realities of the situation made the imposition of parliamentary constraints on the powerful executive a chimera. At best, compromise with Bismarck, as practiced by Lasker, was the narrow path to the enhancement of legislative power.[47]

Nowhere is the compromise relationship between Lasker and Bismarck so clearly visible as in the administration's press policies. A study of them provides a good measure of the extent of the power available to the chancellor in dealing with the opposition. During the Conflict Era, the left vigorously protested the administration's blatant use of the state apparatus against its political enemies, usually liberals. There is no doubt that Bismarck constructed, used, and benefited immensely from government influence over and even control of the press during this period. From the beginning, he saw the need to use the official press (the *Staatsanzeiger, Amtsblätter*, and *Kreisblätter*) as political organs. Eventually the government combined this use of the official press with the practice of granting advice and information to "friendly" papers and refusing to unfriendly papers both government advertising and delivery by government-owned railroads. What rankled liberal legislators most was the administration's policy of requesting fiscal support from the Landtag and Reichstag for this administration-oriented and controlled press in the form of funds whose use did not have to be reported.[48]

Table 5.5

Reichstag Roll-Call Votes on Bills to Weaken the Federal Executive,
1868–1881

Bill Id	Content (Date)	In the Reichstag		In the NL Party		In the NL Exec. Comm.			RvB[b]	EL[c]
		Yes	No	Yes	No	Yes	No	Abs.[a]		
	(1)	(2)	(3)	(4)	(5)	(6)	(7)	(8)	(9)	(10)
32	To indict debt officials (April 22, 1868)	131	114	67	1	13	0	0	Y	Y
166	To limit power of emperor in Alsace-Lorraine (March 18, 1873)	72	171	2	81	17	2	8	N	N
200	Right to punish Foreign Office staff (January 29, 1876)	179	120	127	0	22	0	1	Y	Y
216	To exclude advice of chancellor of imperial appointments (March 8, 1878)	79	201	100	0	21	0	3	Y	Y
217	Third reading of Bill no. 216 (March 11, 1878)	171	101	98	0	18	0	4	Y	Y
255	To call parliament in October (May 16, 1881)	147	132	47	1	16	0	3	Y	Y[d]

Source: Roll-call votes are taken from the *Generalregister*. See Table 4.1.
Note: The "Bill Id" was assigned by the *Generalregister* to bills in chronological sequence.
[a]Abs. = absent
[b]RvB = Rudolf von Bennigsen
[c]EL = Eduard Lasker
[d]Lasker was now a member of the Liberale Vereinigung.

During the Era of Conflict Lasker made a name for himself on the issue of the press by attacking bureaucratic influence in politics in extreme terms. The people, he said, should not pay for the government's propaganda, although he would have no objection if government propaganda were used exclusively in foreign affairs. He made much of the government's disciplinary action against an estate owner serving the functions of the local police office. For not subscribing to the *Amtsblatt*, he had been fined three talers. Although the courts erased the fine, the estate owner had been instructed to subscribe in the future. Lasker argued that no official possessing public trust and power ought to use any newspaper for his political advantage.[49]

The year 1867 and the new constitution wrought a real change in Lasker's attitude toward the use of *Geheime Fonds* (secret funds) by the government. In 1868, and on a number of later occasions, he asked critics for proof of the government's complicity in misuse of the secret funds. When evidence was not forthcoming, he restated his opposition to secret funds but voted for the specific requests (see Table 5.6). In 1871 Lasker even defended the grant of secret funds, arguing that only some were truly secret. In any case, Lasker recognized the government's right to use such funds.[50]

In 1874 Lasker announced that he would vote for the secret funds, as he had since 1867, because no one could *prove* misuse. He explained that between 1867 and 1874 the government had become more and more pro-liberal: "We have, therefore, no need to give it a vote of no confidence in this regard." But he admitted freely that Twesten had been right in 1867; the government had used the press against the liberals in an abuse of power. In 1877 his statement was brief, but interesting: "If we wished to follow a politics of impulse, we would let ourselves strike this item [the secret funds], due to one or the other article in the *Provinzial Korrespondenz*; but since we, as the representatives of the people, must give the government those agencies which no government can do without, we will vote today for this item, as we have done for years." Lasker never again had an opportunity to speak or vote against the funds, since he lost every race for election to the Landtag after 1878—and the government press played a role in his defeat.[51]

The government campaign against the National Liberals in 1878 could have surprised them only by its intensity; administrative use of the official and unofficial press was nothing new. In the period just before the war with France, while the Baden affair still simmered, Bismarck moved to bring Lasker to heel. Moritz Busch, then an official in the press section of the Foreign Office, reports in his diary for April 1, 1870, that Bismarck desired an article on Lasker that would accuse him of being a parliamentary aristrocrat with particularistic tendencies, as compared with Lippe, who was a particularistic aristrocrat with absolutist tendencies. Three days later Busch showed Bismarck the article and was instructed to send it on to the provincial papers.[52]

Although relations between the government and the National Liberal party were relatively peaceful in the early 1870s, a turning point in Lasker's relations with the government occurred in 1874, as reflected in the attitude of the official press. Early in that year, prior to the military bill, Lasker stood for election to the Reichstag in a Frankfurt am Main district against Leopold Sonnemann, head of the Deutsche Volkspartei (German People's party) and the editor of the democratic *Frankfurter Zeitung*. Sonnemann won in a run-off with Lasker, and after the victory his paper published an exposé of the tactics used by the local Lasker committee and the government. All government offices, it charged, used pressure to help Lasker and hurt the opposition, but the post office and the police were especially active. Supporters of Sonnemann who tried to hand out brochures were stopped, questioned, and harassed, while Lasker's men went free. Lasker probably had nothing to do with these actions, as local organization was not his concern. Nevertheless, the incident points up one of the benefits of the National Liberal party's alliance with the government during the 1870s. The government press did not ordinarily attack the National Liberals, even if it did not praise them; it *did* attack opponents of the National

Table 5.6

Prussian Landtag Roll-Call Votes on Bills to Grant Secret Funds
to the Government, 1866–1877

Date	Landtag		NL Party			
	Yes	No	Yes	No	RvB^a	EL^b
	(1)	(2)	(3)	(4)	(5)	(6)
November 11, 1866	146	123				N
December 4, 1866	153	150				Y
January 20, 1874	205	141	134	1	Y	Y
January 28, 1874	220	151	144	1	Y	Y
February 18, 1876	173	131	11	4	Y	Y
January 31, 1877	213	157	138	5	Y	Y

Source: All roll-call votes in this table were taken from the *Wörtliche Berichte über die Verhandlungen des preussischen Abgeordnetenhauses* (Berlin, 1865–1877).
[a]RvB = Rudolf von Bennigsen. Hannover, his home, was not Prussian until 1867.
[b]EL = Eduard Lasker

Liberals—Catholics, Progressives, and Social Democrats—although not primarily out of a desire to aid the National Liberals.

The 1874 *Septennat* required stiff government pressure on the National Liberals to ensure passage. Friedrich Zabel, editor of the National Liberal organ, the *National Zeitung*, called it a "shameless" use of government power. "What worries me," he wrote to Lasker, "is the vehemence of the government's action and their organs in pursuit of their agitation for the military bill." On April 3 Lasker wrote Stauffenberg: "It is unbelievable what distortions the press performs and how contrived the official comprehension is." Later, during the penal code debate, the government press, led by the *Norddeutsche Allgemeine Zeitung*, attacked the National Liberals. The *Frankfurter Zeitung* gleefully pointed out the irony of a polemic against the National Liberal party at the same time that the party organ, the *National Zeitung*, declared that there was no longer an official press in Prussia. The one assurance was worth about as much as the other.[53]

The axe fell in 1878. During the affair over the antisocialist law, the official as well as the unofficial press concentrated attention on Lasker and the left wing of the National Liberal party. Although all papers attacked the opponents of government policy, the ideological lead was taken by the *Norddeutsche Allgemeine* and the conservative *Kreuzzeitung*, which argued that liberalism led to socialism. The *Norddeutsche Allgemeine* also suggested that a new election would be Lasker's fault, because of his opposition to the antisocialist Law, an argument that frightened the National Liberals. The *Frankfurter Zeitung* described this press war against the National Liberals as a war of annihilation reminiscent of the Conflict Era. Adalbert Falk,

Prussian minister of religion and education, related that in July 1878 Bismarck told Hahn, head of the State Press Office, that he again wished to leak an article on his views of the National Liberal party, naming Lasker and Bamberger specifically, as well as to air his views on the tax question. He wanted, Falk recalled, to free Bennigsen from Lasker. Many of the party's left wing, most notably Stauffenberg, were damaged by the offensive, and the party lost at least twenty-seven seats in the Reichstag, although Lasker easily survived in his Meiningen district.[54]

From 1878 on, the government used the press against Lasker, who quickly regained his earlier distaste for such activity. The most he could do, though, was to expose the government's misuse of its power. He criticized the state railroad's refusal to carry the general political news sections of the *Frankfurter Zeitung* while still accepting its business sections. In 1880 he took up Puttkamer's remark that government advertisements were not placed in opposition newspapers, but his complaint sounds overly partisan since the practice was certainly not new. More important, it had become apparent that the National Liberal compromise with Bismarck had been one-sided. During the 1870s the liberals stopped criticizing the government's use of the press, but the government did *not* stop misusing it, although it did direct its attacks toward different foes.[55]

Lasker could do little about Bismarck's control of the press after 1878 because of his own meager power in both the party and the Reichstag and his exclusion from the Landtag. Moreover, he lacked credibility among his new allies on the left. As the *Frankfurter Zeitung* explained: "Had the liberal press protested against that practice when it was directed against democratic and ultramontane papers, had they accepted the only correct position which is our permanent principle—that the public should be considered first in these issues and that the political position of a paper is irrelevent—then we could find in their present complaints more than a tactical move." While men like Herbert von Bismarck plotted against him, using even his father as well as goverment influence and the press, Lasker could only protest, a tactic that Siemens considered very poor indeed. In Lasker's opinion liberals should ignore the "pinpricks" of the government and, "if Haenel answers: 'an eye for an eye, a tooth for a tooth,' he forgets that '*quod licet Jovi, non licet bovi.*'" Even after Lasker's death, Bismarck tried to continue to use the press against him, instructing the *Norddeutsche Allgemeine Zeitung* to criticize him. Its editors, however, showed better taste than Bismarck and for once declined. Holstein noted a few weeks later that Bismarck's maxim was: "Courtesy in diplomacy, rudeness in the press."[56]

The Community

Lasker supported the concept of a federal state and fought Bismarck in order to liberalize it. But he also saw another possibility for progress in constitutional development at the lower levels of the state structure. Since the reforms of 1807–1815, liberals of all colors had supported changes pointing in the direction of local self-government. The movement was explicitly antiabsolutist, aiming at the elimination of the old aristocratic power in the countryside and of the tremendous influence of the monarchical bureaucratic appointees, most notably the *Landrat* (district magistrate). In place of the aristocratic-rural-royal power, liberals hoped to substitute a new combination of the rising town-dwelling burghers and a state-oriented progressive gentry.[57] The major factor in local reform would be extension of the suffrage, coupled with the growth of a more and more urbanized population.

To Lasker's liberal eye, almost any legislation intended to secure local self-government was good, but he never assigned it any more than secondary status as a weapon in the war for constitutionalism. He hoped to see self-government replace the arbitrary and paternalistic bureaucratic police power, and he sharply criticized the government's proposal for reform in 1869 because it seemed to reaffirm the old police powers of 1850. Self-government implied the solution of problems on the local level with local means, and by 1873 Lasker referred to it specifically as decentralization within the Reich. He told a campaign crowd that by accepting the duties of citizens they would weaken bureaucracy and strengthen the state. In 1875 Lasker expressed his desire to unburden the state: "Our state structure suffers from congestion in the head; that is, much too much is assigned to the central government. Our task is now completely directed to using all means which take away this overconcentration on the central government and to disperse it appropriately to separate institutions." In the long run, local involvement in running the state might one day produce dividends in the form of a stronger liberal political base. But Lasker never intended self-government to be a substitute for the centralized state: "The bureaucratic government defines itself—this is the beginning of self-government wherein someone among the governed is called to participate to a certain degree in this government; but, in this capacity, he acts under the discipline, the outlook, and in the name of the state."[58]

In determining which state services should fall under the jurisdiction of community, county, or municipality, the ideal that Lasker pursued was simple. Wherever a local form of government could solve the local problems, the national government ought to stay out, he argued before the Constituent Assembly of 1867. In a discussion of the costs of education in 1869, he suggested that the *Gemeinde* try to bear the cost first, to be superseded by the county or the state only if the *Gemeinde* was unable to do so. The people were to exercise their citizenship by bearing the burden of government at their own level, with the state as a last resort for problems too great for the locality.[59]

To ensure self-government truly free from state interference, Lasker constantly urged full integration of the police with the communal structure and exclusion of full-time state officials from local positions. He particularly disliked the idea of using the *Landrat*'s office to carry out functions of the communal government. Police officials should be part of the new structure; all officials should be salaried, since they were as essential to the state as the army; and state functionaries should be appendages to local self-government rather than dominant over it.[60]

Lasker's most controversial stand on self-government was his opposition to the extension of universal suffrage to localities. Indeed, his position might well have appeared perverse to many of his audiences, since he consistently described self-government as a process of drawing on the whole community for support of the governing process. The key to understanding Lasker's position is contained in his conception of the function of local government as simply administrative. In 1869 he stated: "Government should be nothing more than adherence to its laws." He resisted granting the county the power to levy taxes, since such decisions were not part of its executive role. In his speech against universal suffrage in the community, he noted that local government dealt mainly with expenditures and concluded: "We cannot allow those who pay no taxes to decide which costs should be paid and to what extent taxes should be levied." To Lasker, self-government on the local scale simply meant *administration*; as in the case of the administration of the law, officials were required only to carry out accurately the decisions of others. All local inhabitants should participate in carrying out these decisions, but not all of them deserved a voice in their making.[61]

In fact, Lasker almost never spoke of "the people" in relation to local government, though he usually made free use of the term. He desired participation in the community and county by the "talented men," including the landowners. "The present *Kreisordnung* is an experiment," he said in 1872, "to test whether a genuine aristocracy is present in Prussia and whether these elements can come together to acquire power through service and not simply through presumption." Later that same year he added that the most serious weakness of local government was its failure to encourage participation by its most vigorous members. Too many aristocratic landowners and too few burghers meant one-sided and often corrupt administration. But he also feared the power of the special interests, whether landed, industrial, or unionist. Ironically, he felt that the best defense against corruption was *limited* suffrage coupled with free and unbiased elections.[62]

By 1875 local administration had not changed much, and Lasker was still complaining about the arbitrary power of the *Landrat* and the police. In 1876 he recognized that his appeal to landowners had failed and had in fact produced the opposite result: where previously the landowners controlled only the police, they now controlled the entire communal structure. By 1878 he had become very pessimistic about the power of the special interests, which had begun to organize politically. They were, to Lasker's mind, a key part of the new conservative reaction.[63]

Few of the legislative crises in which Lasker confronted constitutional issues were clear-cut. In some of the most important instances the substance was not specifically constitutional, yet it somehow affected constitutional practice. This was the case with the military bills, the duration of which was the real issue. Moreover, few bills were referenda on the entire future of an aspect of constitutional practice. Lasker had to decide instead in what way and how far a given bill or clause would affect the *direction* of constitutional practice. This was the tactic adopted by most liberals like Lasker in 1866 and 1867 and reiterated in 1871: the constitution itself need not spell out all the solutions; it need only establish the process—parliamentary control— that would solve specific problems in the future.

In Lasker's case, his prolific and lengthy legislative career provides the historian with the material needed to evaluate these constitutional decisions. By the end of his political career, in every major field of constitutional change, Lasker's efforts proved fruitless. Having accepted an imperfect document in 1867 on the grounds that it could later be amended and improved, he found it next to impossible to effect substantive change in the 1870s. His gamble was predicated upon belief in a liberal future, a future that seemed tantalizingly near in 1874 but never materialized. Lasker had erred in his judgment and failed in his legislative attempts to realize his goal of a balanced constitutionalism. He was not unique: many of his allies in the National Liberal party made the same choices. What changed after 1867 was the economic and social structure of German society, and in this change lies much of the explanation of liberal failures in the constitutional and political fields.

VI

The Crisis of Liberal Economics

"Freedom of property is the foundation of all state order."

Eduard Lasker, 1862

"If anything is to be desired from the Prussian people, it is [for them] to beware of an economy in which the obliging banker plays the leading role in the state."

Eduard Lasker, 1866

In the second half of the nineteenth century, the German economy experienced rapid growth and fundamental change. In railroads, heavy metals, chemicals, and the machine tool industry, the economy burst the records of the first half-century with breathtaking ease. Close upon the successes of large-scale industry came the almost equally rapid development of light industry and consumer manufacturing. In the onrush, industrial capital replaced landed wealth in the economic hierarchy. The aristocracy lost its power, and rural Germany, slowly at first and then more and more rapidly, gave up its inhabitants to the cities, which doubled and sometimes trebled their size. Factory and industrial workers grew daily in numbers and soon dominated all other groups in the lower classes. For better or worse, economic and social change seemed to be the order of the day.[1]

Between 1867 and 1893 per capita income and real wages rose almost uninterruptedly in Germany. The financial depression of 1873 did not materially affect most Germans. The decline in prices by about one-third from 1873 to 1896 contributed largely to the increase of real wages. Thus, the economic problems of the 1860s, 1870s, and 1880s were not those of the "Hungry Forties."[2]

Distribution of income and wealth, rather than basic subsistence, was the major cause of societal friction in this era.[3] Workers, irritated by their lack of power in society, were not content with higher wages: they desired a higher percentage of the nation's total wealth. While craftsmen declined in numbers and wealth, an ever larger lower middle class developed with the growth of retail trade, public and private bureaucracy, and lower-level managerial positions in industry. Whereas the artisans had fought factory manufacturing, the new *petite bourgeoisie* simultaneously resented the financier, stockbroker, and large store owner and feared descent into the proletariat. The middle class became more and more industrial-commercial and less and less professional. Added now to the traditional import-conscious burghers of Hamburg, Lübeck, Bremen, and Danzig were the production and export-conscious manufacturers of the Rhineland, Saxony, and the South. Sugar beet and pig production rose to replace the diminished wheat and sheep production, but the agricultural sector in general did not prosper.

The indebtedness of large and small farmers increased steadily. All sectors of the economy re-cognized the power of the banker-financier who underwrote the great ventures and controlled the flow of money.[4]

Into this highly complex economic maelstrom plunged the doughty Lasker, possessed of fine intentions but with almost no expertise in economics, social analysis, or political economy. In this respect he was typical of many nineteenth-century liberal lawyers who turned to politics out of genuine public interest but without the necessary training in economic or administrative prob-lems. Not all were doctrinaire liberals jealous of governmental interference in the "free" mar-ketplace, but certainly most sympathized strongly with laissez-faire ideas. That the economic and social problems of the time forced many of these men, including Lasker, to reappraise and modify their beliefs is testimony to the extent of the change that overtook the German economy in this period.

It is interesting to recall that Lasker began his political activities in the early 1860s in the Berlin Handworkers' Association as chairman of its educational commission. In later years he always argued that education was at least a partial solution to the country's problems. He backed education for women, supported increased expenditure for universities, and urged tech-nical training for workers. He regarded universal suffrage as educational in its contribution to civic virtue.[5] Above all, Lasker hoped that education would encourage and help members of the lower class to move into the middle class.

Early in his career Lasker declared: "Freedom of property is the foundation of all state order. . . ." He never deviated from this belief, but he expanded and modified his original con-cept under pressure from economic and social realities. In the 1860s Lasker thought in terms of equality of opportunity for all citizens to engage in the economic life of the nation. But in 1868 he complained self-righteously about the workers' criticism of the liberal record. Had not the liberal party done all it could, he asked, to remove restrictions and to equalize privileges for the workers, both legally and socially? Lasker resented the accusation that the liberals were a bourgeois party acting primarily for middle-class interests.[6] He did not object to liberals working for labor's cause, and he hoped that those who did so would work *with* the workers and not just for their equal rights. Liberalism had to support equal rights and oppose "status or occupational privileges of any type" as the basis for the development of culture.[7] Legal equity rather than economic equity dominated Lasker's thinking in the 1860s.

In his attempts at social-historical analysis in the later 1870s, Lasker clearly revealed the theoretical underpinnings of his political activity. One collection of his articles, *Means and Objectives of Cultural Development*, exhibits little philosophical or historical sophistication. The essays are poorly reasoned and replete with high-flown phrases supported by little factual content. Yet, despite their theoretical and stylistic inadequacy, they tellingly expose his ideas. Lasker fervently believed in progress, in the gradual development of civilization to ever higher levels, and in the need to raise the economic and educational level of the lower classes. Although law, trade, and other social institutions bound into civilization a humanity torn be-tween animalism and benevolence, the individual was the basis and the beginning point of all progress. "In the continuing task of self-education which the adult practices, in the experiences which ease the self-education of each succeeding generation, lies the gain," he wrote. For Lasker, language, rather than economics or politics, was the most important foundation for ci-vilization and culture.[8]

In "Cosmopolitan and National Wisdom" Lasker recognized the upheavals that had been gaining momentum for a century, but he refused to speculate on how society would evolve in the future. Whatever direction it might take, he denied that progress simply meant increasing wealth and power: rather, society must become more elevated in areas such as language, history, and artistic sensibility. For Lasker, the establishment of associations of all kinds and types—corporations and cooperatives, workers' unions and employers' organizations, international and religious societies—were all attempts to find new principles for the solution of society's problems. Most of these organizations were motivated, according to Lasker, by self-interest and competed vigorously among themselves. Nevertheless, these same organizations had helped to establish freedom in order to secure beneficial results and not, he emphasized, "in order to release a destructive or obstructive struggle." He was more dubious about the value of economics as a guide to social organization because it lacked a factual basis: "We have no data about public ownership, no accurate conception of the movement of labor, and little usable knowledge of the movement of capital; moreover, the taxation of income has no foundation in recognizable facts."[9]

Increasingly aware of this absence of basic knowledge in these areas, Lasker in the late 1870s, after nearly twenty years of public activity, decided to study economics and social theory. That he did so is commendable, but that he waited until 1877 suggests the low priority he gave it. There can be little doubt that he finally embarked on the study only because he feared the socialists. He told his friend Franz von Stauffenberg that he was beginning to know something of the opposition's field of battle. He had uncovered little that was wholly new, but he had found many clearer conceptualizations, many useful limitations, and, incidentally, some good suggestions. His discovery that socialists defined "ideal" as not realizable (*verwertbar*) in the real world is intriguing because it so closely mirrors Lasker's own outlook. A month later he repeated to Stauffenberg that he was finding little that was either new or usable in his study of socialism: "But the work is hard; and, for the moment, its use is not very satisfying. The tendencies and opinions are still too diverse and immature."[10]

Lasker tended to view economic and social problems from a layman's viewpoint and in vague categories. He never approached these issues systematically, almost always treating them as parts of larger problems relative to the state. His stand on the role of cooperatives illustrates his attitudes well.

In addition to giving lectures to artisan groups in Berlin in the 1860s, Lasker strongly supported the cooperative idea encourged and led by Hermann Schulze-Delitzsch. Schulze-Delitzsch's cooperatives were designed to be voluntary savings and credit institutions serving all individuals who possessed some surplus capital. Later, consumers' cooperatives sprang up to accommodate a less affluent segment of the population. The principle guiding both types of cooperatives was to pool small resources to obtain lower rates on goods and loans. In 1866 Lasker reported to the Prussian Landtag the results of a commission's study of the cooperatives. According to Lasker, they were "one of the most beautiful blooms of culture," a victory of clear thinkers over foggy minds. Impressed by the size of the movement—350,000 members and capital assets of twenty-eight million marks—he declared it to be growing rapidly and to represent the kernel of the German *Bürgertum* (middle class). He wanted cooperatives treated under essentially the same commercial regulations as limited liability corporations, denying that they were a weak economic organization simply because most depositors placed all of their money in this one source. Cooperatives were better than large banks, he concluded, because banks threatened to monopolize money.[11]

Lasker's support for cooperatives was matched by his admiration for skilled workers, especially for the craftsmen and artisans who were under heavy economic pressure from more modern means of production. In fact, skilled craftsmen constituted the largest single group participating in cooperatives. Lasker favored skilled laborers over factory workers because they were, in his view, more individualistic. He supported state appropriations for training institutions in the form of trade schools, museums, and technical institutes, whose purpose would be to instruct those who wanted to obtain special skills. His concern for the artisan's individuality was evident in his argument against the introduction of stereotyped work rules. In a variety of ways, Lasker attempted to preserve the remnants of the artisan class against the economic onslaught of the factory.[12]

Freedom of association was a necessary preliminary condition for the wider establishment of cooperatives and for the growth of the smaller and more radical trade union movement. Lasker supported the right of workers to combine, but he did so as much on legal and moral grounds as on economic and social ones. "Is it not our sacred, moral duty," he asked his colleagues in the Reichstag in 1867, "to establish the personal freedom of combination of all citizens, of the employees just as much as the employers?" When the Conservative Hermann Wagener objected that such freedom would lead to social war, Lasker dissented emphatically, countering that the present lack of legal rights for employees *was* war. To grant equal rights would prevent future conflict. He disagreed fundamentally with the prediction that the next major movement would be social.[13]

On bills for the right of workers to associate and against restrictive legislation aimed at trade unions, Lasker, the National Liberal party, and its parliamentary Executive Committee consistently supported freedom for the worker (see Table 6.1). By the end of the 1867–1870 legislative session, cooperatives and trade unions had won legal sanction through the efforts of middle-class liberals like Lasker and Schulze-Delitzsch and of aristocrats like Bennigsen. But the conservatives on the party Executive Committee were consistently absent for these votes, probably indicating latent opposition within the National Liberal party to the legislation on behalf of the working class.

Among the functions of the cooperatives that impressed Lasker was their encouragement of saving and thrift. To supplement the relatively limited amount of capital available through the cooperatives, Lasker supported another Schulze-Delitzsch measure for the extension of state-financed small loans to individuals. Here, too, Lasker's moral concern must be balanced against his concern for economic progress: he believed that it was immoral to charge high interest rates for money needed to sustain life. As late as 1879 he regarded the legislation establishing such loans as a positive and enduring benefit of liberal legislative action.[14]

Lasker did not feel as well disposed toward trade unions as he did toward cooperatives. He saw them as too narrowly working class in orientation, and, because they were aligned closely with the socialists, they presented a possible source of class war. In 1866 the Prussian government introduced a bill granting freedom of association but prohibiting workers from using force, such as threats, ostracism, or violence, to compel support for a strike. Although the liberals, including Lasker, opposed that bill as authoritarian and restrictive, they accepted a similar bill in 1869. Karl Erich Born argues convincingly that the liberals changed their minds between 1866 and 1869 because they had lost control of the workers' movement and were rapidly losing that source of voting support. In the 1870s liberals like Lasker faced a major predicament in the growing size and political strength of the workers. Lasker alternated between sympathy and irritation. In 1872 he was clearly worried: "If we allow the unfettered construction of associations that have the express intent of organizing war between worker and employer, we will work contrary to the public interest." Convinced that the social question could not be solved by social war, he even naively suggested self-regulation by the unions so that they might oppose capital only on "just" issues.[15]

Nevertheless, Lasker's Hobbesian revulsion at the thought of domestic strife of any kind did not prevent him from defending either the new trade unions or the necessity of struggle as a vehicle of progress. As early as 1874 he spoke in support of the progressive workers' regulations (*Gewerbeordnungen*) of 1870, arguing that they had not yet had time to prove their worth. At

The Crisis of Liberal Economics 91

Table 6.1

Reichstag Roll-Call Votes on Bills Relating to Worker Freedom,
1867–1869

Bill Id	Content (Date)	In the Reichstag		In the NL Party		In the NL Exec. Comm.			RvB[b]	EL[c]
		Yes	No	Yes	No	Yes	No	Abs.[a]		
(1)		(2)	(3)	(4)	(5)	(6)	(7)	(8)	(9)	(10)
23	Freedom of association; second reading (October 14, 1867)	136	70	58	1	11	0	3	Y	Y
24	Final vote on No. 23 (October 15, 1867)	126	71	62	1	11	0	3	Y	Y
41	Restrictions on unions (May 1, 1869)	79	100	4	48	1	9	6	Abs.[a]	N

Source: Roll-call votes are taken from the *Generalregister*. See Table 4.1.
Note: The "Bill Id" was assigned by the *Generalregister* to bills in chronological sequence.
[a]Abs. = absent
[b]RvB = Rudolf von Bennigsen
[c]EL = Eduard Lasker

the same time, he suggested that strikes against public monopolies in large cities ought to be punishable, as in England, and that trade unions should have a means of distinguishing between loyal and hostile strikes. Organized struggle was not unusual, he reasoned. Just as the Reichstag and government clashed in the process of reconciling opposing interests in order to find truth, so did society. The object was to have both sides work together. The workers had just emerged from bondage with bitter memories; the employers still fondly remembered their former privileges. In Lasker's view, the situation called for reconciliation.[16]

Three years later, again in a discussion of the workers' regulations, Lasker addressed the same issue with identical arguments—but with much improved rhetoric. If the workers now become a bit exuberant in the style of social democracy, he said, it is only the "awakening of universal human feeling which we have called forth and nourished by our legislation." It was entirely natural to find recently freed men uncertain and lacking balance, but these reactions, he reminded the Reichstag, had been predicted during the earlier discussions: "We must suffer through this stage. It is not the fault of freedom, but rather of long slavery, that proper moderation is not quickly discovered."[17]

The year 1878 witnessed a profound change in union activity of all kinds. The antisocialist law nearly included workers' associations and unions, and the government turned quickly to state socialism to defuse workers' demands. Lasker now had to decide whether to support state welfare. Though strongly attracted to it, Lasker never quite made the transition from the liberal program of the 1860s to the newer goals of social democracy in the 1870s and 1880s.

With the possible exception of a change in attitude in the last few years of his life, Lasker consistently advocated worker-employer cooperation, freedom of occupation, and self-help rather than any form of socialism. Hence, it is hardly surprising that he strongly disliked private restraint of trade, including monopolies, cartels, and the influence of large banks, though it ordinarily remained a secondary element in his politics. Reflecting his negative attitude to banks and banking, he commented in 1866 on the issue of paper currency: "I am not saying that we could suddenly commit economic suicide, but a beginning could be made; and if anything is to be desired from the Prussian people, it is [for them] to beware of an economy in which the obliging banker plays the leading role in the state. That is a danger for our whole Fatherland: not merely for its financial life, but also for its morality, for the constitution, and for the law."[18]

Lasker distrusted bankers and stockbrokers, albeit without either the fervor or the bias of the socialists, well before his exposure of illegal and unethical corporate practices in 1873. Because he could not accept special privileges and the silence surrounding them, he favored control—not abolition—of stockbrokers. As always, he regarded the advantages allowed to some merchants and not to others as inequitable. In the spring of 1870 he argued before the Reichstag that commercial credit was stretched too far, that it was surrounded by too many privileges, and that the secrecy in commercial relations as conducted by businessmen was unhealthy.[19]

Lottery bonds (*Prämienanleihen*) and a state central bank received substantial attention from Lasker during the 1870s. In Germany at this time, states that found it difficult to sell bonds frequently offered to pay off some of the bonds in a particular series at par value well before maturation, and the specific bonds so favored were chosen by lottery. Lasker criticized the practice as deceptive: it attracted risk capital into long-term, low-yield bonds, thereby hurting currency circulation.[20] When his banker friend Bamberger charged that opponents of such bonds were "a brotherhood of aristocrats, policemen, and communists," Lasker asked into which category he fell.[21]

During the 1874–1875 debates over the establishment of a state bank of issue for the Reich, Lasker again found himself at odds with Bamberger. Although both men supported the central bank, Lasker took a more conservative posture and demanded a much higher reserve quota than Bamberger, who saw lower reserves as freeing more currency for investment in the economy. Another intriguing part of the discussion over an imperial bank concerned state monopolization of the power to issue bank notes and paper currency. In a partial shift away from his principles of 1848, Lasker joined many other liberals in support of the state monopoly. He contended that the issuance of currency was not an activity subject to free competition: it was a power and privilege peculiar to the state. It is understandable that liberals like Lasker did not wish to allow private banks extensive powers in the years immediately following the railroad crisis and depression of 1873.[22]

One major aspect of the rapid growth of big business and high finance in Germany was the construction of railroads in nearly every corner of the Reich and in much of Eastern Europe. Lasker recognized clearly in the spring of 1871 that railroads differed from all other undertakings in one important respect: they were immediately regulated by the state through its railroad department. Lasker warned then that government regulation, in liberal theory, demanded equitable treatment for all, but by autumn he noted with intense irritation that one railroad company had advertised that its director was none other than the "privy councillor [*Vortragender Rat*] in the imperial chancellor's Office for Railroad Affairs." In late autumn 1872, Lasker spoke critically of the corporations, the stock market, and embezzling entrepeneurs. "If the right to prosecution were not a public monopoly, there would certainly develop, as in England, associations which accept the duty of prosecuting fraudulent activities of this type—and perhaps I would belong to such associations," he declaimed, adding that the banks had no excuse for not recognizing fraudulent and inequitable conditions.[23]

Spurred by his earlier anxieties about railroad companies, Lasker continued to dig into the connection between the government and railroads. He questioned the relation of the entrepreneur Henry Bethel Strousberg to the Ministry of Commerce, headed by Heinrich Graf von Itzenplitz, and accused Hermann Wagener, Prince Putbus, and Prince Biron of receiving special favors from the Prussian government. Lasker probably did not anticipate the bitter reaction to his charges that erupted in January 1873, and the small, fiery politician responded by devoting all his time and energy to the subject. He was aided immeasurably by the expertise of his friend and political ally Bamberger, a former banker, who advised Lasker for a week and helped to draft his speech.

On February 7 Lasker put his material before the Landtag in an oration covering seventeen double-columned pages. He named names, cited sources, and accused the railroads of overvaluing their assets and attempting to acquire working capital by the sale of inflated stock. In addition to violating several sections of the 1870 law that required publication of a company's financial condition, this practice hurt everyone who invested at falsely inflated prices in companies that later failed. The crime was compounded by government connivance in approving incorporation of undercapitalized companies and in granting railroad concessions. By the time he sat down, Lasker had exposed the greatest scandal of his era. General Albrecht Graf von Roon, now minister-president of Prussia, was literally speechless before facts that, he claimed, were all new to him.[24]

Bamberger reported to his wife that all Berlin was in an uproar. The *Frankfurter Zeitung* stated on February 10 that all other news—"the laws on the Church, the military requests, Bismarck's conversations, and the rest"—was obscured by Lasker's speech. With the exception of the conservative *Kreuzzeitung*, the leading German newspapers showed general astonishment and widespread praise for Lasker. The interest and uproar continued into late spring. Bamberger's letters to his wife reveal a growing difference of opinion between him and Lasker because of the latter's naiveté and increasing fanaticism on the evil character of the business world. Bamberger saw a difficulty in reconciling what he referred to as Lasker's moral bigotry with his own latitudinarian character. But the first reaction by most Germans catapulted Lasker to the heights of public popularity, next to Bismarck himself. So many Germans wanted Lasker's judgment of their local political candidates' possible involvement in corruption that he published an open letter stating that he did not have such knowledge in all cases and that the data must be carefully evaluated because of their sensitivity and complexity. Although he declined to sit in judgment, Lasker nonetheless urged public interest and control of such economic activity.[25]

The effect of Lasker's speech was partially obscured by the major financial depression that struck Germany, most of Europe, and the United States in the autumn of 1873. It seems implausible to argue, as several of Lasker's opponents did, that the exposure of railroad corruption contributed to the collapse. Lasker himself stated in the Landtag in May 1874 that poor working conditions were due "in a not unessential measure" to the haphazard and financially unsound establishment of the railroads. Since liberal free traders and advocates of business freedom and expansion had helped to pass the new laws on incorporation in 1869 and had worked closely with Bismarck and Rudolf von Delbrück, it was natural that blame should fall on liberals as well as on conservatives for the depression. In his 1876 defense against the Conservative Otto von Diest-Daber, who attacked him because of his speech exposing railroad corruption, Lasker admitted as much.[26]

Conservatives quickly and even successfully accused liberals, especially economic liberals, of contributing to the corruption. Conservative publicists, both respectable and vulgar, acted to avert the political damage posed by Lasker's speech. But the conservatives were not immediately successful at the polls. The National Liberals gained thirty-two new seats at the next Reichstag election in 1874, reaching their highest level of all time, and Lasker's speech and fame certainly helped. What success the conservative polemics achieved can be attributed to several factors. Economic liberalism promoted competition, growth, and change, which many Germans linked with the opportunity for unethical and unsound business practices. Many liberals were connected with banking, which in turn was intimately tied to the railroads. Some of the most important National Liberals, men like Lasker and Bamberger, were Jews, and a growing segment of German society associated them with banking, the stock exchange, and sharp practice. For publicists like the vulgar Otto Glagau, it was relatively easy, and nearly irrefutable, to argue that Lasker had accused the conservatives of corruption in order to shift attention away from the sins of his own colleagues, "a gaggle of bankers, businessmen, and Jews."[27]

Franz Perrot, a liberal turned vehement Conservative and anti-Semite, specifically criticized Lasker for his unquestioning support of the 1869 law easing requirements of incorporation. That law, he argued, led to the increase in swindles. There was some truth in this charge. Lasker had said little and had voted for the law despite his concern about the moral and legal quality of German business life. This action probably indicates Lasker's insufficient grasp of the realities of German economic life rather than weak convictions. In 1870 Otto von Diest-Daber viciously took advantage of the situation to argue that Lasker had accused his own National Liberal colleagues, specifically Johannes Miquel, of collusion during the debate over lottery bonds. Lasker finally replied in 1876 with a brochure entitled "Justification and a Few Words to a Disinterested Reader," in which he charged that Diest-Daber had slandered him by using carefully selected material taken out of context. Comparison with the speeches in 1870 shows Lasker to be correct, but Diest-Daber's charges echoed through the conservative press of the 1870s. They even caused problems within the National Liberal party between Lasker and some of his more conservative colleagues.[28]

Nevertheless, it strains credibility to assume that Lasker's exposure of the railroad stock promoters (*Gründer*) represented a shock severe enough to have catalyzed the economic crisis. The basis for the scandal had been prepared by the economic growth of the 1860s and early 1870s, just as the depression originated in inflation and overproduction. Lasker's exposure of the railroads added to the economic crisis of the 1870s, but its more lasting result must be sought in the development of the railroad system and in the government's relation to private industry.

Von Roon's initial judgment that Lasker had assaulted the entire bureaucracy, rather than just the railroads, was true enough. Lasker had attacked two of his lifelong foes: public immorality and the impropriety and often the illegality of special privilege. The *Frankfurter Zeitung* saw this tendency clearly as early as April 7, 1873, when it editorialized that Lasker rejected both the Conservative and the Social Democractic solutions. His liberal preference for state control through reasonable and equitable laws was a subtly different solution than the Progressive party's doctrine of free competition. In both Landtag and Reichstag, Lasker worked for such control and investigation, although his efforts produced results only toward the end of the decade.[29]

Lasker promoted a bill in the Prussian Landtag to make it illegal for a state official to be a member of a private corporation without the approval of his department head. Such a position was not to be held at all if the official received any direct or indirect reimbursement. However, the bill soon became irrelevant with regard to railroads because of the move toward nationalization. In an earlier discussion of the railroad problem in the Reichstag, Lasker had mentioned possible solutions, and his old standby, better and more tightly written laws, received top billing; but his speech trailed off into confusion and ambiguity. After explaining some of the tricks used by business, such as false books, secret agreements to buy and sell so as to alter market values artificially, and connivance with the Prussian government, Lasker concluded that the only solution was to publicize all the essential facts of business practices and public corruption. But he offered no new or efficient method of obtaining such information on a regular basis.[30]

By May 1873 Lasker had turned his attention to consideration of the relation of railroads to the state. Originally, railroads developed by means of private capital; but now, Lasker argued, railroads were no longer a private matter. Much of his speech was an attack on unfettered free enterprise, which did not consider the state's interest in its desire for unhindered commercial activity. Railroads, he argued, were analogous to state highways and should be run for the public good rather than for the profit of the individual or the state treasury. In early 1874, in a debate over a bill to allow the government to lease a railroad, Lasker stated that the abuses of competition often moved him to agree with those who wanted to substitute overall planning for individual chaos. His reluctance in 1874 to agree to this principle stemmed from a lack of knowledge about government control of industry and doubts about the organization of such state corporations. Who would be responsible for the debts, and who would supervise the management, the government or the parliament? It was obvious that state control or ownership had become very real options for Lasker.[31]

The king appointed an investigative commission that included Lasker to look into his charges of corruption in the railroads. Its findings assisted in the dissection of the dealings of the Northern Railroad Corporation and especially of the activities of Princes Putbus and Biron. Lasker criticized the reluctance of both the railroads and the state Railroad Office to provide information, but he also began to question the economic motivation of the administration. He could not understand how responsible officials could believe that *any* railroad, sound or not, was economically beneficial. Because the possibility of government intervention was always there, subsidies for failing enterprises tended to produce laxity in business affairs. When the government justified subsidies on the ground that the railroads would not be built otherwise, Lasker rejoined that weak ventures should not be promoted. He went on record against a bill to rescue the Northern Railroad Corporation because there was no public good involved: it would be better to have either a wholly new corporation or state ownership. Finally, Lasker expressed irritation at the failure of rich men like Putbus, Biron, and the duke of Mecklenburg, not to mention the Berliner Bank, to pay for the collapse of a company they had formed, even though, in accordance with the law of 1869, their liability was limited. In any case, Lasker thought that the state should buy out a failed company only if there was no private purchaser.[32]

Lasker suffered politically from his exposure of the railroad swindles as well as from his support for a state rail system. By 1875–1876 he was an outspoken advocate of state ownership of railroads. But the attempt to construct an imperial railway system irritated the small states, who saw it as another example of Prussian dominance over Germany. Several of Lasker's National Liberal colleagues informed him of popular feeling against the Imperial Railroad Bill, and he warned of trouble at the polls. Julius von Hölder, who later contributed to the split in the National Liberal party, stood among the most vigorous of the bill's opponents. Bismarck was irate at Lasker's criticism of Wagener, a close lieutenant, and the continuing pressure undoubtedly contributed to Bismarck's dislike and distrust of the left wing of the National Liberal party. When the press and individuals appealed to him for advice on who was or was not corrupt, Lasker declined to provide such information but was nonetheless accused of character assassination by men like Diest-Daber and by the right-wing press. As a famous Jew he attracted more than his share of the rising wave of anti-Semitism. August Bebel, expressing the viewpoint of the socialists, concluded that Lasker had introduced a weak reform of corporations that was buried after two long years of investigation; meanwhile, the *Gründer* merely waited for the next opportunity. Until 1879 Lasker stuck to his position; then he began to press for legal guarantees against misuse of the state's power over the railroads. The move toward state control or ownership of the rail system, which resulted in control of 90 percent of the railroads by 1912, was well begun in 1879.[33]

It is entirely possible that the rift between Eduard Lasker and Otto von Bismarck caused Lasker to retreat from his advocacy of government control of industry. This assessment is in line with the evidence provided in the affairs surrounding the tariff shift and the workers' insurance crisis (discussed below). But Lasker's encounter in 1881 with Franz Perrot indicates that there were strong natural barriers to his drift toward state intervention in the economy. Perrot, Lasker's colleague in the Reichstag, proposed a bill to abolish joint-stock companies. Lasker sympathized with Perrot's dislike of limited liability companies but thought that abolition was impractical at the time. Modern society needed this particular method of large-scale capital accumulation because Schulze-Delitzsch's cooperatives, the only other new source of credit, were neither sufficient for business needs nor geared to large capital growth. Lasker never even considered socialism as an alternative. Like many nineteenth-century liberals, he supported greater freedom of occupation and credit but disliked some or all of the results. Raised in an economic world where the extremes were the crafts and the financial-commercial giants, Lasker favored the former and never either understood or liked the latter.[34]

In the crisis of the mid-1870s Lasker first had to find some way of restraining rampant corruption without violating liberal principles of free enterprise within a state that cooperated ever more closely with corporate as well as landed wealth. Simultaneously, the growing support for protective tariffs directly threatened the free-trade beliefs of a large portion of the National Liberal party. Protective tariffs did not become an issue until the late 1870s, paralleling the rise of Lasker's interest in direct taxes. Between 1865 and 1873 Lasker was generally regarded as a free trader, though not so doctrinaire as some of his colleagues in the National Liberal party. Lasker worried more about unity and the *Rechtsstaat* during these years than he did about tariffs. He supported the Zollverein, which combined free trade in Germany with protection against English competition, but only because he saw the Zollverein as leading to unity and centralization, which he favored. In retrospect, Lasker does not appear to have been a doctrinaire "Manchester man."[35]

In 1873 discussion on the economic condition of Germany presented Lasker with a dilemma: he disagreed with the Progressive Eugen Richter that Germany was in financial difficulty, but he did think the state needed more revenue in order to finance necessary social reforms. Income for the confederation, and later the Reich, came from two sources: member states made yearly contributions, and the central government itself collected revenue from tariffs and excises. The only significant alternative source of revenue was direct taxation, especially income taxes. Lasker's turn to direct taxes as the solution is noticeable only after 1870 and seems to be closely linked to his understanding of the need for more national revenue, to his desire to avoid raising tariffs to protective levels, and to his anger at the inequity of excise taxes. What began as a tariff problem gradually became an issue involving Germany's entire tax structure.

In 1871, upset at the Prussian finance minister's lack of initiative in reforming tax laws, Lasker called for the establishment of a "single tax in the sense that at a given level of income the obligation to pay taxes begins." He argued that the existing Prussian system of mixed direct and indirect taxes subjected the wage earner to a tax rate of between 4 and 5 percent while the wealthy paid at a much lower 1 1/2 percent rate. Notwithstanding the attraction of a new and perhaps more efficient source of revenue that would produce almost as much income as indirect taxes, it is clear that Lasker favored direct taxes for their more equitable distribution of the tax burden. Here, as in so many other areas, he demonstrated a strong sense of justice. In February 1872 Lasker advised passage of the Prussian budget but cautioned against abolition of a common tax, the *Mietsteuer* (a tax on rentals), which would exclude many individuals from the lowest class of voting rolls. In Prussia only taxpayers were eligible to vote, and their votes were weighted according to their place among the upper, middle, or lower third of all taxpayers in terms of amount of *direct* taxes paid. Indirect taxes were not only an unequal economic burden, Lasker explained, they were also politically discriminatory; the poor, who paid excises and tariffs with nearly every purchase, received no credit for these taxes in the Prussian tax-based electoral system.[36]

Nevertheless, Lasker refrained from advocating immediate substitution of direct for indirect taxes on the grounds that direct taxes alone would probably not be sufficient to meet state needs. Despite caustic criticism from August Bebel, Lasker did nothing until 1878. It was only when the government finally began to shift to protective tariffs that Lasker both protested the increase and urged direct taxation.[37]

After the turn to protection in 1879, Lasker attacked imperial financial policies along broader lines and based much of his polemics during his last years on the concept of direct taxation. In a major speech in the spring of 1881 he compared the German tax system with those in use in the rest of Europe, noting the much heavier reliance on direct taxes in all but the United States. He criticized the government's antagonism to increased direct taxation, though he still did not ask for a system based exclusively on direct taxes. Yet he eloquently decried the hardship that indirect taxes worked on the poor: "I see the entire system of the new fiscal policies—I hear so much said of the desire to protect the poor man, that one wants to help him in every way—only as an aristocratic policy to help the well-off and the highest classes."[38]

Lasker's support for direct taxation secured no real advances during his own lifetime, but eventually both Germany and Prussia passed reforms in this area. The Prussian system raised the income level below which one paid no taxes from 420 to 900 marks per year, and in 1891 a progressive income tax devised and written by Lasker's old political ally Miquel took effect. A progressive property tax followed in 1893. The Reich waited longer: an inheritance tax was introduced in 1906, a tax on unearned income in 1911, and a direct tax on property and income in 1913.[39]

The major economic controversy of the late 1870s turned on protective tariffs. Germany's economic situation changed in the 1870s as foreign grain and manufacturing began to hurt German sales and after the financial damage of the 1873 depression. Moreover, the industrial and agrarian interests, increasingly in favor of protection, had organized and developed lobbies where none had existed in the 1860s. By the end of the decade the revenues of the imperial government, derived substantially from tariffs, were increasingly inadequate. Whether or not free trade was still practical, it was definitely no longer politically powerful and faced a major crisis in 1878–1879.[40] The initiative in the movement toward protection was, of course, Bismarck's. By the early spring of 1879 the Reichstag was immersed in a bitter debate over the government's protective tariff proposal. The fight over the second antisocialist bill in October and November of the previous year was not forgotten, but it had been supplanted as the main source of contention by tariffs on wheat, rye, iron, timber, oil, and even goose fat.[41]

Protection was a hot issue, Lasker wrote to his friend Karl Baumbach in April 1879, but he intended to enter the fray unbeholden to any party line. This promise was certainly easy to keep, since Lasker was no longer on the National Liberal Executive Committee, had cut himself off from most party activities, and, after defeat in the Prussian Landtag elections, could devote his whole effort to the Reich. Moreover, the debate over the tariff ended before Lasker gave serious thought to the formation of a new party. Lasker was therefore a *Wilder* (loner) in late 1879 and 1880. Infuriated by the government's attacks on himself and on his few left-wing friends after the passage of the second antisocialist bill, he began to vote his own mind. Throughout the ensuing tariff debates Lasker pursued several points consistently: he deplored the taxation of necessities, argued against a system that made the poor pay more than the rich, sympathized with the need for protection in some areas of the economy, and attacked the emergence of economic interest groups in politics.[42]

Behind Lasker's factual arguments was an enduring hostility to the government and to Bismarck. In his opening speech on the Tariff Bill, Lasker noted that by its own admission the government was responsible for the failure of the 1870s. Why, he asked, should the Reichstag trust such a government's economic plan for the future? Coming from a man who had worked closely with Bismarck for years, such statements did not persuade most members of the Reichstag or the National Liberal party, but they indicate a decision on Lasker's part to discard his earlier policy of compromise.[43]

Bismarck argued that, in actuality, tariffs were taxes paid not by German consumers but by foreign merchants. Lasker, however, saw clearly that tariffs meant higher prices for the consumer, chiefly the poor and the workers. In any case, he argued, how could the government propose to tax food but not beer? The needs of the consumer, he wryly commented, were seldom mentioned in parliamentary discussions, which centered only on commercial interests. His speech against the oil tariff was almost totally devoted to this problem. Oil was increasingly a basic consumer item rather than a business expense, and most of the revenues would be taken from the common man. Citing the German economist Etienne Laspeyres, Lasker argued that prices would rise more than the amount of the tariff itself, thus hitting the consumer even more heavily. Tobacco and spirits were worthwhile tax objects, according to Lasker, but oil was not. "All taxes," he told his Meiningen constituents, "come from the people's pocket, but which class of the people? That alone is the question."[44]

Bismarck, Lasker charged, had created class warfare through his support of indirect taxes in the form of tariffs and excise taxes. Lasker could never agree to use indirect taxes as the means to obtain the 500–600 million marks Bismarck requested for workers' accident insurance. In early 1880 Lasker resigned from the National Liberal party and by late summer had helped to organize the new Liberal Union (Liberale Vereinigung). His message to voters for the new party was: The new state economic policies might help a few great capitalists but not the small owner, the craftsman, the wage laborer, the teacher, or the official; the common man would bear the largest burden of the 130 million marks in new taxes.[45]

Though willing to admit that there was some damage to native German industries from foreign competition, Lasker could find few concrete examples. Nor did he see any use for agricultural tariffs, though he conceded that they might apply in the case of the sugar beet industry. He saw the agricultural protective tariff simply as an attempt to end one failure through another. Initially, he declared that he would examine the administration's requests with an open mind, and in 1881 he recalled that he and others had been prepared to support protective tariffs in cases in which an industry could show proof of damage. Under no circumstances, however, would he support a system of protection. But the government simply moved too fast for Lasker.[46]

What really frightened and embittered Lasker about the introduction of the 1879 Tariff Bill was its political implications. In addition to setting the rich against the poor, Lasker wrote,

Bismarck's tariffs seemed to set city against country, region against region, and interest against interest. In Lasker's view, the scrambling for personal, corporate, or regional gain at the cost of the people and the nation demeaned politics. More than anything else, he preached the message of opposition to "interest politics" during this last period of his career. As early as May 8, 1878, he predicted that the alliance of industry and agriculture would not last: each had temporarily given in to the other in order to acquire immediate gain, but they were basically incompatible. Lasker did not regard the agricultural tariffs as analogous to the Corn Laws in England, but he felt that their results might be the same: the political separation of the city from the country. At the height of the debate in June 1879 Lasker wrote, "We are in the middle of a war of interests provoked by political goals," and he accused the administration of waging a highly tendentious campaign.[47]

In Lasker's estimation, setting blacksmith against estate owner and grower against baker was the "divide and conquer of tax politics." Publicly Lasker accused the government and its political allies, the Catholic Center and the Conservatives, of pursuing a policy of "interest politics." Moreover, Lasker expressed his fear of the power of commerce in tones reminiscent of his 1866 invectives against bankers: "No nation that remains dependent in public affairs and trade on private organizations and persons will endure."

The second Reichstag session of 1879 was the most painful of his career, he reported, because it was dominated by the blatant politics of the iron and rye interests. Their victory was a victory for particularism and the Catholic Center party. The chancellor, too, in Lasker's opinion, had deserted his own nationalist policy: Bismarck's support for the protective tariff bill demonstrated his lust for power at any price. The Zollverein, Lasker argued, had already proved that special interests did not bring automatic prosperity and a world market. The tariff was dividing the country.[48]

The iron and agricultural tariff bills were complex, detailed pieces of legislation that necessitated roll-call votes on each major item (presented in Tables 6.2 and 6.3). Lasker's record clearly shows him supporting free trade and opposing protection in both industry and agriculture. Only his 1873 vote against immediate elimination of the current iron tariff (No. 170) appears to be an exception. Yet this seeming vote against free trade is deceptive. Lasker did not want to cut state revenues drastically and was not opposed to a revenue tariff. He always voted in agreement with the majority of the National Liberal Executive Committee, and only once (No. 169 deviated from the majority of the party itself. But twelve of the sixteen votes were victories for protection, which won a hard-fought legislative struggle. It is apparent from the tables that the National Liberal party was unable to present a united front in the Reichstag on tariff issues—eloquent testimony to the effect of the economic changes of the 1870s on the political fortunes of Germany's largest party.

The tariff debate of 1879 shows Lasker's economic views to have been motivated by considerations other than purely economic ones. The judgment of contemporary economist Gustav Schmoller that Lasker was not a doctrinaire free trader seems well justified by his action on the tariff of 1879, despite a voting record that any free trader could respect and admire. He voted his moral and national convictions as much and perhaps more than his economic beliefs. It was, for Lasker, immoral and unethical to tax some people more than others, especially when those highest taxed were also those poorest paid. It seemed to Lasker in 1870 to be antinational to pursue a policy that played off one group against another. He opposed protective tariffs even though his Meiningen electoral district would benefit from them. Liberals could not, he wrote to Miquel after the protective tariffs (*Schützzoll*) were accepted, think of economics: "We are not simply businessmen, despite how highly I value the work of individuals and the commercial life of the nation. The demands of liberal politics are much broader, permeating the

Table 6.2

Reichstag Roll-Call Votes on Bills Relating to the Iron Tariff,
1873–1879

Bill Id	Content (Date)	In the Reichstag		In the NL Party		In the NL Exec. Comm.			RvB[b]	EL[c]
		Yes	No	Yes	No	Yes	No	Abs.[a]		
	(1)	(2)	(3)	(4)	(5)	(6)	(7)	(8)	(9)	(10)
169	To decide on iron tariff in 1876 rather than 1877 (June 24, 1873)	114	119	27	55	9	7	9	N	Y
170	Immediate abolition of the iron tariff (June 24, 1873)	98	134	20	63	8	9	8	N	N
208	To extend iron tariff to 1/1/1879 (December 13, 1876)	116	201	23	100	0	21	3	N	N
214	Equalization of tariff on iron (April 27, 1877)	111	211	32	81	0	22	2	A	Y
224	To lower iron tariff from 1 M to .5M/kg. (May 16, 1879)	125	192	57	25	15	1	4	Y	Y
225	To raise tariff on iron to 1 M/kg. (May 16, 1879)	218	88	35	44	3	11	6	Y	N
238	Final vote on 1879 tariff bill (July 12, 1879)	217	117	19	63	1	15	4	N	N

Source: Roll-call votes are taken from the *Generalregister*. See Table 4.1.
Note: The "Bill Id" was assigned by the *Generalregister* to bills in chronological sequence.
[a]Abs. = absent
[b]RvB = Rudolf von Bennigsen
[c]EL = Eduard Lasker

Table 6.3

Reichstag Roll-Call Votes on Bills Relating to Agricultural Tariffs,
1879–1883

Bill Id	Content (Date)	In the Reichstag Yes	No	In the NL Party Yes	No	In the NL Exec. Comm. Yes	No	Abs.[a]	RvB[b]	EL[c]
		(2)	(3)	(4)	(5)	(6)	(7)	(8)	(9)	(10)
	(1)									
227	To raise tariff on rye from .5 to 1 M/100 kg. (May 23, 1879)	161	173	7	76	0	15	4	N	N
228	To raise tariff on wheat, etc., to 1 M/ 100 kg., but keep rye at .5 M/kg. (May 23, 1879)	226	109	35	49	3	12	4	Y	N
229	To tax timber at .1 M/100 kg. (May 28, 1879)	172	88	8	54	0	8	11	Abs.[a]	N
230	To tax woodbark at .5 M/100 kg. (June 16, 1879)	140	86	10	47	0	10	9	Abs.[a]	N
231	To tax pork and goose fat at .1 M/100 kg. (June 24, 1879)	184	79	14	49	1	11	7	N	N
232	To tax coffee at 40 M/100 kg. (July 5, 1879)	174	97	17	56	1	11	7	N	N
233	To tax oil at 6 M/100 kg. (July 5, 1879)	171	92	17	52	1	10	8	N	N
268	To eliminate tax on pork and goose fat at .1 M/100 kg. (June 7, 1882)	120	130	32	1	6	3	2	N	Y
269	To tax asbestos at 60 M/100 kg. (June 9, 1882)	150	165	1	31	0	8	3	N	N

Table 6.3 (cont.)
Reichstag Roll-Call Votes on Bills Relating to Agricultural Tariffs,
1879–1883

| | | Number Voting | | | | | | | | |
| | | In the Reichstag | | In the NL Party | | In the NL Exec. Comm. | | | | |
Bill Id	Content (Date)	Yes	No	Yes	No	Yes	No	Abs.[a]	RvB[b]	EL[c]
	(1)	(2)	(3)	(4)	(5)	(6)	(7)	(8)	(9)	(10)
284	To tax building wood at .3 M/100 kg. commerical wood at .7 M/100 kg. (May 8, 1883)	150	178	2	39	0	9	2	N	N

Source: Roll-call votes are taken from the *Generalregister*. See Table 4.1.
Note: The "Bill Id" was assigned by the *Generalregister* to bills in chronological sequence.
[a]Abs. = absent
[b]RvB = Rudolf von Bennigsen
[c]EL = Eduard Lasker

whole of public life. The liberal party will not wish to sacrifice its politics to free trade."[49] To be sure, Lasker was trying to prevent a split in the party by arguing that it was founded not only on free trade; but it is also apparent that the economic crisis of the 1870s and the resulting establishment of protection awakened him to the social and economic discontent in German society.

Lasker's record on tariffs and taxation provides clear proof of his desire to eliminate economic, as well as legal and political, inequity. As early as the 1860s, when he ardently supported Schulze-Delitzsch's cooperatives, Lasker developed a keen interest in helping and encouraging the poorer classes. Despite strong hostility to Bismarck and to the state after 1878–1879, Lasker voted for most of the social insurance measures the chancellor submitted to the Reichstag. He never shared Bismarck's motives for the legislation, which were far more political than genuinely social or economic, but he did accept politically motivated legislation when he thought it might help the people and the nation.[50]

In 1868 Lasker warned that the problem faced by the poor could not be solved by private philanthropy; money for this purpose in Germany could not begin to match that available in England. Only the state could help. Lasker originally thought of state assistance in the form of loans and aid to the cooperatives, but as early as 1871 he spoke in favor of workers' insurance. Lasker was concerned that most workers had neither the time nor the awareness to save enough to make themselves secure in case of injury or sickness. The solution he suggested in 1871 envisioned employees and employers working together to remedy the situation. Moreover, such cooperation need not be a burden on the employers. It was undoubtedly statements such as this, coupled with Lasker's relatively open attitude toward free trade and his angry frustration at economic corruption, that induced the new Association for Social Politics (Verein für Sozialpolitik) to invite Lasker to its first organizational meeting in 1872.[51]

What began as an ordinary invitation to participate in private discussions about "the social question, especially concerning the trade unions, strikes, factory laws and housing problems," became a question of loyalty to the National Liberal party. H. B. Oppenheim hoped Lasker would not attend, adding that he and Karl Frenzel, a writer and an editor of the *National Zeitung*, agreed that Lasker should be Friedrich Zabel's successor as editor of the largest party press organ, the *National Zeitung*. Whether or not this was really an obvious attempt to "buy" Lasker away from the Association, Lasker replied that he was not going as an invited member and only wanted to see how these people thought. Oppenheim retorted that attendance would result in misuse of his name and prestige. He made it a choice between Adolf Wagner and Gustav Schmoller of the Association or John Prince-Smith, Otto Michaelis, and Karl Braun of the National Liberals. Lasker could not accept such advice and assured Oppenheim that he would guard against any misuse of his name.[52]

Bamberger then added his voice to Oppenheim's. He had read a recent book on unions by Lujo Brentano, founder of the Association, and found it riddled with the message of class hate. Bamberger was convinced that an attack upon capital and freedom of occupation would damage society and the workers. Finally, Lasker begged off in a friendly and apologetic letter to Schmoller. He exused himself on the grounds that the meeting was becoming a kind of congress and that he had no wish to participate in such an assembly: "I have so far stayed away from this type of thing, because I expect no real or fruitful discussion of the tough questions from such random assemblies."[53]

In one regard Oppenheim and Bamberger were correct: the Association was critical of the traditional liberal economic position. By 1875 Schmoller was proclaiming that liberalism no longer served the lower classes and that it had overlooked the connection between politics and social problems. But Brentano, at least, did not abandon the attempt to include Lasker, if only on an informal basis. "When I was in Berlin with Lasker," Brentano wrote to Schmoller in 1875, "the idea was explained to him, he agreed eagerly, and promised to agitate among the economists for it, and write to me." That Lasker did not write may have been due, Brentano suggested, to fear of publicizing the goals of the Association. Brentano jogged Lasker's memory two days later and evidently received Lasker's doubts about Schmoller and his excessive willingness to work through the state. Soon Bamberger bitterly attacked the members of the Association, and Brentano wrote to both Schmoller and Lasker. He told Schmoller that they could not have an informal agreement with men who desired perfection and complete security from any impolitic action. If Lasker had any interest in an alliance, he would have to show trust for their sense of honor. In his letter to Lasker, he likened the attack to Perrot's articles against liberals and Jews. There could be no alliance on such a basis; if Lasker agreed, he should do what he could to "save our honor," or else the alliance would be seriously endangered. He had turned to Lasker, Brentano added, out of trust and a common desire for an alliance of two groups. But nothing was done, and Lasker remained aloof from the Association and its programs.[54]

If the Association for Social Politics could be ignored, social problems could not. In the later 1870s poor relief and especially workers' assistance became national issues. Lasker doubted the efficacy of poor relief, which was almost entirely a communal and municipal operation in Germany. He maintained that anyone who accepted relief would feel so restricted in his economic individuality that he would turn to workers' associations and trade unions. The inability of workers to protect themselves against sickness and accident was obvious to Lasker, but he worried that welfare would induce apathy. In order to make welfare less attractive, the state should deny citizenship rights to those accepting it for as long as three years. Out of fear of losing his rights, the worker would redouble his efforts to avoid economic disaster. To Lasker's mind this kind of coercion was a valid use of state perogatives for a purely economic goal. He at least emphasized that acceptance of poor relief was not a crime.[55] But communal poor relief was a last-ditch measure that held little attraction for men like Lasker because of its feeble attempt to effect a cure merely by alleviating symptoms.

Accident and sickness insurance appealed to Lasker more than relief. Although he questioned technical aspects of Bismarck's accident insurance plan, his only major criticism was that it would be administered by the state. A review of Lasker's speeches and memoirs after 1878–1879 shows him to have been so critical of Bismarck and the state that he simply could not vote for an otherwise acceptable program. He declared at the outset that he liked the government's plan, except for some minor points; he felt that security against accidents was a legitimate state activity, although he deplored the low levels of compensation. Lasker also supported the attempt to require employers to bear the total cost. Insurance was a sound and peaceful way to solve social problems, but it should not be entrusted to state agencies.[56]

At the second reading of the accident insurance law, Lasker reiterated his support but warned that he and his friends would not vote for it if it was to be administered by the state or an imperial monopoly. He would rather wait than pass a bad law. Here Lasker emerged as a spokesman for decentralization. Earlier in his career he had supported the state out of a combination of personal patriotism and political pragmatism. His desire for unity so pervaded his politics in the years immediately after unification that he had been more conscious of threats to unity than of threats to personal welfare from the state. Politically, Lasker had yearned for a stable party system in which liberalism would not only dominate but also cooperate positively with the government. By 1881 the thrill of unity had faded, cooperation with the government was a debacle, and Lasker's power and his party had shrunk. The accident insurance law passed easily over Lasker's opposition on June 15, 1881.[57]

In defense of his vote, Lasker admitted the importance of accident insurance but argued that the liberals had prepared the way for social reforms through freedom of movement, work, and association. He would continue to work for self-help, but now the state was the obstacle: "The state wants, so far as we know, to transfer all concern and responsibility to itself and deliberately wishes to make its initiative and good will visible, almost to force upon a small fraction of the workers a government subsidy, in return for state control of the organization of labor. We want no preference for any class of workers, we want no direct control of the struggle for existence by the state, we want no state tutelage for the economic drive of grown men." This insurance law, Lasker maintained, would limit personal freedom and not solve economic problems.[58]

In the next Reichstag session, as leader of a new party that had achieved moderate success at the polls, Lasker continued to defend the liberal record of the 1870s. His support for laws that regulated factory conditions was tempered with a call for caution. In supporting reform of the laws on the responsibilities of the employer in heavy industry, he also looked forward to adequate protection for the old and the disabled. Furthermore, he began to voice a principle that had not previously appeared in his arguments: workers should have the opportunity to associate in order to provide their own insurance. Lasker argued that the state should provide the basic necessities and thereafter allow for self-help by the workers, as in England. Legislation alone, Lasker thought, would not solve the problems of social reform.[59]

The 1882 sickness insurance bill differed from the accident insurance bill in that workers would pay two-thirds of the cost of the plan and participate in its administration. Lasker felt that it did not go far enough, but he recognized that it answered a desperate need. Moreover,

Table 6.4

Reichstag Roll-Call Votes on Bills Relating to Worker's Insurance,
1881–1883

Bill Id	Content (Date)	In the Reichstag		In the NL Party		In the NL Exec. Comm.			RvB[b]	EL[c]
		Yes	No	Yes	No	Yes	No	Abs.[a]		
		(2)	(3)	(4)	(5)	(6)	(7)	(8)	(9)	(10)
	(1)									
257	Employers to pay 2/3 of accident insurance, employees pay 1/3 (June 2, 1881)	39	185	1	28	0	11	8	Abs.[a]	N
261	To establish an imperial insurance corporation (June 15, 1881)	105	161	41	1	12	0	7	Y	Y
262	Final vote on accident insurance (June 15, 1881)	145	108	3	37	0	11	8	N	N
285	To include agriculture and forestry in sickness insurance bill (May 25, 1883)	136	134	31	2	10	0	1	Y	Y
290	Final vote on sickness insurance bill (May 31, 1883)	216	99	11	26	5	5	2	Y	Y

Source: Roll-call votes are taken from the *Generalregister*. See Table 4.1.
Note: The "Bill Id" was assigned by the *Generalregister* to bills in chronological sequence.
[a]Abs. = absent
[b]RvB = Rudolf von Bennigsen
[c]EL = Eduard Lasker

he agreed that it must be compulsory: it was the state's right to require individuals to prepare against illness, just as it compelled them to go to school. He did not think that the bill would encourage socialism. Not only did Lasker support the final bill, he also voted for its extension to agriculture and forestry. The final Reichstag vote was overwhelmingly favorable, 216 to 99 (see Table 6.4).[60]

Lasker saw no irony in his post–1878 record of hostility to the centralized state he had worked so hard to establish. A shift in his thinking is more clearly evident in the field of economics and social insurance, since these two areas comprised the largest portion of legislation in the post–1878 period. The law codes were formulated, the *Kulturkampf* was over, budgetary votes were infrequent, the country was territorially unified, and constitutional changes, other than the perennial *Diäten*, had faded into the background. In the industrial age economic and social problems seemed permanent. Lasker did not see, or was not willing to accept, what the more perceptive Treitschke described in 1881: "The program of liberalism is fulfilled. Meanwhile the adolescence of the German state has produced a new series of tasks, which have nothing in common with the old party teachings and sooner or later must destroy our party activity—the threefold tasks of finances, economics, and social-political reform."[61]

VII

Lasker and the Collapse of the National Liberal Party

> "I want to settle the past peacefully, I want to estab-
> lish the present securely, but I do not want to com-
> promise the future."

> Eduard Lasker
> April 5, 1867

The year 1878 marked a turning point for Eduard Lasker and the National Liberal party. Both found it impossible to continue politics as usual under Bismarck's insistence on antisocialist and protective tariff legislation. Rejection of the first antisocialist bill infuriated the Iron Chancellor, and the second assasination attempt gave Bismarck his opportunity to alter the political makeup of the Reichstag by persuading the Kaiser to prorogue parliament and call immediately for new elections.

In many areas Lasker and the left wing became the primary issue in the election. The *Schleswiger-Nachrichten* predicted (incorrectly it turned out) that the local candidates Paul Hinschius and Willichs would win in Schleswig-Holstein because they were opponents of Lasker. The National Liberal party appeared chaotic, with a Treitschke group here and a Lasker group there; many party members promoted the slogan "away with all Laskerism." The *Frankfurter Zeitung* wondered what the National Liberal party was: Lasker, Bennigsen, or Treitschke? All crossed themselves with the sign of the National Liberal party, it editorialized, but that meant little.[1]

Lasker foresaw a tough campaign and was already tired. Bennigsen was clearly torn between his belief that the people wished to fight the Social Democrats and his knowledge that his party wanted to fight the chancellor. In Hannover peasants reportedly believed that Lasker now controlled Bennigsen. Elsewhere Eduard Stephani urged cooperation with Bismarck and criticized Lasker's harmful influence on the campaign literature emanating from Berlin. In Stephani's opinion a war between Lasker and Bismarck would not only lose seats but also split the party. The election results confirmed the serious damage to the party, including the decimation of the Bavarian contingent and the defeat of its left-wing leader Franz von Stauffenberg.[2]

The real effect of the 1878 elections was to promote internal change in the National Liberal party. The left wing did not immediately opt for secession; rather, Lasker and his allies felt a vastly increased pressure from the right, and talk of a split became more and more common. In the short term the left needed to secure Stauffenberg's re-election from a "safe" constituency in the first available by-election, since he was indispensable to the National Liberals in the South and to the relations between the two wings of the party in the Reichstag. Lasker recognized that Stauffenberg, as a personal ally, was vital to his own position as well as to that of the National Liberal party in general.

Although Franz von Stauffenberg eventually won in Braunschweig, the party remained torn, and Lasker operated more and more independently. Julius von Hölder's diary from the fall of 1878, the most complete record of activities at the time within the National Liberal party, portrays Lasker as obstinate (*hartnäckig*) and increasingly isolated. There were bad feelings in the caucus and a general bitterness toward Lasker and his compatriots. Stauffenberg, along with Max von Forckenbeck and Ludwig Bamberger, stuck with Lasker, obliging Bennigsen to work alone in the Reichstag in the autumn and especially during the debates on the second antisocialist bill. By mid-November Lasker was tired and disappointed: "I have lost the double confidence that either the party wants me or that my membership in it is useful." If he could do nothing significant, he would retire. After all, he asked Stauffenberg, was he not entitled to some rest? Moreover, he doubted whether an attempt at greater party organization would do anything more than produce a split: "If only some convinced, independent men came forth, much could be won. Too much strength is lost in 'understandings' among ourselves and with the government." But Lasker remained pessimistic about the chance for fruitful party activity and looked forward to a future of independent action.[3]

Still, the National Liberal party held together in the face of constant predictions of dissolution by almost all elements of the party and the press. Lead articles in papers of both right and left prominently featured the possibility of a new National Liberal party without Lasker. Several party leaders still hoped for some kind of agreement on the government's proposed tariff legislation. Lasker, on the other hand, suggested that separating economics and politics might achieve unity on noneconomic issues. But such unity meant political opposition to Bismarck over budget control, ministerial responsibility, and the antisocialist law—equally impossible. Bennigsen wavered before a choice that would probably split the party for good. Stauffenberg retained no hopes for a new party organization, and Bamberger refused to act without Forckenbeck, who was convinced that separation was inevitable and who stayed at home during this crucial period.

By late June, Lasker foresaw a final confrontation in the party but emphasized to Stauffenberg that he was no great proponent of a new formal party. Bennigsen, too, had now decided that a separation was necessary. Lasker said much the same in July to Hölder, who recorded that the new party would probably be named the Liberal Imperial party (Liberale Reichspartei). But an actual split still seemed to depend on Bennigsen, whom Lasker tried to win for the opposition. Bennigsen, watching the party crumble (Volk, Schauss, and twelve others on the right seceded on July 14), decided to resign. Ironically, his temporary resignation seemed to clear the air, and again the split failed to materialize.[4]

Beginning in August 1879, Lasker and the National Liberal party devoted most of their political attention to the October elections to the Prussian lower house. During that summer and fall Lasker modified his political vocabulary, substituting "liberal" for "National Liberal." He even harbored hopes for stronger organization and discipline in a "Liberal Party" as a preliminary to the reacquisition of power. He did not mourn Bennigsen's loss too much, because the Hannoverian aristocrat would be useful only as an opponent of the government, and he refused to go that far. This period also marked the beginning of Lasker's emphasis on the need for unity among liberals: "All 'staunch liberals' should hold fast to the decision to organize resistance to the pressure of reaction."[5]

Lasker's new mild enthusiasm and optimism were neither evident among other National Liberal leaders nor reflected in the Prussian election results. Johannes von Miquel, Robert von Benda, and Rudolf Bennigsen on the right found it almost impossible to work with Lasker, and the left-wing leaders also nourished personal goals and grievances that prevented unity within the National Liberal corpse. Miquel told Benda that if Lasker were elected there was reason to instigate a "clear confrontation," even if it caused a split. On the other hand, Stauffenberg told Lasker that he feared Bennigsen's cooperation with Bismarck if Bennigsen accepted a mandate. The lines of demarcation became much clearer after the Prussian electoral disaster. The party fell from 169 to 85 seats in the lower house, a 50 percent decline. Lasker himself lost in Magdeburg, Breslau, and Frankfurt am Main. He never again returned to the Prussian Assembly, where he had begun his career in 1865.[6]

The defeats of 1879, coming as they did on the heels of the trauma surrounding the antisocialist bills of 1878, led Lasker to remark sourly that "some former friends did not appear dissatisfied with the results." He believed that interest groups controlled the party, that a liberal-conservative alliance already existed, and that Bismarck enjoyed complete mastery of the situation. He discussed establishment of a new political newspaper but admitted to a strong disinclination to engage in political activity. A future in journalism interested him, but only in the periodical press, because "I believe that it is now more important to inspire the educated circles to recognition and awareness." He was in no hurry to decide where to run in the next campaign. Two months earlier Forckenbeck, concerned over Lasker's optimism, had written: "I almost fear that he wants to familiarize himself with the quiet contemplativeness of old age that he prizes and loves so much." But Lasker regained some vigor, and by early 1880 the press began to report rumors of the formation of a Lasker-Rickert or a Lasker-Rickert-Forckenbeck group. Again, talk of a split grew. In early March Lasker led the Reichstag fight against the Stosch system in the navy, and the *Frankfurter Zeitung* predicted that he would soon be called a "loner."[7]

Not surprisingly, Lasker finally resigned from the National Liberal party in mid-March, motivated, he said, by the overall situation. He obviously would have liked company, but Bamberger would leave only if Forckenbeck and Stauffenberg did, and Forckenbeck could not decide. Lasker announced his resignation and the reasons for it to his supporters in Meiningen in a formal brochure and to the Executive Committee of the party in the Reichstag. He cited as his basic reason for leaving the lack of harmony in the party, for which he had no hope of improvement. The Executive Committee expressed regret over his decision but accepted his resignation with no attempt to persuade him to reconsider. Lasker's close friend Berthold Auerbach privately predicted that this action foreshadowed Lasker's retirement. But Lasker probably did not intend immediate withdrawal. It is improbable that he would write and publish such a carefully worded apologia to his supporters in Meiningen as a prelude to retirement.[8]

There is no doubt that the left wing of the National Liberal party, or at least its foremost leaders, had little hope of remaining within the party much longer. Delay in following Lasker or in organizing a group secession seems to have stemmed from concern for style rather than difference in principle. The left-wing leaders were concerned about the type of program to be issued, the possible need for a party convention, and the relation to the Progressives. Bamberger, for example, felt that perhaps the tide had finally begun to turn in their favor; but he cautioned against any public agitation for a new party, feeling that it should develop spontaneously. Lasker confided to Stauffenberg that he had planned a trip to America because his activity at home appeared to be completely unproductive, but recent events had heartened him. He especially noted dissatisfaction in the party and widespread recognition of the need for a new liberal party. Still, Lasker was unwilling to give up his quiet life unless he felt he could really help; he would remain in Berlin to see what developed. He foresaw two possibilities: a return to the National Liberal party or the establishment of a new party that could and should ally with the Progressives.[9]

Lasker spent the remainder of July and all of August 1880 in negotiations with his friends in the left wing over the best possible basis for secession. Essentially, the plan was to begin with secession and then to attempt a union with the Progressive party. Heinrich Rickert became a key figure in these exchanges. He represented the narrow free-trade interests of seaports such as his own Danzig, he was otherwise moderate, and he possessed power and talent in political organization. Rickert wrote Lasker on July 19, 1880, that he agreed with the position of the Progressive Albert Haenel and felt a real need for a political electoral organization to include *all* liberals. He was not, he stressed, interested in a formal convention with the Progressives, but he was concerned about control of the press. He could accept a new party only if it were "generally" liberal.[10]

Lasker responded immediately by contacting Haenel and E. A. Müller, whom he considered to be sympathetic Progressives. He supported the steps taken to form a new party and emphasized the relation to the Progressives as a key element. In his opinion, he told Haenel, not only was there no obstacle to merger and the construction of a great liberal party, but union should occur quickly so as to capitalize on the mood of the moment. Solidarity with the Progressives was necessary to the growth of a strong liberal party. Müller resonded favorably, but could do little as a Progressive. He deplored the narrow factionalism that he evidently detected within his own party and that he feared might harm the liberal cause. If a program for a new party was to be issued, Müller warned, everything would depend on what it said. Not surprisingly, in view of the suddenness of the merger plan, nothing came of the attempt.[11] The Progressives stayed aloof from the left-wing secession during the early days of its existence.

The actual secession from the National Liberal party took shape during August. Rickert played down secession in itself, focusing attention instead on the need for action. The new political group must be positive, must align with the Progressives, and, above all, must organize at every level. Lasker agreed and argued for a clear and simple campaign program, which Stauffenberg drafted. Stauffenberg wanted the secessionists to concentrate on repudiation of the Conservatives and to avoid criticism of the change in Bismarck's personal politics. The new party must, he emphasized, advocate only what everybody could understand immediately.

Forckenbeck played an active role in August, writing to Rickert and talking with Lasker and Theodor Wilhelm Lesse in Berlin, Bamberger in Switzerland, and Stauffenberg in Munich. He now felt the National Liberal party to be useless and no longer a party; the solution was to secede and form a new party. On the one hand, Forckenbeck thought that Rickert placed too much emphasis on party organization and structure; on the other hand, he recognized the left-right polarization in the party but thought they were caused primarily by events external to the party.[12]

Certainly, the "awful organization of the party" aided the dissolution. Unlike Forckenbeck, Rickert wanted positive action and organization. The draft program was acceptable to him, but it said nothing about structure. He therefore requested counter-signature by as many supporters as possible. He continually returned to the practical questions of control of newspapers and formation of electoral committees. By August 14 the *Frankfurter Zeitung* knew of Rickert's involvement and registered its surprise; the participation of a man from the party center (except on tariff issues) made the secession look far more viable. By this time Rickert had supplanted Lasker as the party organizer and had substituted public political action and organization for Reichstag debate and program formulation. Rickert was by far the most active leader of both the nearly defunct National Liberal party and the incipient Liberal Union.[13]

The details of secession were complete by August 15, when Lasker wrote his friend and campaign manager in Meiningen, Karl Baumbach, of the move: "You will have to decide. . . . whatever you do, do it with your whole heart." He emphasized Rickert's demand for strong party organization and a positive program in the country. He had hoped to lead it, but he had to conserve his energy. To Stauffenberg, Lasker confessed a lack of interest in the form of the declaration of secession; only politicians would understand it anyway, he remarked. Again, he repeated Rickert's message, adding his own strong support for positive action.

Rickert formally notified Bennigsen of the resignation of nineteen National Liberals on August 17. The *Frankfurter Zeitung* referred to them as the *Sezessionisten* or "Secession" throughout the rest of the month. On the thirtieth, the nineteen issued a formal public declaration of secession. The long-predicted separation was completed.[14]

The original members of the new Liberal Union (Liberale Vereinigung) were few in number, although several were men of national stature with power and ability to garner votes at the polls and with lengthy parliamentary experience. Their program, short and vague, offered support for liberalism in general, resistance to reaction, reform of taxation, opposition to indirect taxes and tariffs, and support for religious freedom if controlled by the state. The Progressive Eugen Richter quickly wrote Lasker that the Liberal Union seemed promising for the liberal cause and agreed with some, but not all, of the important points of its program. But he concluded that the Progressives would have to wait and see how far they could cooperate politically with the former National Liberals. The Progressives obviously wanted more solid evidence than a printed declaration.[15]

The withdrawl of the nineteen placed new pressure on the remainder of the National Liberal party. Stephani advised public cooperation with the *Sezessionisten*, although he feared that Lasker and his allies would fall more and more into the clutches of Eugen Richter. Benda felt that if the "renegades" wished more seats they would have to fight the Progressives rather than the center and the right wings of the old National Liberal party. Such a clash would mean political disaster for the Progressives, the Liberal Unionists, or both. The Unionists lost little time in attacking the National Liberals, prompting Bennigsen to warn Rickert of the danger posed by Richter and to refuse to share control of the *Deutsche Korrespondenz*, a National Liberal paper. Rickert understood Bennigsen's fear but defended the agitation against the National Liberals as politically necessary; the cities were moving leftward and would otherwise be dominated by the Progressives.[16]

The Liberal Union had its problems in the winter of 1880–1881. Lasker suffered a resounding setback in a Landtag contest in Magdeburg in which the Progressives played a hostile role. Baumbach worried over Lasker's strength in Meiningen under a new and little understood party label. Furthermore, the Liberal Union experienced difficulty in securing a journal to be used as a national organ of party opinion and information; eventually it bought the Berlin *Tribune*, a move that proved financially and politically unsuccessful. Stauffenberg was irate at the Progressive's simultaneous pressure for support from and attacks on the Liberal Union. He predicted his own loss in Erlangen because the Peoples' party (Volkspartei) would back a Progressive; nothing could be done, he urged, without the banner of a great liberal party. On the other hand, both Ludolf Parisius, secretary of the Progressive party, and Richter had occasion to complain about Liberal Unionists who supported National Liberal candidates over Progressives and continued to run their own candidates except in local areas. Even electoral cooperation on the lowest level did not come easily.[17]

In trying to annoy as few liberals as possible and to be as simple as it could in appealing to the people, the Liberal Union created other problems for itself. The *Weserzeitung* took the party to task for refusing to publish a positive program. The party's June statement—that it needed no program because the people knew what the new party stood for—was essentially Lasker's position. The *Frankfurter Zeitung* correctly called the program illusory and deceptive; it was only personal representation based on faith, not a system. References to an all-liberal party were greeted by the democratic paper as harmless naiveté.[18]

In *Fünfzehn Jahre*, probably written about the time of the split, Lasker expressed real concern over the unwillingness of liberals to unite. The lesson of the 1878 election failure was that liberals must work together. Lasker provided several examples of political cannibalism among liberals. Even if an all-liberal party could not agree on everything, it would be better than the inefficiency of division, as practical experience demonstrated. Lasker was in fact so concerned about the necessity of alliance or merger that he began a serious attempt to find a basis for cooperation with Bennigsen and the National Liberals in the last few weeks before the Reichstag election of October 27, 1881.[19]

Lasker first broached the subject to Bennigsen on September 3, 1881. He was interested in cooperation of some kind or, at least, desired a frank discussion of the elections and the parliamentary future. He was willing to go to Hannover for a meeting. Bennigsen agreed to talk but held out no hope in light of the opposition of the Progressives and the Liberal Union. At the same time, he told his close political associate Benda of Lasker's bid, which had been accompanied by a complaint about a dearth of good candidates. Benda talked to Lasker and wrote Bennigsen of the results. Lasker had emphasized the need for unity through an electoral coalition and especially a joint declaration of unity. When Benda asked how that might be achieved with such wide differences, Lasker suggested a series of similar, but not identical, public statements. Benda saw some value in this but wanted to discuss it first with Bennigsen. Lasker stressed that the issue of support for either the National Liberal or Progressive parties was a local question and on September 14 asked for more discussions, urging opposition to Bismarck as the primary goal and playing down the specific form unity would take. This proposal resembled the Liberal Union's arrangement with the Progressives, but nothing came of the discussion.[20]

A campaign speech in Meiningen on October 9, 1881, reveals Lasker's frustration at not producing a workable electoral alliance. Much of his political message to the Thuringian voters was a plea, in tones reminiscent of 1862–1866, to oppose the reactionary government and its bureaucracy. For this purpose, a union of all liberals was necessary, but an all-liberal party could not be established on past history: the old conflicts between the Progressives and the National Liberals must be forgotten. There had been progress toward such a party, Lasker claimed, but the task was difficult. He accused conservatives of attempting to identify him with the Progressives so as to split off the moderate liberals. Lasker countered: "The truth is, however, that we are agreed on entering the present elections without respect to any fractional differences and in an undivided condition." The object was to elect as many liberals as possible and to avoid conflict with them whenever possible.[21]

The 1881 elections gave the Liberal Union a slight edge in the Reichstag over the National Liberals, 47 to 45, and the Progressives increased their seats to 59. Overall, these figures represent a 240 percent increase in seats for the Liberal Union and a 220 percent increase for the Progressives. The National Liberals lost 30.7 percent. Yet Bennigsen interpreted the elections negatively for the Progressives and Liberal Unionists. He felt that Richter was incorrigible and that "Friend Lasker" probably was too. "The dream of a liberal absolute majority, which would be wholly divided within," he opined, "is probably gone, even with the imaginative and sanguine à la Lasker." Bennigsen saw hope only in a center party, one that did not include the Catholic Center, however. Lasker did not agree and wrote Bennigsen on November 8 that a coalition could still be built even if not strongly unified and more difficult to establish. The voters had demonstrated their opposition to reaction. He counted 150 to 160 liberal votes in the Reichstag, to which political negotiation could add 15 or 20. Hold out till next election and increase this total, Lasker urged. Past differences must be forgotten. Neither concrete cooperation nor a new party was now the main point; instead, the government and its allies must recognize the liberals as capable of real action.

Bamberger was more pessimistic, but he had much earlier agreed that the success of the new party or any all-liberal party would depend on the extent to which the people recognized the danger from reaction. Bennigsen remained unmoved by Lasker's prose or by the Progressives' attitude, especially Richter's, during the campaign. He wrote Lasker that he could not speak for his colleagues prior to the meeting of the Reichstag. Lasker responded that the Progressives Haenel and Rudolf Virchow, the famous pathologist, could be depended upon and that Richter would cooperate in a crisis. Lasker even raised the possibility of cooperation with the Free Conservatives and called for an end to the infighting that cost all of them seats. Even if an alliance did not work, the effort at collaboration might reveal the obstacles to merger. On December 6, however, the National Liberals decided to allow for local electoral arrangements with the Liberal Union while retaining full independence as a party.[22] This action effectively killed plans for a wide-ranging electoral alliance.

When Lasker referred to the nation as "liberal" in the Reichstag in late November, Bismarck immediately rose to ridicule the idea that a majority of Germans were liberal. Lasker weakly replied that he had meant the "liberals in the nation," affirmed that they were not purely negative, and predicted that the all-liberal party would give them the power to work positively. Lasker was mistaken. The Progressives were torn by their own problems, and the National Liberals and Progressives had little in common. Lasker left for America in June 1883, and Bennigsen retired in September. In 1884 other men constructed a merger between the Liberal Union and the Progressives under a new name, the German Freethinking party, which led an uneasy and unsuccessful existence until it also split in 1893.[23]

VIII

Eduard Lasker and German Liberalism

Many historians today still identify the last one hundred years of German history with the misfortunes of liberalism: World War I, Hitler, and World War II do not readily evoke memories of a liberal past. Lasker and many of his liberal colleagues would undoubtedly agree with this assessment. Only in the wake of the cultural and social destruction wrought by Hitler and World War II was liberalism widely accepted in Germany. In the prewar period, most historians contend, German liberalism was never vital enough to acquire power, or, more seriously, it failed as early as the revolutions of 1848, the Indemnity Bill of 1866, or the constitution of 1867.[1]

Yet, despite its long-range weaknesses, it would be inaccurate to conclude that German liberalism died a stillbirth in the events of 1848 or 1866–1867. Each of these episodes in fact produced significant liberal changes: a written constitution and elections after 1848, and a new constitution with broader powers based on universal suffrage after 1867. If such results are taken as measures of success, then liberalism in Germany won some significant victories.[2] Although many Progressives and Democrats saw the events of 1866–1867 as a setback, most liberals in Germany, who were far more numerous than their critics to the left, viewed them as generally liberal and were optimistic about the future. In this respect Lasker represented the main thrust of liberal expectations after the war of 1866 and the founding of the North German Confederation.

Like almost all liberals, Lasker desired the unification of Germany, and when Bismarck and the army achieved it, he was properly appreciative. Lasker and most of his liberal colleagues strongly supported the North German Confederation and the German Empire. Even if Lasker worked harder than most liberals to secure the merger of South Germany, he was hardly unique. Bismarck never failed to remind his fellow citizens that he and the military had secured German unity. Indeed, he went much farther, falsifying history by trying to make liberals like Lasker appear to be opponents of national unity. Despite vigorous protests, this myth grew throughout Bismarck's chancellorship.

One cannot realistically argue that liberals should have opposed unity in the 1860s because the later national development of Germany was detrimental both to Germans themselves and to all of Europe. National unity was part of the liberal program from the early decades of the century, and Lasker merely followed the lead of earlier liberals—democrats and radicals alike—when he embraced unification both as a liberal goal and as the practical beginning of a liberal state. One may question the tactics used by men like Lasker, but only in particular cases. That is, one may ask whhether any specific compromise with the government was worthwhile, but the answer should not depend upon later German history. Lasker and the majority of liberals agreed to end the Conflict Era by voting for the indemnity, but they did not do so in a vacuum. Not only were they under political pressure from the electorate, but they also had a not unreasonable expectation of being able to work with the government within a substantially new and favorable context, a constitutional democracy similar to that of England. There is no evidence, moreover, that Lasker or most of his colleagues abandoned any of their liberal goals in 1867.

Nor is it accurate to portray Bismarck as an ardent enemy of liberalism and liberal programs. Despite opposition to much of what the liberals said and did, he worked with them, compromising when he had to, at least in the period between 1867 and 1878. Even after 1878, Bismarck continued to cooperate with a substantial minority of the National Liberals. If compromise was a political tactic of liberals like Lasker, it was also a favorite Bismarckian method. And where critics on the left attacked Lasker for his compromises, those to Bismarck's right criticized him on similar grounds. What was at issue was not the methods each used but the success achieved in employing those methods.[3]

In this connection, with respect to both Lasker and liberalism, it is important to be clear about who their opponents were. In fighting for their political goals, liberals like Lasker clashed with other political parties, with the regime, and sometimes with both together. The historical lesson of the period 1867–1884 is that liberalism could not succeed when it faced the combined opposition of its political enemies and Bismarck's administration. In the halcyon days of the New Era and the Era of Conflict, liberalism in the form of the Progressive party was by far the dominant political movement; its only recognizable foe was a weak Conservative party. By contrast, the 1870s witnessed the rapid growth of political Catholicism, reformed Conservatism, and Social Democracy, while the Progressive party split into a small but vocal group of Progressives and a large National Liberal party. Lasker represented many liberals in the latter group who expected a liberal future and did not foresee the emergence of such broad-based political opposition.

Facing a powerful state led by the dynamic Bismarck and a gaggle of apparently insubstantial fledgling political parties, Lasker and the National Liberals chose to compromise with the tougher opponent while attempting either to defeat or to overawe the new parties. In retrospect this choice was politically understandable but historically disastrous. Should Lasker have foreseen the rapid growth of antiliberal political parties? Perhaps. Few, if any, political observers were so prophetic in the 1870s. By the time Lasker and others recognized what had occurred, it was too late. Nor was it reasonable to expect men like Lasker to subordinate their programmatic ambitions to the "higher" goal of driving Bismarck from office and forcing a liberal administration on Germany. Even had it been possible for the liberals to defeat Bismarck with the help of anti-Bismarckian parties like the Center, it is doubtful that the nonliberal parties would have allowed a liberal administration. More important, it is unrealistic to think that Lasker and his allies might have attacked Bismarck with the support of anti-national parties. Most liberals, after all, were patriots and could not conceive of working with the enemies of the Reich. Certainly Lasker could not.[4]

The best example of the liberals' lack of vision is provided in their analysis of the German economy. Rapid economic growth after 1848 transformed Germany from a predominantly rural and agrarian state into a heavily urban and commercial-industrial one. Liberal economic theory not only failed to predict the changes this development produced, but it also failed to offer guidelines in the face of a whole new set of economic, social, and political problems. Liberals effectively abdicated leadership in one of the most important aspects of German social development and consequently could not but lose political support to parties that claimed to possess a solution. Although this conclusion stands as an indictment of Lasker's economic program and that of liberalism generally, it should be noted that liberal parties throughout Europe foundered on the same question in this period. In Germany the failures of liberal economic theory produced a split within the movement, and Lasker's membership in the Liberale Vereinigung after 1880 betrayed his reluctance to desert the traditional free-trade basis of German liberalism.

If we grant that 1848 and 1866–1867 did not mark irrevocable turning points, that liberals like Lasker made errors in political judgment, and that misunderstanding of economic development was a common liberal failing, we can understand more clearly the liberal politics of the 1860s and 1870s, but we have yet to explain the failure of liberalism as such. Liberalism's failure in Germany can be traced in its political history and occurred in a traditional and prosaic fashion—at the polls and in the legislature.

The demise of the National Liberal party and the catastrophic decline in Lasker's popularity and power at the polls were both quick and final. Tables 3.1, 3.2, and 3.3 document the abrupt electoral decline of support for him and his programs between 1877 and 1881. The record on legislation is complex and confusing, but it explains much of the National Liberal "success" and "failure" in the 1867–1881 era. Although not always successful in passing legislation, the National Liberal party won far more Reichstag and Landtag battles than it lost (see Appendixes E and F). Its record of success on the most important legislation was consistently high. The party record on the most hotly debated and divisive bills (see Table 8.1) shows a remarkable level of internal unity and success in passage of legislation.

Yet this record is illusory. The most notable triumphs were the votes on the seven-year military budget (Bills 187 and 188) and on the first and second antisocialist laws (Bills 221 and 223). But the *Septennat* was Bismarck's victory; it was neither Lasker's policy nor that of liberalism to abdicate budget control over the military for seven years. The nearly unanimous vote against the first antisocialist law was impressive but costly, for it damaged the National Liberals' public image, while the unanimous vote supporting the second bill won no new friends and embittered left-wing allies among the Progressives, Democrats, and Social Democrats. The four-year military budget of 1867 (Bill 10) was an administration victory that served as a prototype of the 1874 *Septennat*. The paper-thin victory on travel and expense pay for members of the Reichstag (Bill 9) died a quiet death waiting for government approval. The anti-Jesuit law (Bill 155) was originally Bismarck's legislation, but when the chancellor ended the *Kulturkampf*, the Catholics still remembered the very solid support it had received from liberals. The liberal position in the *Kulturkampf* was always a liability in Catholic areas. The bills raising tariffs to protective levels (Bills 237 and 238) were pyrrhic victories that immediately caused the secession of the left wing of the National Liberal party. Ironically, the largest numerical split within the party occurred over the death penalty (Bill 20), but it was quickly forgotten and had no perceptible effect on liberal unity or popularity in 1870 or later.

To be sure, one can point to liberal successes in a variety of areas. These have been described above with specific reference to Lasker's career. But they were not as important as the legislation mentioned above and found in Table 8.1. Legislation such as the *Septennat*, the antisocialist laws, and the protective tariffs involved fundamental questions about liberal progress versus antiliberal government policies. When success meant agreeing with such a government, as it did in most cases, victory turned into defeat. In the final analysis Lasker and many liberals voted for legislation that was contrary to liberal principles because of their reluctance to provoke a new Conflict Era by denying Bismarck a budget or other vital legislation. Lasker's rationale for his important compromises was not only that half a loaf was better than none but also that cooperation would produce a bigger slice of the loaf in the future. In acting on this assumption, Lasker tragically underestimated Bismarck's capacity for domestic *Realpolitik*.

Eduard Lasker and his fellow liberals pursued the goal of a liberal Germany long after 1867; they did not surrender their principles piecemeal after hearing the news from the Bohemian battlefields. But neither Lasker nor most liberals saw the necessity for acquiring effective government power through control either of the chancellor or of the budget. The 1870s and early 1880s proved this decision to be an error in political judgment fraught with fateful consequences for the future of liberalism.

Table 8.1

Reichstag and National Liberal Party Voting Records on Ten
Important Roll-Call Votes, 1867–1878

Reichstag Importance Ranking[a]	Bill Id	Description (Date)	Number of Votes				Win or Lose
			Reichstag		National Liberals		
			Yes	No	Yes	No	
(1)		(2)	(3)	(4)	(5)	(6)	(7)
2	9	Travel expenses and daily pay for RT Members (March 30, 1867)	136	130	64	12	Win
5	10	Four-year military budget (April 5, 1867)	137	127	67	6	Win
11	223	Final vote on 2nd anti-socialist law (October 19, 1878)	221	149	95	0	Win
12	237	To raise tariff on rye from .5 to 1 M/ 100 kg. (July 11, 1879)	186	160	8	77	Lose
15	187	Seven-year budget clause of 1874 military bill (April 14, 1874)	222	146	145	0	Win
20	92	To include death penalty in penal code (May 23, 1870)	127	119	22	44	Lose
40	188	Final vote on military bill of 1874 (April 20, 1874)	214	123	140	0	Win
47	238	Final vote on tariff bill of 1879 (July 12, 1879)	217	117	19	63	Lose
125	155	Final vote on anti-Jesuit law (June 19, 1872)	181	93	84	3	Win

Table 8.1 (cont.)

Reichstag and National Liberal Party Voting Records on Ten
Important Roll-Call Votes, 1867–1878

			Number of Votes				
Reichstag Importance Ranking[a]	Bill Id	Description (Date)	Reichstag Yes	No	National Liberals Yes	No	Win or Lose
(1)	(2)	(3)	(4)	(5)	(6)	(7)	
189	221	Final vote on first anti-socialist law (May 24, 1878)	57	251	1	90	Win

Source: Roll-call votes are taken from the *Generalregister*. See Table 4.1.

Note: The "Bill Id" was assigned by the *Generalregister* to bills in chronological sequence.

[a]"Importance" is calculated quantitatively from the number of members present and voting and the closeness of the vote. It is called the Riker scale and is described in Lee F. Anderson et al. *Legislative Roll-call Analysis* (Evanston, Ill., 1966), pp. 81–86. It is widely known and used. Two assumptions are involved: legislators are present in large numbers for crucial bills, and "close" votes indicate controversy. When both conditions are fulfilled, it generally indicates a very important piece of legislation or legislative action. A coefficient was generated for each bill, and all bills were ranked by their coefficients; the higher the coefficient, the greater the bill's "importance." These ten bills were chosen because of their importance to Lasker's own career and to that of the National Liberal party. All but the ninth and tenth also rated quite high quantitatively and all were, indeed, important. The votes on the anti-Jesuit law and the first antisocialist law were not close numerically, but this surface agreement concealed bitter in-fighting in the National Liberal party.

For Lasker personally the last years of his life were filled with change. Illness prevented him from playing his characteristically vigorous role in the new party, and other members, especially Heinrich Rickert, supplanted him as chief organizer. More and more, he took positions on issues individually rather than as a party member. He still held his seat in the Reichstag, but there too he was not nearly as active as he had formerly been. The Liberal Union, his hope for a new liberal party, was soon torn by inner tension and showed signs of serious weakness. It was within this context of personal frustration and poor health that Lasker planned a lengthy trip to the United States to visit his brother Morris, who lived in Galveston, Texas, but also, as he told Bennigsen, to seek a "renaissance of the spirit."[5]

Lasker's ship sailed from England on the fourteenth of July 1883 and entered the thriving port of New York on the twenty-second. His visit was also an introduction to the United States. He traveled to many of the major cities and through numerous areas, including, of course, Texas and the West. The Northern Pacific Railroad inaugurated its transcontinental service, and Lasker was among the dignitaries who enjoyed the first trip to San Francisco. As a visiting foreign politician of note, he was entertained and invited to speak to many groups on numerous occasions. Little is known of his personal reaction to his brother's chosen land, but the indications are that he was attracted to much that he saw. In his last letter from America, to his friend Ludwig Bamberger, he praised the free-trade system of the United States.[6]

A few days before his departure on the return trip to Germany, after an evening at the house of the prominent Jewish banker Jesse Seligmann in New York City, Lasker suffered a sudden heart attack and died while on the way home. Memorial services were held in New York. Carl Schurz, the German-American politician, and Andrew D. White, the president of Cornell University and a former diplomatic representative to Prussia, gave commemorative speeches in his honor. Then Lasker's body was returned to Germany for still another series of memorials and eulogies, including one in the Reichstag, which sparked an emotionally critical response by Otto von Bismarck. Lasker was finally buried in the Jewish cemetery in Berlin, where, years later, he was joined by Ludwig Bamberger, his lifelong friend and political ally.[7]

Whether Lasker personally might have contributed to the political life of Germany in the 1880s, 1890s, and after is speculation. He was not old at fifty-five and might have remained politically active for many more years. Death claimed him just at the threshold of the precipitous decline of liberal political power. It may well have prevented his own equally speedy decline in an increasingly illiberal epoch. German liberalism's only significant claims to success had come in the late 1860s and 1870s, and those years were gone forever.

Appendixes

Appendix A
The Executive Committee of the National Liberal Reichstag *Fraktion*, 1871–1878

Name	Members' Electoral Districts	Years in Prussian Landtag	Occupations		Sessions on Exec. Comm.
			Occupation in General Register	Other Occupations	
	(1)	(2)	(3)	(4)	(5)
Bamberger	Hessen No. 8 Hessen No. 9		Person of private means	Banker	1871 1874 1877
Benda	Magdeburg No. 6	1867–98	Noble estate owner		1874 1877 1878
Bennigsen	Hannover No. 19	1867–83	Head of federal bureaucracy in a province; privy councillor		1871 1874 1877 1878
Biedermann	Sachsen No. 15		Professor	Editor	1871
Braun	Wiesbaden No. 2 Reuss j.L. Liegnitz Nos. 3/4	1867–79	Honorary title for lawyers (*Justizrat*)	editor; lawyer	1871 1874
Bunsen	Düsseldorf No. 3 Liegnitz	1867–79	No occupation	Estate owner	1871 1877
Dernburg	Hessen No. 5		Chief editor		1874 1877
Forckenbeck	Magdeburg No. 5	1867–73	Lord mayor		1871 1874 1877
Forkel	Coburg No. 1		Honorary title for lawyers, professors, and officials (*Justizrat*)	Lawyer	1878
Fries	Sachsen-Weimar No. 1		Lawyer		1871
Hennig	Marienwerder No. 3	1866–73	Town councillor	Estate owner; man of private means	1871
Kapp	Magdeburg No. 1	1873–76	Author	Lawyer	1874 1877
Kiefer	Baden No. 6		Judicial official		1877 1878
Lasker	Berlin No. 1 Meiningen No. 2	1867–79	Lawyer		1871 1874 1877
Marquardsen	Mittelfranken No. 2		Professor		1877 1878
Miquel	Hannover No. 4 Waldeck	1867–82	Lord mayor	Lawyer	1871 1874 1877
Oetker	Kassel No. 1	1867–81	Lawyer	Editor	1871

Appendix A (cont.)
The Executive Committee of the National Liberal Reichstag *Fraktion*, 1871–1878

Name	Members' Electoral Districts	Years in Prussian Landtag	Occupations		Sessions on Exec. Comm.
			Occupation in General Register	Other Occupations	
	(1)	(2)	(3)	(4)	(5)
Oppenheim	Reuss a.l.		Author		1871 1874 1877
Pogge (Str.)	Mecklenburg-Strelitz		Noble estate owner		1877
Rickert	Danzig No. 3	1870–86	Retired head of provincial self-government	Journalist	1874 1877
Stauffenberg	Oberbayern No. 1 Braunschweig No. 3 Mittelfranken No. 2		Estate owner	Public prosecutor	1874 1877
Stephani	Sachsen No. 12		Deputy mayor (retired)	Lawyer	1877 1878
Techow	Düsseldorf No. 1	1866–80	High school director	Church and town councillor	1874 1877
Unruh	Magdeburg No. 4	1866–71	Administrative adviser board of works (retired)	Merchant	1871 1874 1877
Vahl	Stralsund No. 2	1873	Lawyer; notary	Estate owner	1877
Wachs	Schleswig-Holstein No. 4	1873–79	Estate owner	Doctor	1877
Weber	Coburg-Gotha No. 1 Magdeburg No. 4	1868–82 1884–97	Town councillor		1878
Wehrenpfennig	Waldeck Kassel No. 3	1868–79	Administrative advisor	High school director; editor	1874
Weigel	Kassel No. 2 Kassel No. 8		Honorary title for lawyers (*Justizrat*); lawyer	Merchant	1874 1877 1878
Wolffson	Hamburg No. 3		Lawyer		1878
Zabel			Editor		1871

Source: Information on the electoral district and occupation of each Executive Committee member was taken from the *Generalregister zu den stenographischen Berichten über die Verhandlung und die amtlichen Drucksachen des constituierenden Reichstages, des Reichstages des norddeutschen Bundes, des deutschen Zollparlamements und des deutschen Reichstages vom Jahre 1867 bis einschliesslich der am 24. Mai 1895 geschlossenen III. Session 1894/95* (Berlin, 1896). Information on other occupations, on membership in the Prussian Landtag, and on the number of sessions served on the Executive Committee was taken from Georg Hirth, ed., *Parlamentsalmanach* (Berlin, Leipzig, and Munich, 1867 and 1877); *Allgemeine Deutsche Biographie* (56 vols., Leipzig, 1875–1912); and Adalbert Hes, *Das Parlament dass Bismarck widerstrebte. Zur Politik und sozialen Zusammensetzung des preussischen Abgeordnetenhauses der Konfliktszeit (1862–1866)* (Cologne and Opladen, 1964), pp.138–50. Max Schwarz, *MdR. Biographisches Handbuch der Reichstage* (Hannover, 1967), provides, with a few exceptions, the same information as in the *Generalregister*.

Appendix B

Occupational Distribution of Reichstag Members, 1871–1884

Occupation	Number Elected and Percentage					
	1871	1874	1877	1878	1881	1884
Noble estate owners	84	82	87	98	97	100
	(21)	(20)	(21)	(24)	(23)	(25)
Estate owners	27	36	30	24	27	21
	(7)	(9)	(7)	(6)	(6)	(5)
Farmers	4	8	8	7	9	19
	(1)	(2)	(2)	(2)	(2)	(5)
Peasants	0	0	0	0	1	0
	(0)	(0)	(0)	(0)	(1)	(0)
Tenant farmers	1	2	1	3	3	5
	(0)	(0)	(0)	(1)	(1)	(1)
Ministers (state officials)	21	12	13	12	7	4
	(5)	(3)	(3)	(3)	(2)	(1)
Heads of provincial Bureaucracy	30	11	17	17	15	7
	(8)	(3)	(4)	(4)	(4)	(2)
High-level state officials and Landräte (district magistrate)	18	20	14	17	16	15
	(5)	(5)	(3)	(4)	(4)	(4)
Retired officials	8	11	7	9	6	7
	(2)	(3)	(2)	(2)	(1)	(2)
Middle-level state Officals	2	1	1	1	0	0
	(1)	(0)	(0)	(0)	(0)	(0)
Military	3	6	3	5	2	5
	(1)	(1)	(1)	(1)	(1)	(1)
Lower-level state Officials	1	0	2	1	2	0
	(0)	(0)	(1)	(0)	(1)	(0)
Mayor	7	6	8	6	11	7
	(2)	(2)	(1)	(1)	(1)	(2)
Chief judge	14	9	14	15	6	4
	(3)	(2)	(3)	(4)	(1)	(1)
Judicial advisers	22	24	27	26	29	20
	(5)	(6)	(6)	(6)	(7)	(5)
Judicial officials (retired)	10	14	12	9	7	5
	(2)	(3)	(3)	(2)	(2)	(1)
Town councillor	4	6	4	5	5	1
	(1)	(2)	(1)	(1)	(1)	(0)
University professors	16	17	14	20	17	11
	(4)	(4)	(3)	(5)	(4)	(3)
Secondary school teachers	9	8	6	6	6	4
	(2)	(2)	(2)	(2)	(2)	(1)
Archivists and librarians	3	6	5	1	3	2
	(1)	(2)	(1)	(0)	(1)	(0)
Elementary school teachers	0	0	0	0	0	2
	(0)	(0)	(0)	(0)	(0)	(0)

Appendix B (cont.)
Occupational Distribution of Reichstag Members, 1871–1884

Occupation:	Number Elected and Percentage					
	1871	1874	1877	1878	1881	1884
Protestant clergy	1	0	0	1	1	1
	(0)	(0)	(0)	(0)	(0)	(0)
Catholic clergy	15	22	20	20	20	17
	(4)	(6)	(5)	(5)	(5)	(4)
Physicians	4	4	4	2	5	7
	(1)	(1)	(1)	(0)	(1)	(2)
Lawyers	38	37	30	29	27	22
	(10)	(9)	(7)	(7)	(6)	(5)
Architects and engineers	0	1	4	4	6	3
	(0)	(0)	(0)	(1)	(1)	(2)
Shopkeepers	15	8	11	16	16	15
	(4)	(2)	(2)	(4)	(4)	(4)
Bankers	4	5	6	7	4	3
	(1)	(1)	(2)	(2)	(1)	(1)
Innkeepers	0	0	0	1	1	1
	(0)	(0)	(0)	(0)	(0)	(0)
Retailers	0	0	0	2	1	3
	(0)	(0)	(0)	(0)	(0)	(1)
Printers and publishers	2	3	3	3	2	1
	(0)	(1)	(1)	(1)	(0)	(0)
Authors	9	11	10	7	15	15
	(2)	(3)	(2)	(2)	(4)	(4)
Industrialists	7	15	17	28	36	33
	(2)	(4)	(4)	(7)	(8)	(8)
Trustees of cooperatives	2	1	2	1	1	2
	(0)	(0)	(0)	(0)	(0)	(0)
Trustees	3	4	4	3	5	2
	(1)	(1)	(1)	(1)	(1)	(0)
Bailiffs and forest rangers	1	0	0	0	0	1
	(0)	(0)	(0)	(0)	(0)	(0)
Persons of private means	11	14	15	14	14	16
	(3)	(3)	(4)	(3)	(3)	(4)
Title without occupation	2	5	5	5	2	3
	(0)	(1)	(1)	(1)	(0)	(1)
Craftsmen and workers	1	6	6	4	4	11
	(0)	(2)	(2)	(1)	(1)	(3)

Source: Willy Kremer, *Der Soziale Aufbau der Parteien des deutschen Reichstages von 1871–1918* (Cologne, 1934), pp. 79–80.

Appendix C

Absenteeism in the Reichstag and in the National Liberal *Fraktion*, 1867–1884

Session	Reichstag			National Liberal *Fraktion*		
	No. Seats	Avg. No. Absent	Avg. % Absent	No. Seats	Avg. No. Absent	Avg. % Abs.
	(1)	(2)	(3)	(4)	(5)	(6)
Constitutional Reichstag (1867)	297	32	10.7	80	7	8.75
North German Confederation (1867–70)	297	102	34.3	78	25	32.0
Reichstag (1871–74)	382	126	32.9	120	34	28.6
Reichstag (1874–77)	397	103	25.9	152	29	19.3
Reichstag (1877–78)	397	108	27.2	127	29	23.2
Reichstag (1878–81)	397	118	29.7	98	25	25.8
Reichstag (1881–84)	397	109	27.4	45	12	26.6

Source: Data are from the *Generalregister*. See Appendix A.

Appendix D
Absenteeism Among Members of the National Liberal Executive Committee in the Reichstag,
1867–1884

Member	Total No. of Roll-Call Votes During Tenure	No. Absent	% Absent
	(1)	(2)	(3)
Bamberger	128	8	6.25
Benda	203	26	12.8
Bennigsen	236	46	19.4
Biedermann	48	30	62.0
Braun	224	72	32.1
Bunsen	177	51	28.8
Dernburg	140	22	15.7
Forckenbeck	224	86	38.3
Forkel	146	41	28.0
Fries	144	18	12.5
Hennig	144	14	9.7
Kapp	74	12	16.0
Kiefer	48	22	45.8
Lasker	224	12	5.3
Marquardsen	140	7	5.0
Miquel	186	57	30.6
Oetker	224	157	70.0
Oppenheim	42	6	14.2
Pogge (Str.)	184	63	34.2
Rickert	80	6	7.5
Stauffenberg	128	47	37.0
Stephani	203	30	14.7
Techow	99	19	19.1
Unruh	212	52	24.5
Vahl	51	4	7.8
Wachs	92	45	48.9
Weber	24	0	0.0
Wehrenpfennig	201	59	29.3
Weigel	236	10	4.2
Wolffson	140	10	7.1

Source: Data are taken from the *Generalregister*. See Appendix A. Note: Variations in total number of roll-call votes are due to variations in length of tenure as an elected member of the Reichstag.

Appendix E

National Liberal and Liberale Vereinigung Wins and Losses in the Reichstag,
1867–1884

Legislative Period	Party	Roll-Call Votes		
		Won	Lost	% Won
	(1)	(2)	(3)	(4)
1867	NL	12	5	70.5
1867–70	NL	50	29	63.3
1871–74	NL	34	14	70.8
1874–77	NL	32	10	76.1
1877	NL	7	2	77.0
1878–81	NL	19	22	46.3
Total	NL	154	82	65.2
1878–81	LV	8	4	66.6
1881–84	LV	12	20	37.5
Total	LV	20	24	45.4

Source: Data are taken from the *Generalregister*. See Appendix A. Notes: Wins are counted when the majority of the National Liberal party voted with the majority of the Reichstag; losses are when the majority of the party voted with the minority of the Reichstag. It would be profitable to compare the National Liberal record with that of other parties in the Reichstag, but until the relevant data are collected and this method applied to them, such treatment is impossible. For a use of this method only for the 1867 Constitutional Reichstag, see James F. Harris, "Politische Parteibereinstimmung in Konstitutionellen Reichstag des Norddeutschen Bundes von 1867," in Konrad Jarausch, ed., *Probleme und Möglichkeiten des Quantifizierung* (Düsseldorf, 1975), pp. 168–85. The Liberale Vereinigung or Liberal Union, was formed during the 1878–1881 session as a secession from the National Liberal party.

Appendix F

National Liberal Roll-Call Wins and Losses in the Prussian Landtag,
1867–1884

Legislative Period	Roll-Call Votes		
	Won	Lost	% Won
	(1)	(2)	(3)
1866	4	0	100.0
1867–70	52	16	66.6
1870–73	34	3	91.8
1873–76	35	4	89.7
1876–79	8	5	61.5
Total	133	28	82.6

Source: *Wörtlicher Berichte über die Verhandlungen des preussischen Abgeordnetenhauses* (Berlin, 1865 *et seq.*).

Note: Wins are counted when the majority of the National Liberal party voted with the majority of the Landtag; losses are counted when the majority of the party voted with the minority of the Landtag.

Notes

I. From Jarotschin to New York

1. Thomas Peck Ochiltree, "The Late Dr. Eduard Lasker," March 19, 1884, in *Speeches of the United States 48th Congress*, Vol. V, no. 15 (Washington, D.C., 1884), pp. 1–11, includes excerpts from eulogies by Carl Schurz and Dr. Andrew D. White (president of Cornell), and the correspondence of the State Department. Louis Snyder, "Bismarck and the Lasker Resolution," *Review of Politics* 29 (Jan. 1967): 41–64.

2. Aron Heppner and Izaak Herzberg, eds., *Aus Vergangenheit und Gegenwart der Juden und der jüdischen Gemeinden in den Posener Landen* (Koschmin and Breslau, 1909), pp. 503–4.

3. Ludwig Bamberger, *Bismarcks Grosses Spiel. Die Geheimen Tagebücher Ludwig Bamberger*, ed. Ernst Feder (Frankfurt am Main, 1932), pp. 282–84. This is still the best, and very nearly the only, source for information about Eduard's childhood and family.

4. Ibid., pp. 283–84. See also Gordon R. Mork, "The Making of a German Nationalist: Eduard Lasker's Early Years, 1829–1847," *Societas* 1 (1971): 23–32. Tobias Cohn, "Eduard Lasker. Biographische Skizze von Dr. Tobias Cohn, Rabbiner zu Potsdam," *Jahrbuch für die Geschichte der Juden und des Judentums* (Leipzig, 1869), ignores such problems.

5. Bamberger, *Bismarcks Grosses Spiel*, pp. 283–84; Gustav Mayer, *Briefe von und an Lassalle bis 1848*, vol. 1 of *Ferdinand Lassalle. Nachgelassene Briefe und Schriften* (reprint: Osnabrück, 1967), p. 26. See Lassalle's letters from school, which include a protest against his failure to obtain the *Abitur* (school-leaving certificate) because of discrimination.

6. Salo W. Baron, "The Jewish Question in the Nineteenth Century," *Journal of Modern History* 10 (March 1938): 51–52; P.G.J. Pulzer, *The Rise of Political Anti-Semitism in Germany and Austria* (New York, 1964), p. 9. See also M. Laubert, "Die Stadt Posen in neupreussischer Zeit, 1815–1847," in Gotthold Rhode, ed., *Geschichte der Stadt Posen* (Neuendettelsau, 1953), p. 106.

7. J. Perles, "Geschichte der Juden in Posen," in *Monatsschrift für Geschichte und Wissenschaft des Judentums*, ed. Zacharias Frankel (Hildesheim and New York, 1972), a reprint of the periodical published originally in Breslau, vol. XIV (1865), p. 207, note 6, shows an increase of Jews in the city of Posen from 3,367 in 1799 to 7,361 in 1855. But Eugen von Bergmann, *Zur Geschichte der Entwicklung deutscher, polnischer und jüdischer Bevölkerung in der Provinz Posen seit 1824* (Tübingen, 1883), pp. 44, 51, 53, states that there were 33,000 fewer Jews in the province in 1871 than in 1824; there were only 18,790 fewer Christians, who outnumbered Jews more than 20 to 1. The law of 1833 is well described in Perles, "Geschichte," pp. 214–15. Also see Mork, "Making of a German Nationalist," pp. 25, 27–28.

8. Bergmann, *Entwicklung*, pp. 34–35; Gotthold Rohde, "Posen von der Revolution des Jahres 1848 bis zur Gründung des Deutschen Reiches," in Rohde, ed., *Geschichte*, pp. 122, 126. Also see Richard Breyer, "Die Stadt Posen in südpreussischer und herzoglich Warschauer Zeit (1793–1815)," in ibid., p. 87. For Breslau see *Kleines Statistisches Taschenbuch für die Stadt Breslau* (Graz and Breslau, 1928), p. 12. P. H. Noyes, *Organization and Revolution: Working-Class Association in the German Revolution of 1848–1849* (Princeton, 1966), p. 19, notes that only Hamburg and Berlin were larger than Breslau in 1848.

9. Paul Wentzcke, "Glaubensbekenntnisse einer politischen Jugend. Beiträge zum Lebensbild Ludwig Aegidis und Eduard Laskers," in Wentzcke, ed., *Deutscher Staat und deutsche Parteien. Beiträge zur deutschen Partei- und Ideengeschichte. Friedrich Meinecke zum 60. Geburtstag dargebracht* (1922; reprint Aalen, 1973), pp. 87–88.

10. Arnold Ruge, *Briefwechsel und Tagebuchblätter aus den Jahren 1825–1880*, ed. Paul Nerrlich (Berlin, 1886), 2: 13–14, 48. The early years are described in Helmut Köster, "Aus Laskers politische Frühzeit" (Ph.D. diss., University of Leipzig, 1924), pp. 7–8. Anton Bettelheim, *Berthold Auerbach. Der Mann, Sein Werk, Sein Nachlass* (Stuttgart and Berlin, 1907), p. 214, states that Lasker met Auerbach in 1848. See also Adolph Kober, "Jews in the Revolutions of 1848 in Germany," *Jewish Social Studies* 10 (1948): 155–56.

11. Wentzcke, "Glaubensbekenntnisse," pp. 87–92.

12. Noyes, *Organization*, pp. 214–15; Wentzcke, "Glaubensbekenntnisse," p. 88, citing Leonhard Muller, *Die Breslauer politische Presse von 1742–1861. Nebst einem Überblick über die Dekade 1861–1871* (Breslau, 1908), which is replete with evidence that Wentzcke is correct.

13. Paul Wentzcke, "Aus Eduard Laskers sozialistischen Anfängen," *Archiv für die Geschichte des Sozialismus und der Arbeiterbewegung* 11 (1925): 207–14. Since publication, these letters appear to have been lost. See Rudolf von Gottschall, *Aus meiner Jugend. Erinnerungen* (Berlin, 1898), pp. 123–24, who describes the "Breslau Opposition" as

more philosophical and less practical than that in Königsberg. Gottschall makes no mention of Lasker, but he names as members Dr. Otto Lindner and Dr. Möcke, later editors of the *Vossische Zeitung* (Berlin) and *Schlesische Zeitung* (Breslau). He notes that Esenbeck turned to mysticism and spiritualism in his later years.

14. Wentzcke, "Glaubensbekenntnisse," pp. 92–93. Lasker, "Wort und Tat," in Lasker, *Wege und Ziele zur Kulturentwicklung* (Leipzig, 1881), p. 249, wrote that it was difficult to establish an assembly in non-German Vienna. Hans Blum, *Die deutsche Revolution 1848–49. Eine Jubiläumsgabe für das deutsche Volk* (Florence and Leipzig, 1897), pp. v, 372, states only that Lasker registered with Blum as a volunteer. In *Vorkämpfer der deutschen Einheit. Lebens und Characterbilder* (Berlin, 1899), p. 29, Hans Blum, Robert's son, added some detail, describing Lasker as a "small, slender, eighteen-year-old student of mathematics from Breslau" and citing conversations with Lasker and Bamberger. Moritz Hartmann and Julius Fröbel made no mention of Lasker. See Moritz Hartmann, *Revolutionäre Erinnerungen*, ed. H. H. Houben (Leipzig, 1919), pp. 43–96, which has an excellent description of the fighting, and Julius Fröbel, *Ein Lebenslauf. Aufzeichnungen, Erinnerungen und Bekenntnisse* (2 vols., Stuttgart, 1890), 1: 189, 208.

15. The source for Lasker's readmittance to the university is Köster, "Laskers politische Frühzeit," pp. 8–9. Unfortunately some of the documentation is no longer extant.

16. Noyes, *Organization*, p. 215, note 37.

17. Köster, "Laskers politische Frühzeit," p. 11, cites a letter from Dr. Wilhelm Cohn warning Lasker of the king's opposition to state careers for Jews. For the conditions of education and employment of Jews, see Ernst Hamburger, "Jews in Public Service under the German Monarchy," *Leo Baeck Institute Yearbook* 9 (London, 1964): 221–24; for the specific problem of a career in law, see John Gillis, *The Prussian Bureaucracy in Crisis, 1840–1860: Origins of an Administrative Ethos* (Stanford, 1971), pp. 189–90, who notes that even in 1862 only 86 of 868 assessors (10%) were paid allowances.

18. Köster, "Laskers politische Frühzeit," p. 10, also cited in part by Wentzcke, "Glaubensbekenntnisse," pp. 93–94, citing the *Nachlass* in Erich Brandenburg's possession.

19. The Wilhelm Cohn-Eduard Lasker letters are in the Lasker Nachlass in the Zentrales Staatsarchiv in Potsdam (hereafter cited as LNP). EL to Cohn, Aug. 11, 1853, broached the subject; EL to Cohn, Aug. 29, 1853, confirmed his intention to go. As early as Oct. 20, 1853, Lasker appeared depressed by his job and was slow in answering Cohn's queries of Jan. 12 and March 11, 1854, about his future prospects. On Dec. 24, 1854, Eduard gave full expression to his disenchantment with the business life, and his letters turned away from the "money market" and toward his future. The material on Lasker's stay in England is largely from "Über Laskers Aufenthalt in England," by Dr. A. Asher in *Familien-Blatt. Feuilleton-Beiträge der Israelitischen Wochenschrift*, no. 5 (1884), pp. 10–11. The original document of his elevation to the second degree in the Masonic Order is in the Leo Baeck Institute Archives in New York. John Gunther's *Taken at the Flood: The Story of Albert D. Lasker* (New York, 1960), is about Morris's son, Eduard's nephew, and the facts about Eduard are often inaccurate (see, e.g., pp. 22–23). There seems no doubt (pp. 18, 22, 54, 88–89) that Morris's family revered Eduard long after his death. Morris hoped that his son would follow in Eduard's footsteps, but Albert had both talent and love for the business life that his uncle abhorred.

20. Lasker told of his poetic ambitions in a letter to Wilhelm Cohn dated July 5, 1855, in LNP. The émigré community and the Kinkel family are well described in Julius Rodenberg, *Erinnerungen aus der Jugendzeit* (2 vols., Berlin, 1899), 2: 65–70, 167, 238, 296–97). The letter from Kinkel to Lasker is in Wentzcke, "Glaubensbekenntnisse," pp. 94–95.

21. Lasker, *Erlebnisse einer Mannes-Seele*, ed. Berthold Auerbach (Stuttgart, 1873), pp. 46–48.

22. Köster, "Laskers politische Frühzeit," p. 12, is unclear as to date, but probably late 1855 or early 1856.

23. Wentzcke, "Glaubensbekenntnisse," p. 95.

24. Ibid., p. 96.

25. Theodore S. Hamerow, *The Social Foundations of German Unification 1858–1871*, vol 1, *Ideas and Institutions* (Princeton, 1969), pp. 301–5.

26. The best description in English is Eugene N. Anderson and Pauline R. Anderson, *Political Institutions and Social Change in Continental Europe in the Nineteenth Century* (Berkeley and Los Angeles, 1967), pp. 314–18.

27. H. B. Oppenheim to EL, June 23, 1861, in LNP. Later letters refer to Eduard's work for the *Jahrbücher*; see Oppenheim to EL, Aug. 24, 1861, and Sept. 8, 1863. For discussion of the *Deutsche Jahrbücher*, see Otto Westphal, *Welt- und Staatsauffassung des deutschen Liberalismus. Eine Untersuchung über die preussischen Jahrbücher und den konstitutionellen Liberalismus in Deutschland von 1858 bis 1863*, Historische Bibliothek, 41 (Berlin and Munich, 1919), pp. 167–68; Lasker, *Zur Verfassungsgeschichte Preussens* (Leipzig, 1874).

28. Literature on the conflict is vast; the best description is still Eugene N. Anderson, *The Social and Political Conflict in Prussia, 1858–1864* (Lincoln, 1954). Otto Pflanze, *Bismarck and the Development of Germany: The Period of Unification, 1815–1871* (Princeton, 1963), is indispensable for Bismarck's role.

29. Köster, "Laskers politische Frühzeit," pp. 22–24; Julius Rodenberg, "Briefe an Eduard Lasker," *Deutsche Rundschau* 38 (1884): 443; Siemens to Lasker, an invitation to a *Besprechung* at Meser's salon on April 17, dated April 15, 1862, in LNP. Four other notices from Siemens exist in LNP, concluding on May 8, 1862. Ludwig

Bamberger, *Eduard Lasker. Gedenkrede gehalten am 28. Januar 1884 im Saale der Singakademie zu Berlin* (Leipzig, 1884), p. 18.

30. See Lawrence D. Steefel, *The Schleswig-Holstein Question* (Cambridge, 1932).

31. Lasker describes this situation well in *Fünfzehn Jahre parlamentarische Geschichte 1866–1880*, which composes most of the volume entitled *Aus Eduard Lasker's Nachlass*, ed. Wilhelm Cahn (Berlin, 1902), pp. 1–136 (hereafter cited as *AELN*).

32. Analysis of Lasker's role in this and other significant areas may be found in Chapters II-VII.

33. Bamberger, *Eduard Lasker*, p. 19; Chlodwig Fürst zu Hohenlohe-Schillingsfürst, *Denkwürdigkeiten* (2 vols., Stuttgart and Leipzig, 1907), 2: 78, dated Berlin, May 10, 1872; Heinrich Ritter von Poschinger, *Fürst Bismarck und die Parlamentarier* (3 vols., Breslau, 1894–1896), 3: 12–13, citing Karl Braun, *Dreissig Parlamentsbriefen. Zur Physiologie und Pathologie der Parteien im Reichstage* (Sept. and Oct. 1878). Fritz Stern, *Gold and Iron. Bismarck, Bleichröder, and the Building of the German Empire* (New York, 1977), p. 117; In March 1870 Bleichröder offered Lasker a very lucrative position which he declined in order to maintain his freedom.

34. Poschinger, *Fürst Bismarck*, 1: 209, dated March 22, 1881; Gustav Schmoller, "Hermann Schulze-Delitzsch und Eduard Lasker," *Jahrbuch für Gesetzgebung, Verwaltung, und Volkswirtschaft im Deutschen Reich* 8 (1884): 251; "Laskers Beziehung zu Frankfurt," *Frankfurter Zeitung*, Jan. 14, 1884, no. 14, Morgenblatt, p. 1.

35. Bamberger, *Eduard Lasker*, pp. 29–34, felt that Lasker died of overwork. "Eduard Lasker," *Preussische Jahrbücher* (1884), pp. 198–204, probably by Constantin Rössler; see esp. p. 199. See also Robert von Mohl, *Lebenserinnerungen, 1799–1875* (2 vols., Stuttgart, 1910), 2: 420, 424, 426; Otto Elben, *Lebenserinnerungen, 1823–1899* (Stuttgart, 1931), pp. 78–79; Jakob Auerbach, ed., *Berthold Auerbach. Briefe an seinen Freund Jakob Auerbach* (2 vols., Frankfurt am Main, 1884), 2: 269–70, Berthold to Jakob, Berlin, Jan. 4, 1876, commenting on Lasker's leadership and the assistance he gave to young members.

36. Mohl, *Lebenserinnerungen*, 2: 175–76, 166; Bennigsen to his wife, Berlin mid-Feb. 1868 and Jan. 16, 1870, in ABRB (1906), p. 321, and (1907), p. 31; Elben, *Lebenserinnerungen*, pp. 178–79. An American observer, Herbert Tuttle, incorrectly described Lasker as the "accepted and natural leader of the National Liberal party" in his study *German Political Leaders* (New York, 1876), p. 114.

37. Friedrich Boettcher, *Eduard Stephani. Ein Beitrag zur Zeitgeschichte, insbesondere zur Geschichte der Nationalliberalen Partei* (Leipzig, 1887), pp. 104, 108, 125; Max Cornicelius, ed., *Heinrich von Treitschkes Briefe* (3 vols., Leipzig, 1913–1920), 3: 276; Wilhelm Wehrenpfennig to Treitschke, Berlin, Dec. 22, 1869, ibid., 1: 447; Karl Helffreich, *Georg von Siemens* (3 vols., Berlin, 1923), 3: 163; Otto Bähr to Friedrich Oetker, Berlin, Dec. 17, 1873, HW, 2: 95.

38. Bamberger, *Bismarcks Grosses Spiel*, p. 284. Lasker's *Erlebnisse* clearly does not fit Bamberger's description, but this may be another example of the public-private dichotomy in Lasker's life.

39. Hohenlohe, *Denkwürdigkeiten*, 2: 78; Rodenberg, "Briefe," pp. 441, 451, 457. Lasker received some advice on what to read from friends like Oppenheim, who, in a letter of July 3, 1868 (LNP), criticized two of Renan's works and discussed the literary merits of Bagehot, Runclin, Frenzel, Laboulaye, and Lafrey.

40. Arnold Ruge to his son Richard, Nov. 2, 1872, Ruge, *Briefwechsel*, 2: 376; Johannes Miquel to EL, Feb. 13, 1879, LNP. Also see Julius Duboc, "Ein dunkler Philosoph," *Die Wage, Wochenblatt für Politik und Literatur*, ed. Dr. Guido Weiss, in the Archives of the Leo Baeck Institute; Julius Eckardt, *Lebenserinnerungen* (2 vols., Leipzig, 1910), 1: 146–47; *Frankfurter Zeitung*, Nov. 16, 1877. Adolph Oppler's letters to EL from April 2, 1866, to Dec. 25, 1868, LNP, all provide information on education. See E. B. Brockhaus to EL, Jan. 19, 1873, LNP, which was obviously a reaction to Lasker's sudden national popularity. Most of the articles appeared under the title *Wege und Ziele zur Kulturentwicklung* in 1881.

41. Marx to Engels in Ramsgate, Karlsbad, Aug. 19, 1876, in Karl Marx and Friedrich Engels, *Briefwechsel* (4 vols., Berlin, 1947), 4: 528; Rodenberg, "Briefe an Eduard Lasker," p. 452. Adolph Oppler wrote to Lasker from London on May 15, 1873, concluding with a comment on the appearance of the book and noting that it must refer to Lasker; Oppler to EL, LNP.

42. Lasker, *Erlebnisse*. See p. 8: "So I watched her leave and I did not request her hand."

43. Ibid. See especially the conclusion, pp. 119–20.

44. Ibid., pp. 46–48.

45. Ibid., pp. 81, 86, 94, 96, 100, 107.

46. Asher, "Über Laskers Aufenthalt in England"; Lasker, *Erlebnisse*, pp. 73–74.

47. Lasker, *Erlebnisse*, p. 108.

48. Bamberger, *Bismarcks Grosses Spiel*, pp. 271–73.

49. Hugo to Florina Feilchenfeld, Sept. 6, 1940, Leo Baeck Archives; Cohn, "Eduard Lasker," p. 5; Selmar Speier, "Jewish History as We See It," *Leo Baeck Institute Yearbook* 1 (London, 1956): 3–14. For Breslau, see S. W. Baron, "The Impact of the Revolution of 1848 on Jewish Emancipation," *Jewish Social Studies* 2 (1949): 200–201. For more detail on all aspects of Lasker's relation to Judaism, see James F. Harris, "Eduard Lasker: The Jew as National German

Politician," *Leo Baeck Institute Yearbook* 20 (London, 1975), pp. 151–77.

50. LT, April 20, 1865, 2: 1078, Nov. 30, 1866, 2: 784, Dec. 15, 1868, 1: 769–71; H. Baerwald to EL, Jan. 13, 1867, LNP, giving permission to use his name if necessary.

51. RT, March 21, 1867, 1: 313.

52. *Allgemeine Zeitung des Judentums*, April 2, 1867, pp. 276–77; Cohn, "Eduard Lasker," pp. 75–76; LT, Feb. 1, 1869, 2: 1390; RT, Feb. 28, 1870, 1: 113.

53. LT, Jan. 9, 1873, 1: 449, 684–690.

54. LT, March 19, 1873, 3: 1750–53. For Lasker's speech, see ibid., pp. 1755–57.

55. LT, May 26, 1876, 3: 1724–26.

56. Pulzer, *Political Anti-Semitism*, pp. 18–22; Hans Rosenberg, *Grosse Depression und Bismarckzeit. Wirtschaftsablauf, Gesellschaft und Politik in Mitteleuropa* (Berlin, 1967), pp. 88ff.

57. Constantin Frantz, *Der Nationalliberalismus und die Judenherrschaft* (Munich, 1874), pp. 42, 63–64 and passim; Franz Perrot, *Bismarck und die Juden. "Papierpest" und "Ara-Artikel" von 1875*, comp. Karl Perrot, ed. with an Introduction and Epilogue by L. Feldmuller-Perrot (Berlin, 1931), pp. 17, 18–19, 118–19, 122; Otto Glagau, *Des Reiches Noth und der neue Culturkampf* (Osnabrück, 1879), pp. 1, 21, 22–27, 58–59.

58. EL to Hermann Baerwald, Berlin, Sept. 12, 1881, HW, 2: 382–84. Lasker stated after the election that he could not use the same tactics as the anti-Semites; speech printed in the *Frankfurter Zeitung*, Oct. 6, 1881, p. 1; EL to Berthold Auerbach, Berlin, Dec. 29, 1881, HW, 2: 389–90.

59. RT, May 22, 1872, 1: 472; N. M. Gelber, "The Intervention of German Jews at the Berlin Congress 1878," *Leo Baeck Institute Yearbook* 5 (London, 1960), pp. 221–47. See the correspondence from the Alliance to Lasker's family after his death; Lasker Nachlass, Brandeis University (hereafter LNB).

60. Bamberger, *Bismarcks Grosses Spiel*, pp. 271–73.

61. Lasker's speech, with no title, is in the Leo Baeck Archives.

62. Jakob Toury, *Die politische Orientierung der Juden in Deutschland. Von Jena bis Weimar*, Schriftenreihe wissenschaftlicher Abhandlungen des Leo Baeck Instituts, 15 (Tübingen, 1956), p. 148.

63. *Die Jüdische Presse*, Jan. 10, 1884, p. 2, and Jan. 24, p. 39; *Israelische Wochenschrift*, Jan. 10, 1884, p. 9; "Curiosum," *Familien-Blatt*, Jan. 17, p. 12; "Eduard Lasker," *Allgemeine Zeitung des Judentums*, Jan. 22, 1884, pp. 52–53, and March 4, pp. 147–51. For more interesting comments, see "Berthold Auerbach and the Antisemitismus," also in the *Allgemeine*, April 29, 1884, pp. 283–85. For the eulogies, see P. F. Frankl and S. Maybaum, *Geistliche Reden, gehalten am 29. I, 1884, an der Bahre von Eduard Lasker* (Berlin, 1884), which contains both Frankl's "Rede gehalten in der Synagoge," pp. 5–13, and Maybaum's "Rede gehalten auf dem Friedhof," pp. 17–20; Ludwig Stein, *Es werde Licht. Eine Denkpredigt zur Charakteristik Eduard Laskers*, (Berlin, n.d.), pp. 3–4; S. Bloch, *In der Heimat! Rede bei der Enthüllung der dem Andenken Dr. Eduard Laskers gewidmeten Denktafel, gehalten in der Synagoge von Jarotschin am 8. III. 1884* (Posen, 1884) pp. 5–9.

II. The Patriot

1. Robert M. Berdahl, "New Thoughts on German Nationalism," *American Historical Review* 77 (Feb. 1972): 65–80.

2. August Ludwig von Rochau, *Grundsätze der Realpolitik. Angewändet auf die staatlichen Zustände Deutschlands* (Stuttgart, 1853), pp. 223–24; Otto Hintze, "Machtpolitik und Regierungsverfassung," *Staat und Verfassung. Gesammelte Abhandlungen, zum allgemeinen Verfassungsgeschichte*, ed. Gerhard Oestreich (Göttingen, 1962), p. 433, and "Liberalismus, Demokratie und Auswärtige Politik," in *Soziologie und Geschichte. Gesammelte Abhandlungen zur Soziologie, Politik und Theorie der Geschichte*, ed. Gerhard Oestreich (Göttingen, 1964), pp. 200, 202; Erich Brandenburg, "Zum älteren deutschen Parteiwesen," *Historische Zeitschrift* 119 (1919): 70; Theodore Schieder, ed., *Reichsgründung, 1870–71. Tatsachen, Kontroversen, Interpretationen* (Stuttgart, 1970), p. 450. See also Wilhelm Mommsen, "Zur Beurteilung der deutschen Parteigeschichte," *Historische Zeitschrift* 138 (1928): 543.

3. Gustav Mayer, "Die Trennung von der bürgerlichen Demokratie in Deutschland (1863–1870)," *Archiv für die Geschichte des Sozialismus und der Arbeiterbewegung* 2 (1911): 25–27.

4. V. Böhmert to Bennigsen, Bremen, Oct. 24, 1864, in ABRB (1906): 154–55.

5. On this subject also see T. S. Hamerow, *The Social Foundations of German Unification 1858–1871*, vol. 1, *Ideas and Institutions* (Princeton, 1969), pp. 144, 397–98; Friedrich Meinecke, "Zur Geschichte des älteren deutschen Parteiwesen," *Historische Zeitschrift* 118 (1917): 50–51; Brandenburg, "Parteiwesen," p. 69.

6. "Eisenacher Erklärung des Deutschen Nationalvereins," Aug. 1859, in Wilhelm Mommsen, ed., *Deutsche Parteiprogramme* (Munich, 1964), p. 131. Hermann Oncken, *Rudolf von Bennigsen. Ein deutscher liberaler Politiker* (2 vols., Stuttgart, 1910), 1: 341–42, citing H. V. von Unruh to Bismarck, Sept. 12, 1859; Mommsen,

Parteiprogramme, p. 133.

7. Bennigsen to V. Böhmert, Oct. 26, 1864, and Bennigsen to Böhmert, Nov. 9, 1864, in ABRB (1906): 156, 157–58.

8. Duncker to Staatsrat Francke in Kiel, May 6, 1865, in Johannes Schultze, ed., *Max Duncker. Politischer Briefwechsel aus seinem Nachlass* (Osnabrück, 1967), p. 389; Karl Twesten to the chairman of the German Convention of Deputies, Berlin, Sept. 28, 1865, HW, 1: 257.

9. Treitschke to Freytag, Oct. 1, 1865, in Max Cornicelius, ed., *Heinrich von Treitschkes Briefe* (3 vols., Leipzig, 1913–1920), 2: 418–19; Böhmert to Bennigsen, Bremen, Oct. 25, 1865, in ABRB (1906): 159; Eugene N. Anderson, *The Social and Political Conflict in Prussia, 1858–1864* (Lincoln, 1954), p. 442; Hermmann Wendorff, *Die Fraktion des Zentrums* (Leipzig, 1916), p. 122; E. W. Mayer, "Parteikrisen im Liberalismus und in der Sozialdemokratie, 1866–1916," *Preussische Jahrbücher* 172 (1918): 177; Martin Spahn, "Zur Entstehung der nationalliberalen Partei," *Zeitschrift für Politik* 1 (1907–1908): 359–60; Ludwig Dehio, "Die Taktik der Opposition während des Konfliktes," *Historische Zeitschrift* 140 (1929): 304–5, 331–33, 336–37; and "Benedikt Waldeck," *Historische Zeitschrift* 136 (1927): 54–56.

10. EL to H. B. Oppenheim, Berlin, Oct. 17, 1865, HW, 1: 256; RT, Jan. 25, 1882, 1: 937. Also see Spahn, "Zur Entstehung," pp. 366–67. All the districts were radical, but the fourth (Lasker's) and the first (Twesten's) were the least radical. EL to Oppenheim, Berlin, Feb. 25, 1866, and Oppenheim to EL, Stuttgart, Feb. 28, 1866, HW, 1: 273–74, 276.

11. Treitschke, "Die Zukunft der norddeutschen Mittelstaaten," *Flugschriften* of July 30, 1866, Berlin, in Treitschke, *Zehn Jahre Deutscher Kämpfe. Schriften zur Tagespolitik* (2 vols., Berlin, 1897), 1: 147. For his earlier views, see "Der Krieg und die Bundesreform," Freiburg im Breisgau, May 25, 1866 in ibid., 1: 88–89. Oppenheim to EL, Nov. 28, 1866, LNP.

12. Eduard Lasker, "Die Mahnung," *National Zeitung*, July 12, 1866, in *AELN*, pp. 138–41.

13. Spahn, "Zur Entstehung," pp. 397–98, citing the *Kreuzzeitung* of July 1, 1866, reporting a speech of June 29, 1866; Lasker, "Nach dem Frieden," in *AELN*, pp. 142–44. Lasker emphasized the union of the nation and the army in a speech in Jan. 1867; see Werner Schunke, *Die Preussischen Freihändler und die Entstehung der Nationalliberalen Partei*, Leipziger Historische Abhandlungen 41 (Leipzig, 1916), p. 77, citing the *National Zeitung* report of a speech in the Halleschen Tor Bezirksverein.

14. Lasker, "Erklärung," Berlin, Sept. 1866, in *AELN*, pp. 153–56.

15. Lasker, "Die Thronrede und die Konservativen," *National Zeitung*, Aug. 10, 1866, in *AELN*, pp. 149–53. See Friedrich Eulenburg's promise of such a bargain (that is, government cooperation in return for approval) in LT, March 27, 1865, 1: 769; K. Rössler to Duncker, Hamburg, Aug. 6, 1866, in Schultze, ed., *Max Duncker*, p. 429; LT, Sept. 3, 1866, 1: 182–84. And see James F. Harris, "Eduard Lasker and Compromise Liberalism," *Journal of Modern History* 42 (Sept. 1970): 342–60.

16. LT, Sept. 3, 1866, 1: 183–84. Lasker kept up the pressure in the autumn; see LT, Nov. 30, Dec. 10, 1866, 2: 786, 1017–18, and Jan. 12, 1867, 3: 1433. For later comments on Lasker's attitude to the indemnity, see Lasker, "Erklärung," Berlin, September 1866, in *AELN*, pp. 154–55; LT, Nov. 21, 1866, 2: 615; RT, April 5, 1867, 1: 564–65; Lasker speech on April 28, 1867, in the first Berlin electoral district, *National Zeitung*, April 30, 1867, cited in Spahn, "Zur Entstehung," p. 392; "Vertrauliche Programm," Berlin, June 1867, in *AELN*, pp. 158–59. See also the excellent analysis by Lasker's close friend and ally Ludwig Bamberger, "Alte Parteien und neue Zustände," in Bamberger, *Gesammelte Schriften* (5 vols., Berlin, 1894–1898), 3: 310–17, and "Die Sezession," Berlin, late summer 1880, in ibid., 5: 65. See also Schunke, "Die Preussische Freihändler," p. 76.

17. *Frankfurter Zeitung*, Dec. 9, 1866, and similarly Dec. 13, 1866. Mayer, "Parteikrisen," pp. 172–73, singled out Lasker, Twesten, and Otto Michaelis for supporting the government during the war. As for the other liberals, Mayer wrote: "Sie vergass das Vaterland über die Partei." Ludwig Bamberger, "Alte Parteien," in *Gesammelte Schriften*, 3: 300; EL to Auerbach, Berlin, Feb. 11, 1867, HW, 1: 367.

18. Gerhard Ritter, "Die Entstehung der Indemnitätsvorlage von 1866," *Historische Zeitschrift* 115 (1915): 17; *Frankfurter Zeitung*, Feb. 23, 1867, lead article entitled "Das Zweite Königgrätz," on the election results.

19. RT, March 11, 1867, 1: 124–27.

20. H. Baumgarten to Fr. Oetker, Karlsruhe, March 31, 1867, HW, 1: 373–74; Bennigsen to his wife, Berlin, March 20, April 8, 1867, and notes from A. L. von Rochau to Bennigsen on April 2, 4, and 7, 1867, in ABRB (1906): 163, 166–67; Forckenbeck to his wife, Berlin, April 7, 1867, in Martin Philippson, "Forckenbecks erstes Debut beim Kronprinzen und beim Grafen Bismarck," *Deutsche Revue* 23 (1898): 13; Paul Wentzcke, "Zur Luxembourger Frage von 1867," *Deutsche Rundschau* 193 (1922): 227–31; RT, April 6, 10, 1867, 1: 606, 685.

21. "Gründungsprogramm der Nationalliberalen Partei, Juni 1867," in Mommsen, *Parteiprogramme*, pp. 147–51.

22. RT, June 8, 1867, 1: 312–13, and especially June 15, 1867, 1: 435–38. The need for a fleet, as Lasker saw it, arose from a military threat from Scandinavia, an amazing concept in itself.

23. Speech in Magdeburg, Oct. 10, 1868, pp. 22–24, in LNB. Earlier parts of the speech dealt with a large variety of domestic political and constitutional problems. The wager, witnessed by Dr. Alfred Woltmann, occurred in 1868 and is a separate document in LNP.

24. LT, Feb. 4, 1868, 3: 1380–83.

25. LT, Nov. 20, 1868, 1: 157–62.

26. LT, Nov. 5, 1869, 1: 362–65; Nov. 24, 1869, 2: 738–40. See also Josef Becker, "Bismarck und die Frage der Aufnahme Baden in den Norddeutschen Bund im Frühjahr 1870. Dokumente zur Interpellation Laskers von 24 Februar 1870", *Zeitschrift für die Geschichte des Oberrheins* 119 (1971): 427–70.

27. From 1868 through 1870 Lasker received a steady stream of letters from friends and politicians in South Germany supporting extension of the confederation. In LNP see the following examples: Widemann to EL, May 20, 1869; Straub to EL, May 7, 1868, and March 18, 1871; Wilhelm Blum to EL, Aug. 8, 26, 1869, Oct. 2, 1869, and Aug. 29, 1871; and Julius von Hölder to EL, April 4, 1870.

28. RT, Feb. 24, 1870, 1: 59–61. This speech obviously occurred before the resounding victory of the Napoleonic plebiscite in May 1870. See also Friedrich Kiefer to EL, Karlsruhe, Jan. 31, 1870, HW, 1: 448–49, stating that Baden and Hesse-Darmstadt backed immediate union. Lasker mentioned Kiefer by name in his speech in regard to his activities in the South on behalf of unity.

29. Bismarck to Count Flemming, Berlin, Feb. 28, 1870, to Bluntschli, Berlin, March 5, 1870, and to Flemming, Berlin, March 12, 1870, admitting the great feeling in Baden, in Otto von Bismarck *Die Gesammelten Werke* (15 vols., Berlin, 1925–1935), 6-c: 264, 165, 276–77; Kiefer to EL, Karlsruhe, March 1, 6, 1870, HW, 1: 460–63; Berthold to Jakob Auerbach, Berlin, Feb. 28, 1870, in Jakob Auerbach, ed., *Berthold Auerbach. Briefe an seinen Freund Jakob Auerbach* (2 vols., Frankfurt am Main, 1884), 2: 11; Baumgarten to Treitschke, Karlsruhe, March 7, 1870, HW, 1: 463–64; Baumgarten to Duncker, March 7, 1870, in Schultze, ed., *Dunckers Briefe*, pp. 449–50; "Die badischen Frage vor den norddeutschen Reichstag," *Frankfurter Zeitung*, March 1, 1870; Mayer, "Parteikrisen," p. 140, commenting that the official press branded Lasker as a firebrand after the Baden incident. Also see Moritz Busch, *Tagebuchblätter* (3 vols., Leipzig, 1899), 1: 24–25.

30. RT, July 20, 1870, 3: 13–15.

31. "Aufruf an das deutsche Volk," Berlin, August 30, 1870, in ALN (May): 167. Cahn, editor of part of the Lasker papers, stated that Lasker was the author of this document, but he was undoubtedly only the primary author.

32. EL to Bennigsen, Berlin, July 23, 1870, in Oncken, *Bennigsen*, 2: 171. Lasker stated that the peace must bring the "staatliche Einheit der Nation."

33. EL to Bismarck, Berlin, Aug. 15, 1870, ALN (April): 51. For Lasker's preparations for the trip, see Forckenbeck to EL, Elbing, Aug. 20, 1870, ibid., p. 60, and note 37 below.

34. EL to Kiefer, Berlin, Aug. 28, 1870, ALN (April): 63–64. Lasker emphasized the need for freedom within a Bund to Marquardsen in a letter of Sept. 20, 1870, in LNP.

35. "Address" and "Aufruf," in ALN (April): 167.

36. Hölder to EL, Stuttgart, Aug. 12, 1870, EL to Bismarck, Aug. 15, 1870, and EL to Hölder, Berlin, Aug. 18, 1870, ALN (April): 49–51, 52–53.

37. EL to Bennigsen, Aug. 18, 24, 27, 28, 1870, in Oncken, *Bennigsen*, 2: 176–79; EL to Hölder, Berlin, Sept. 6, 1870, and Forckenbeck to EL, Aug. 20, 1870, ALN (May): 177, 60; Baumgarten to Duncker, Karlsruhe, Sept. 22, 1870, in Schultze, ed., *Max Duncker*, p. 457.

38. Moritz Busch probably started the rumor; see Busch, *Tagebuchblätter*, 1: 419, Nov. 21, 1870; Bismarck, dispatch to Delbrück, Versailles, Nov. 26, 1870, in *Gesammelten Werke*, 6-b: 600; Bamberger to EL, Nov. 22, 1870, EL to Bamberger, Berlin, Nov. 25, 1870, and Bamberger to EL, Versailles, Nov. 28, 1870, ALN (Sept.): 287–90; 291–94, 296; Bennigsen to his wife, Berlin, Nov. 30, 1870, in ABRB (1907): 162; Chlodwig Fürst zu Hohenlohe-Schillingsfürst, *Denkwürdigkeiten* (2 vols., Stuttgart and Leipzig, 1907), 2: 74, Berlin, Sept. 30, 1871, reporting comments by Lasker after a dinner at Bunsen's; Baumgarten to Duncker, Karlsruhe, Sept. 22, 1870, and Duncker to Baumgarten, Berlin, Sept. 23, 1870, in Schultze, ed., *Max Duncker*, pp. 457, 460; "Vergesst die Freiheit nicht!" *Frankfurter Zeitung*, Sept. 24, 1870, Baumgarten to Heinrich von Sybel, Karlsruhe, Sept. 28, 1870, HW, 1: 480–81; Baumgarten to Duncker, Karlsruhe, Dec. 8, 1870, in Schultze, ed., *Max Duncker*, p. 462.

39. EL to Elben, Sept. 15, 1870, in Otto Elben, *Lebenserinnerungen, 1823–1899* (Stuttgart, 1931), p. 164; EL to Marquardsen, Berlin, Oct. 31, 1870, ALN (July): 78; EL to Elben, Berlin, Nov. 22, 1870, Hölder to EL, Göppingen, Dec. 3, 1870, ALN (Sept.): 283, 300.

40. EL to Hermann Mittnacht, Berlin, Oct. 3, 1870, ALN (June): 306; EL to Eduard Simson, Berlin, Nov. 9, 1870, HW, 1: 484–85. But Kiefer told Lasker that Bavaria would gravitate to Austria and then to France and become a center for anti-Prussian conspiracies; see Kiefer to EL, Mannheim, Dec. 6, 1870, ALN (Oct.): 60–61.

41. RT, Dec. 5, 1870, 3: 81–86.

42. Elben to EL, Stuttgart, Dec. 1, 1870, ALN (Sept.): 299.

43. Kiefer to EL, Mannheim, Dec. 6, 1870, and EL to Marquardsen, Berlin, Dec. 12, 1870, ALN (Oct.): 61–62, 66–67; Heinrich von Poschinger, ed., *Erinnerungen aus dem Leben von Hans Viktor von Unruh* (Stuttgart, 1895), p. 322; EL to Elben, Berlin, Dec. 29, 1870, ALN (Oct.): 76.

44. EL to Riedel, Berlin, Dec. 13, 1870, ALN (Oct.): 65–66.

45. EL to Freytag, Berlin, Dec. 18, 1870, EL to Elben, Berlin, Dec. 29, 1870, and Freytag to EL, Munich, Jan. 9, 1871, ALN (Oct.): 74; EL to Marquardsen, Berlin, Jan. 8, 1871, HW, 2: 5.

46. EL to Marquardsen, Berlin, Oct. 3, 1870, ALN (June): 308; Hölder to EL, Oct. 18, 1870, ALN (Aug.): 68; Bennigsen to his wife, Berlin, Jan. 29, 1871, in ABRB (1907): 307; Bamberger to EL, Mainz, Feb. 9, 1871, ALN (Oct.): 197–98; EL to an unknown recipient, Nov. 30, 1871, LNP.

47. Hölder to EL, Stuttgart, Aug. 12, 1870, ALN (April): 51. For an involved explanation of why a Bavarian liberal did not wish to waste time on the question of Alsace-Lorraine, see Barth to Hölder, Munich, Aug. 18, 1870, ibid., p. 55. See also Paul Wentzcke, "Zur Entstehungsgeschichte des Reichslandes Elsass-Lothringen," *Süddeutsche Monatshefte* 8 (1911): 608.

48. Forckenbeck to EL, Elbing, Aug. 20, 1870, Bennigsen to EL, Hannover, Aug. 22, 1870, and EL to Kiefer, Berlin, Aug. 28, 1870, ALN (April): 61, 58, 63; EL to Forckenbeck, Berlin, Nov. 10, 1870, ALN (Aug.): 164.

49. This assessment agrees favorably with the thesis of Lothar Gall, "Zur Frage der Annexion von Elsass und Lothringen 1870," *Historische Zeitschrift* 206 (1968): 265–326, esp. pp. 290, 293, 298–300, 306–7; H. B. Oppenheim, "Der Siegespreis," in Oppenheim, *Unser wiedergewonnenes Land. Beiträge zur Kenntnis des deutschen Gebiets im Elsass und im Lothringen* (Berlin, 1870), pp. 25–26, 28–31, 33–35.

50. RT, May 20, 1871, 2: 827; Nov. 20, 1871, 1: 375; Dec. 19, 1874, 2: 862–63.

51. See Detlev Albers "Reichstag und Aussenpolitik von 1871–79," *Historische Studien* 170 (1927): 10–12, 17–18, 20–21.

52. RT, April 26, 1877, 1: 786; Irene Fischer-Frauendienst, *Bismarcks Pressepolitik* (Münster, 1963), pp. 161–63. One of Lasker's few discussions of foreign affairs concerned Crispi's Italy, on which he took the Bismarckian position; EL to Bamberger, June 21, 1877, in the Bamberger Nachlass, Zentrales Staatsarchiv Potsdam. Miquel felt much the same and for a longer time. In 1879, when Lasker moved toward secession from the National Liberal party and opposition to Bismarck, Miquel wrote Lasker that he "held a politics of opposition to the person of Prince Bismarck as neither patriotic nor feasible"; Miquel to Lasker, July 29, 1879, LNP.

53. *Extra Beilage zu Nr. 1 der neuen Frankfurter Presse*, Jan. 1, 1874, printing in full the speech by Lasker in Frankfurt am Main on Dec. 19, 1873, in LNB.

54. "The Future of the German Empire," Jan. 18, 1877; English copy in the Leo Baeck Archives, New York.

55. RT, Jan. 25, 1882, 1: 936–39.

56. The correspondence is in LNP and includes over forty separate items. Lasker's acceptance was a letter of May 1881 to the association. He eventually presided for one day at the meeting of the convention in Brussels, and he supported the efforts of the association to organize in Germany in a limited way. His acceptance letter inspired criticism from the Ligue International de la Paix, with specific reference to Alsace-Lorraine; see Lasker's letter of June 21, 1881. He did little actual organizing himself (a Progressive, Ferdinand Giles, did) and served as a figurehead for the association in Germany. His services were appreciated by the English, at least, who later invited him to speak in London.

III. The Rise of the National Liberal Party

1. For organizational studies, see especially Thomas Nipperdey, *Die Organisation der deutschen Parteien vor 1918* (Düsseldorf, 1961), and Ursula Steinbrecher, *Liberale Partei Organization unter besonderer Berüchsichtigung des Linksliberalismus, 1871–1893. Ein Beitrag zur deutsche Parteigeschichte* (Cologne, 1960). For the Prussian lower house, see Adalbert Hess, *Das Parlament das Bismarck widerstrebte. Zur Politik und sozialen Zusammensetzung des preussischen Abgeordnetenhauses der Konfliktszeit (1862–1866)* (Cologne and Opladen, 1964); for the Reichstag, see Peter Molt, *Der Reichstag vor der improvisierten Revolution* (Cologne and Opladen, 1963). Among the very few constituency studies is Hansjürgen Schierbaum, *Die politischen Wahlen in den Eifel- und Moselkreisen des Regierungsbezirks Trier 1849–67* (Düsseldorf, 1960). Analysis of the political leadership may be found in Lenore O'Boyle, "Liberal Political Leadership in Germany, 1867–1884," *Journal of Modern History* 27 (Dec. 1956): 338–52. There have been several sociological analyses, most of them out of date, but see Willy Kremer, *Der Soziale Aufbau der Parteien des deutschen Reichstages von 1871–1918* (Cologne, 1934), and Karl Demeter, "Die soziale Schichtung des deutschen Parlaments seit 1848. Ein Spiegelbild der Strukturwandlung des Volkes," *Vierteljahrschrift für Sozial- und Wirtschaftsgeschichte* 39, no. 1 (1952): 1–29.

2. The most notable exception is Nipperdey, *Organisation der deutschen Parteien*.

3. More recent studies include Erich Angermann, *Robert von Mohl, 1799–1875. Leben und Werk eines altliberalen Staatsgelehrten* (Neuwied, 1962); James J. Sheehan, *The Career of Lujo Brentano: A Study of Liberalism and Social Reform in Imperial Germany* (Chicago, 1966); and Stanley Zucker, *Ludwig Bamberger: German Liberal Politician and Social Critic, 1823–1899* (Pittsburgh, 1975). Bennigsen, Miquel, Forckenbeck, and Stauffenberg have been studied, but only Oncken's work on Bennigsen is thorough, though dated; Steinsdorfer's work on Stauffenberg is the more recent, but it is short, traditional, and unsatisfying. See Hermann Oncken, *Rudolf von Bennigsen. Ein deutscher liberaler Politiker* (2 vols., Stuttgart, 1910); Hans Herzfeld, *Johannes von Miquel. Sein Anteil am Ausbau des deutschen Reiches bis zur Jahrhundertwende* (2 vols., Detmold, 1938); Wilhelm Mommsen, *Johannes von Miquel* (Berlin, 1928); and Helmut Steinsdorfer, *Franz Freiherr Schenk von Stauffenberg (1834–1901) als ein bayrischer und deutscher Politiker* (Munich, 1959).

4. Nearly the only work on the National Liberal party in these years is Dan S. White, *The Splintered Party: National Liberalism in Hessen and the Reich, 1867–1918* (Cambridge, Mass., 1976). Several works treat the National Liberal party or its origins as part of more comprehensive studies. See Heinrich A. Winkeler, *Preussischer Liberalismus und deutscher Nationalstaat. Studien zur Geschichte der deutschen Fortschrittspartei 1861–1866* (Tübingen, 1964); Gerhard Eisfeld, *Die Entstehung der Liberalen Parteien in Deutschland, 1858–1870* (Hanover, 1969); Dieter Fricke, ed., *Die bürgerlichen Parteien in Deutschland* (2 vols., Leipzig, 1968–1970), which contains material in several entries; James J. Sheehan, *German Liberalism in the Nineteenth Century* (Chicago and London, 1978); and J. H. Snell and Hans Schmitt, *The Democratic Movement in Germany 1789–1914* (Chapel Hill, 1976). Older studies of the National Liberal party include Erich Brandenburg, *50 Jahre Nationalliberale Partei, 1867–1917* (Leipzig, 1917); Paul Harms, *Die Nationalliberale Partei* (Berlin, 1907); Hermann Block, *Die parlamentarische Krise der Nationalliberalen Partei 1879–1880* (Münster, 1930); and Julian Borchardt, *Aus Geschichte, Wesen, und Tätigkeit der Nationalliberalen Partei* (Düsseldorf, 1911).

5. Voter participation in Prussia before 1867 was much worse, though it showed signs of improvement; from a low of 16.1 percent in 1855 it rose to a high of 34.3 percent in 1862, falling slightly to 30.4 percent in 1866. See Gertrud Beushausen, *Zur Strukturanalyse parlamentarischen Repräsentation in Deutschland vor der Gründung des Norddeutschen Bundes* (Hamburg, 1926), pp. 87–88. Participation in the electoral process was directly proportional to wealth. Hans Rosenberg, *Grosse Depression und Bismarckzeit. Wirtschaftsablauf, Gesellschaft und Politik in Mitteleuropa* (Berlin, 1967), p. 122, suggests that nonvoting indicated passive resistance; Eugene N. Anderson, *The Social and Political Conflict in Prussia, 1858–1864* (Lincoln, 1954), p. 415, feels that it at least does not indicate apathy or satisfaction. Theodore S. Hamerow, *The Social Foundations of German Unification, 1858–1871*, vol. 1, *Ideas and Institutions* (Princeton, 1969), pp. 397–98, agrees with Anderson.

6. *Die Grenzboten* editorialized in 1867 in "The General and Secret Suffrage before the Reichstag," p. 456: "[It is] not to be believed that one can direct the masses in their many local centers and countless subsections through an electoral committee in Berlin and through brochures, which are of course good tools; without personal action that extends to each village, farm and estate, [it will], as a rule, remain unsuccessful."

7. See Appendix A. The average number of sessions served by National Liberal executive committee members from 1867 to 1881 was 4.13.

8. This is especially true of Heinrich Rickert's rise to power in 1878–1879; see Rickert to EL, letters from Nov. 24, 1879, to Sept. 10, 1881, and especially Aug. 18, 1879, in LNP.

9. Nipperdey, *Organisation der deutschen Parteien*, p. 120.

10. Ibid., pp. 158–60; Brandenburg, *50 Jahre*, pp. 55–56.

11. See, for example, Lenore O'Boyle, "The Middle Class in Western Europe, 1815–1848," *American Historical Review* 71 (1966): 834, 841–43, 884; Eugene N. Anderson and Pauline R. Anderson, *Political Institutions and Social Change in Continental Europe in the Nineteenth Century* (Berkeley and Los Angeles, 1967), pp. 391–92; and John Gillis, *The Prussian Bureaucracy in Crisis, 1840–1860: Origins of an Administrative Ethos* (Stanford, 1971), p. 214. In "The Members of the Reichstag," the *Frankfurter Zeitung* of April 12, 1871, stated that 160 of 376 members derived their primary income from the state, either salary or pension, and that 39 lived in Berlin.

12. For corroboration see O'Boyle, "Liberal Political Leadership," pp. 339–40; for the first attempt (to my knowledge) to use multicoding of occupations. She was probably too cautious; her total number of classifications expanded only from 591 to 656. The *Generalregister* was published as part of the Reichstag debates for the 1895 session; Reichstagsbureau, *Generalregister zu den stenographischen Berichten über die Verhandlungen und die amtlichen Drucksachen des constituierenden Reichstages, des Reichstages des norddeutschen Bundes, des deutschen Zollparlaments und des deutschen Reichstages vom Jahre 1867 bis einschliesslich der am 24. Mai 1895 geschlossenen III. Session 1894/95* (Berlin, 1896).

13. Beushausen, *Strukturanalyse*, pp. 100–101. Fritz K. Ringer, *The Decline of the German Mandarins: The German Academic Community, 1890–1933* (Cambridge, Mass., 1969), p. 45, sees in these figures an abdication of political life by the German middle class compared to England. Rosenberg, *Grosse Depression*, p. 135, asserts that busi-

ness interests gravitated to the National Liberals; the precentage of businessmen-members grew from 11.2 in 1874 to 27.6 in 1878 and to 41.5 in 1890. However, Rosenberg's figures differ radically from those of Hermann Kalkoff, *Nationalliberale Parlamentarier, 1867–1917, des Reichstages und der Einzellandtage. Beiträge zur Parteigeschichte* (Berlin, 1917), and he lists no source for them.

14. Among the National Liberals, 5.5 percent did not list a religious affiliation, or such data were lacking for them; but data were available for all members of the Executive Committee.

15. These figures are from Gerhard Stoltenberg, *Der deutsche Reichstag, 1871–73* (Düsseldorf, 1955), p. 18. But his total for the National Liberals in 1871 is only 113, contradicting his printed sum of 120. In any case, the missing deputies were not from the South.

16. Beushausen, *Strukturanalyse*, p. 106. Rudolf Rocker, *Johann Most. Das Leben eines Rebellen* (Berlin, 1924), p. 40, relates Lasker's comment to Most that had Lasker studied philosophy rather than law he might have become a socialist.

17. The Liberal Union was often referred to as the party of the *Sezessionisten* or "secessionists." The Liberal Group was sometimes called the "Group Schauss-Volk" after its two leaders.

18. Heinrich von Treitschke may at first have been associated with this group. Ludwig Bergsträsser, *Geschichte der politischen Parteien in Deutschland* (Berlin und Leipzig, 1926), pp. 140–41, and Nipperdey, *Organisation der deutschen Parteien*, pp. 164–65, note that Volk left after a bitter argument with Bennigsen involving personality.

19. See Kalkoff, *Nationalliberale Parlamentarier*, p. 24.

20. The *Frankfurter Zeitung*, which seems to have developed a passion for counting, noted on Sept. 3, 1880, that in the previous Reichstag session the 19 members of the National Liberal left wing spoke 181 times while the 69 remaining members spoke 109 times.

21. See James F. Harris, "Eduard Lasker and Compromise Liberalism," *Journal of Modern History* 42 (Sept. 1970): 342–60.

22. August Ludwig von Rochau, *Grundsätze der Realpolitik. Angewändet auf die staatlichen Zustände Deutschlands* (Stuttgart, 1853), pp. 1–2.

23. Ludwig Bamberger, "Über Kompromisse," *Nation*, Oct. 4, 1890, in Bamberger, *Gesammelte Schriften* (5 vols., Berlin, 1894–1898), 5: 310, 312. Bamberger was much taken with John Morley's *On Compromise* (London, 1889), which he hoped would be the model for a book treating the same topic in Germany with reference to the National Liberal party.

24. Wilhelm Mommsen, ed., *Deutsche Parteiprogramme* (Munich, 1964), pp. 141–42, citing a speech by Miquel in Osnabrück after the 1866 war; Hermann Baumgarten, "Der deutsche Liberalismus. Eine Selbstkritik," October 1866, in ibid., p. 145; Treitschke, "Zum Jahresgang," Kiel, Dec. 23, 1866, *Preussische Jahrbücher*, in Treitschke, *Zehn Jahre Deutscher Kämpfe. Schriften zur Tagespolitik* (2 vols., Berlin, 1897), 1: 201; Bennigsen to his wife, March 3, 1867, in ABRB (1906): 159; "Twestens Entwurf," in HW, 1: 500–503; Bamberger, "Kandidaten Rede," Feb. 27, 1868, in *Gesammelte Schriften*, 4: 25, 35; also Friedrich Boettcher, *Eduard Stephani. Ein Beitrag zur Zeitgeschichte, insbesondere zur Geschichte der Nationalliberalen Partei* (Leipzig, 1887), p. 89; *Frankfurter Zeitung*, June 20, 1867.

25. "Vertrauliche Programm," Berlin, June 1867, in *AELN*, pp. 62–63.

26. Bennigsen to his wife, Berlin, Dec. 2, 1867, in ABRB (1906): 315–18; Moritz Busch, *Tagebuchblätter* (3 vols., Leipzig, 1899), 1: 517, Dec. 13, 1870, 3: 70, Dec. 2, 1868; 3: 11, March 4, 1870 (Bismarck would shortly name three bourgeois ministers, but *not* Lasker); 3: 29, April 13-May 28 (Bismarck was sick because of the *Unfug* [mischief] of the Lasker *Fraktion*). George G. Windell, *The Catholics and German Unity, 1866–71* (Minneapolis, 1954), pp. 293–94, writes that the National Liberals threatened an open revolt against Bismarck in the assembly.

27. Max von Forckenbeck to EL, Elbing, April 13, 1868, HW, 1: 416–17; Bamberger, "Vertrauliche Briefe aus dem Zollparlament," Berlin, June 22, 1869, in Bamberger, *Gesammelte Schriften* 4: 147, 151; Bergsträsser, *Geschichte*, pp. 123–24 and, for Lasker, p. 125.

28. See the discussion in Chapter II of the military bill; LT, Jan. 28, 1874, 1: 876; Brentano to Schmoller, Oct. 16, 1874, in Walther Goetz, "Der Briefwechsel Gustav Schmollers mit Lujo Brentano," *Archiv für Kulturgeschichte* 27 (1938): 336.

29. See Bergsträsser, *Geschichte*, pp. 124–25. Otto von Bismarck, *Die Gesammelten Werke* (15 vols., Berlin, 1924–1935), 8: 139, records a talk between von Tiedemann and von Sybel on Jan. 25, 1875, in Berlin. H. B. Oppenheim to EL, Berlin, Nov. 10, 1875, HW, 2: 137–138; Heinrich Ritter von Poschinger, *Fürst Bismarck und die Parlamentarier* (3 vols., Breslau, 1894–96), 1: 101; Oppenheim to EL, Heringdorf, July 7, 1876, HW, 2: 152.

30. Poschinger, *Fürst Bismarck*, 2: 211–12; see also Chapter V. Dietrich Sandberger, *Die Ministerkandidatur Bennigsens*, Historische Studien, no. 187 (Berlin, 1929), pp. 126, 179–82, sees the failure as a catastrophe for the National Liberal party; George Windell, "The Bismarckian Empire as a Federal State, 1866–1880: A Chronicle of Failure," *Central European History* 1 (Dec. 1969): 306–7, assumes that Bismarck would not have become conservative economically if Bennigsen had agreed—an intriguing, but unprovable, claim. See also Helmut Böhme, *Deutschlands Weg zur Grossmacht. Studien zum Verhältnis von Wirtschaft und Staat während der Reichsgründungszeit, 1848–1881*

(Cologne, 1966), p. 489, citing Sächsische Landes Haupt Archiv Dresden, Am. Nr. 1102; 2./10. III 1878 Bericht Nostitz; Eduard Hüsgen, *Ludwig Windthorst. Sein Leben Sein Wirken* (Cologne, 1911), p. 190; Hermann Oncken, "Bennigsen und die Epochen des parlamentarischen Liberalismus in Deutschland und Preussen," *Historische Zeitschrift* 104 (1910): 72, 76; Poschinger, *Fürst Bismarck*, 2: 274, citing Hölder *Tagebuch*, Stuttgart, March 20, 1878. The *Frankfurter Zeitung* of Dec. 27, 1877, suggested that Bismarck's overtures to Bennigsen were proof of the chancellor's rather than the National Liberals' strength. Also see Lasker's speech in Frankfurt, Sept. 29, 1879, p. 10, LNB.

31. Fürst Chlodwig zu Hohenlohe-Schillingsfürst, *Denkwürdigkeiten* (2 vols., Stuttgart and Leipzig, 1907), 2: 256, Berlin, 1878; ibid., pp. 256–57, "Memoire an den Fürsten Bismarck," Berlin, Sept. 18, 1878.

32. See Oncken, *Bennigsen*, 2: 403, citing Hölder, *Tagebuch*, May 1879; RT, May 8, 1879, 2: 1075; EL to Miquel, Berlin, June 29, 1879, HW, 2: 250; Bismarck, *Gesammelten Werke*, 8: 154–57, Berlin, July 3, 1879. See also Block, *Parlamentarische Krisis*, pp. 35–36, 105, who states that the break came on both economic and general political issues.

33. Hans-Georg Schroth, *Welt- und Staatsideen des deutschen Liberalismus in der Zeitalter der Einheits- und Freiheitskämpfe, 1859–1866* (Berlin, 1931), pp. 90–92, 96–97, 101; Andreas Dorpalen, "Emperor Friedrich III and the German Liberal Movement," *American Historical Review* 54 (Oct. 1948): 4–5; Walter Bussmann, "Zur Geschichte des deutschen Liberalismus im 19. Jahrhunderts," *Historische Zeitschrift* 186 (Dec. 1958): 557. Anderson and Anderson, *Political Institutions*, pp. 372–73, 395, say of the liberals that "they should have been the political leaders of the masses." Ernst Schraepler, "Die politische Haltung des liberalen Bürgertums im Bismarckreich," *Geschichte in Wissenschaft und Unterricht* 5 (Sept. 1954): 532, lists the Social Democrats, the Catholic Center, and the state as the main enemies of the liberals; see James J. Sheehan, "Political Leadership in the German Reichstag, 1871–1918," *American Historical Review* 74 (Dec. 1968): 511–28.

34. Ernst Fraenkel, "Historische Vorbelastungen des deutschen Parlamentarismus," *Vierteljahrschifte für Zeitgeschichte* 8 (1960): 335; Eberhard Pikart, "Die Rolle der Parteien im deutschen konstitutionellen System vor 1914," *Zeitschrift für Politik* 1 (1962): 25, 28, 30; Bamberger, "Über Kompromisse," p. 307.

IV. The Role of Law

1. John H. Hallowell, *The Decline of Liberalism as an Ideology with Particular Reference to German Political-Legal Thought* (Berkeley and Los Angeles, 1943), pp. 12–13, 35–49, 53–69, and passim; Guido de Ruggiero, *The History of European Liberalism*, trans. R. G. Collingwood (1927; reprint Boston, 1959), pp. 219–38, 254–60; Otto Pflanze, "Juridicial and Political Responsibility in Nineteenth-Century Germany," in Leonard Krieger and Fritz Stern, eds., *The Responsibility of Power: Historical Essays in Honor of Hajo Holborn* (New York, 1967), pp. 166–67; John Henry Merryman, *The Civil Law Tradition* (Stanford, 1969), pp. 31–33.

2. Heinrich von Sybel, *The Founding of the German Empire by William I*, trans. M. L. Perrin, (7 vols., New York, 1890–1898), 7: 226; Adalbert Wahl, *Beiträge zur Geschichte der Konfliktszeit* (Tübingen, 1914), p. 64; Theodor Schieder, "Das Verhältnis von politischen und gesellschaftlichen Verfassung und die Krise des bürgerlichen Liberalismus," *Historische Zeitschrift* 177 (1954): 50; Friedrich S. Sell, *Die Tragödie des deutschen Liberalismus* (Stuttgart, 1953), pp. 263–64; Heinrich Heffter, *Die deutsche Selbstverwaltung im 19. Jahrhundert. Geschichte der Ideen und Institutionen* (Stuttgart, 1950), p. 414; Ernst Engelberg, *Deutschland, 1871–1897* (Berlin, 1959), p. 63; Eugene N. Anderson, *The Social and Political Conflict in Prussia, 1858–1864* (Lincoln, 1954), p. 50; Leonard Krieger, *The German Idea of Freedom: History of a Political Tradition* (Boston, 1957), p. 352. Hajo Holborn, *A History of Modern Germany* (New York, 1969), 3: 145; on pp. 39–40 he describes the *Rechtsstaat* as non-ideological. See Otto Hintze, "Preussens Entwicklung zum Rechtsstaat," in Hintze, *Regierung und Verwaltung. Gesammelte Abhandlungen zur Staats-, Rechts-, und Sozialgeschichte Preussens*, ed. Gerhard Oestreich (2nd ed., Göttingen, 1967), pp. 97–163 and esp. pp. 160–61 for an admittedly Hegelian analysis; also see Krieger, *German Idea of Freedom*, pp. 253–54. Adolf Laufs, "Eduard Lasker und der Rechtsstaat" *Der Staat. Zeitschrift für Staatslehre, Öffentliches Recht und Verfassungsgeschichte* 13 (1974): 365–82 is a very general description of Lasker's attitude toward the *Rechtsstaat*.

3. Eduard Lasker, *Zur Verfassungsgeschichte Preussens* (Leipzig, 1874), pp. 203–4, 209, 376–97. Wahl, *Konfliktszeit*, pp. 43–44, praised Lasker's articles and his knowledge of law, though from a hostile viewpoint.

4. RT, Dec. 10, 1870, 3: 182, Dec. 18, 1876, 2: 865; Lasker, "Der Mensch und seine Geschlecht," in Lasker, *Wege und Ziele zur Kulturentwicklung* (Leipzig, 1881), pp. 365–87; LT, Jan. 13, 1874, 1: 545. Also see his attitude to the Peace Association, discussed in Chapter II, note 55.

5. LT, Nov. 9, 1869, 1: 418; RT, May 3, 1869, 2: 775; Lasker, "Wort und Tat," in Lasker, *Wege und Ziele*, pp. 235, 246; *Camburger Wochenblatt*, July 8, 1878, reprinting Lasker's speech of July 3, 1878, p. 1, LNB.

6. Heinrich von Treitschke, "Die Freiheit," in Treitschke, *Historische und politische Aufsätze* (4 vols., Leipzig, 1886–1897), 3 :12; John S. Mill, *On Liberty* (1859; New York, 1963), p. 129.

7. LT, May 19, June 10, 1865, 3: 1571–75, 2037; LT, Nov. 27, 1866, 2: 783–84. Reform of the law was a subordinate part of the National Liberal program of 1867; see Wilhelm Mommsen, ed., *Deutsche Parteiprogramme* (Munich, 1964), pp. 157–61.

8. LT, Nov. 27, 1866, 2: 783–84; RT, March 19, 1870, 1: 408.

9. Lasker used the term *Indigenat*, by which he meant "citizenship," and I have used that meaning.

10. RT, March 20, 1867, 1: 284–85.

11. RT, May 4, 1869, 2: 810, 813. See also RT, April 10, 1869, 1: 286, where Lasker first called for such a court and welcomed anything that would lead to a more comprehensive court structure; RT, March 15, 1870, 1: 300–301, May 12, 1870, 2: 833–56, where Lasker requested a common legal system in great detail.

12. RT, March 19, 1870, 1: 408; EL to Barth, Berlin, Oct. 2, 1870, ALN (June): 302.

13. RT, May 10, 1869, 2: 911, May 23, 1870, 2: 1122–24; Merryman, *Civil Law Tradition*, p. 31.

14. RT, April 18, 29, 1872, 1: 95–96, 98–99, 214, June 8, 1872, 2: 841.

15. RT, Dec. 14, 1875, 1: 623, 626.

16. RT, Nov. 17, 1876, 1: 152–53; LT, March 23, 1878, 3: 1946–47; RT, April 29, 1879, 2: 878–79.

17. RT, June 19, 1872, 2: 1123–26; Karl Biedermann to EL, Leipzig, June 12, 1872, EL to H. B. Oppenheim, Berlin, July 1, 1872, and Peter Reichensperger to EL, Berlin, July 8, 1872 (thanking him for his stand and asking him to aid in further work for legal freedom), HW, 2: 53–54, 55, 56.

18. LT, March 19, 1873, 3: 1755–56. I do not mean to imply that there was *no* political pressure: Sybel opposed Lasker in the Landtag, but the bill passed easily. Also, there is evidence that Lasker subsequently lost some Jewish support. See James F. Harris, "Eduard Lasker: The Jew as National German Politician," *Leo Baeck Yearbook* 20 (London, 1975), pp. 151–77.

19. LT, May 24, 1878, 1: 1536–39.

20. *Frankfurter Zeitung*, July 5, 16, 1878. Herbert wanted the press to refer to Lasker and Eugen Richter as if they were rebels; see Fritz Stern, *Gold and Iron. Bismarck, Bleichröder, and the Building of the German Empire* (New York, 1977), p. 198.

21. *Camburger Wochenblatt*, July 8, 1878, reprinting Lasker's speech of July 3, in LNB; *Frankfurter Zeitung*, June 27, Aug. 17, 27, Sept. 2, 12, 1878.

22. RT, Oct. 11, 1878, 2: 183–87.

23. RT, Oct. 12, 14, 18, 1878, 2: 218–19, 251–52, 354–59; *Frankfurter Zeitung*, Sept. 23, 1878.

24. Lasker's speech in Frankfurt am Main on Sept. 29, 1879, pp. 14–15, LNB; Hugo Feilchenfeld, "Gedächtnisserede" (Berlin, 1929), p. 5, and Hugo to Florina Feilchenfeld, Sept. 6, 1940, both in Leo Baeck Archives; *Frankfurter Zeitung*, Feb. 21, 1879 (when two deputies, Fritsche and Hasselmann, were jailed), March 7, 1880, and Jan. 31, 1883, p. v.

25. Lasker, *Verfassungsgeschichte*.

26. LT, Nov. 30, 1866, 2: 785–86. Lippe did not last long, and Leonhardt became the minister of justice within a matter of months. See Merryman, *Civil Law Tradition*, p. 111, for a discussion of career judges in civil law countries.

27. LT, Nov. 30, 1866, 2: 784, Jan. 8, 1868, 2: 707.

28. RT, Nov. 26, 1874, 1: 343–44. The civil law system of investigation and prosecution is described in Merryman, *Civil Law Tradition*, pp. 111–12, 124ff., 137ff.; though not critical of the system, Merryman notes the historical problem of reforming the process by eliminating undue governmental influence and bias. Outside of parliament, Lasker acted in support of the individual in only one case, that of the Society for Legal Protection of German Citizens in England. See Trübner to Lasker, July 31, 1868, LNP.

29. Lasker, *Verfassungsgeschichte*, pp. 181–89, 197; LT, Jan. 21, 1868, 2: 1033; also see LT, Nov. 25, 1869, 2: 786. Lasker later criticized the law of 1842 for establishing a police state; see LT, Feb. 7, 1870, 3: 1965–69.

30. LT, Jan. 11, 19, 1870, 3: 1398, 1545–46; RT, April 8, 1870, 2: 758. By 1870 Gneist had produced four books on English law.

31. LT, Jan. 13, 1874, 1: 546, May 19, 1874, 3: 1823–24; and see LT, June 2, 1865, 3: 1914.

32. RT, April 24, 1874, 2: 1090–93, May 9, 1878, 1: 1180, March 6, 1880, 1: 306–7, May 5, 1882, 1: 17–18.

33. LT, Nov. 30, 1866, 2: 786–88, 798.

34. LT, Jan. 8, 1868, 2: 710–12; and see LT, May 9, 1867, 1: 114–15, Jan. 10, 1868, 2: 778–80. Yet it was Leonhardt who in 1870 named Lasker a state lawyer of the Berlin City Court, the first Jew so designated. See document of appointment dated Oct. 10, 1870, LNP.

35. For examples of Lasker's fruitless calls for reform, see LT, April 4, 1865, 2: 958–60, Oct. 8, 1867, 2: 306, Nov. 9, 1869, 1: 417–18; RT, Nov. 7, 1876, 1: 67.

36. RT, March 19, 1870, 1: 406–8, 418, March 23, 1874, 1: 497–98, May 7, 1878, 1: 1101–2, April 26, 1880, 2: 934–35.

37. RT, May 1, 1869, 2: 728; LT, Oct. 29, 1869, 1: 228; RT, March 18, 1870, 1: 391–93, Feb. 25, 1876, 1: 262.

38. LT, Feb. 10, 1875, 1: 165.
39. RT, Dec. 3, 1875, 1: 386–99.
40. RT, March 4, 1870, 1: 185, Jan. 15, 1875, 2: 1029; LT, Feb. 24, 1876, 1: 224–25. Merryman, *Civil Law Tradition*, p. 38, writes of the civil law concept of the judge: "The net image is of the judge as an operator of a machine designed and built by legislators. His function is a mechanical one."
41. LT, Nov. 30, 1866, 2: 784–85, Jan. 8, 1868, 2: 708; RT, May 4, 1869, 2: 813, Jan. 22, 1876, 2: 841.
42. LT, Jan. 8, 1868, 2: 708; RT, March 4, 1870, 1: 184–85.
43. RT, Feb. 28, 1870, 1: 112–17.
44. RT, Jan. 27, 1876, 2: 954–62.
45. Lasker, "Der Streit um die Justizgesetze" ("The Fight over the Judicial Code"), dated Dec. 1876, pp. 1–12, in LNB; "Eduard Lasker über die Lage," Dec. 24, 1876 (Niederschrift zu eigenem Gebrauch), in HW, 2: 163–64. See August Bebel, *Die Parlamentarische Tätigkeit des deutschen Reichstages und der Landtage von 1874–1876* (Berlin, 1876), p. 107, who says that the Reich law was stricter in some parts than was the Prussian. In *Aus meinem Leben* (3 vols. in 1, Berlin und Stuttgart, 1933), p. 529, Bebel says that the socialists allowed the liberals to fight for them.
46. See Merryman, *Civil Law Tradition*, pp. 145–48.

V. The Power of the Constitution

1. See for example R. R. Palmer and Joel Coelton, *A History of the Modern World* (3rd ed., New York, 1965), esp. pp. 454, 588–89. Paul MacKendrick et al., *Western Civilization* (2 vols., New York, 1968), 2: 385, sees 1848 as a watershed, after which liberal principles and practices spread from Western Europe to Eastern Europe and beyond. Crane Brinton et al., *A History of Civilization* (2 vols., Englewood Cliffs, N.J., 1967), 2: 292–93, and Norman Cantor, *Western Civilization: Its Genesis and Destiny* (2 vols., Glenview, Ill., 1969), 2: 377–78, 399, both agree that constitutionalism moved east, though at a gradually slower pace.
2. The late emergence of German constitutional life has never been seriously questioned, though historians differ over how "new" constitutions really were. For an interesting treatment, see Otto Hintze, "Machtpolitik und Regierungsverfassung," in *Staat und Verfassung. Gesammelte Abhandlungen zur allgemeinen Verfassungsgeschichte*, ed. Gerhard Oestreich (Göttingen, 1962), pp. 427–28; and also Ernst Fraenkel, "Historische Vorbelastungen des deutschen Parlamentarismus" *Vierteljahrshefte für Zeitgeschichte* 8 (1960): 333–34. Franz Schnabel, *Deutsche Geschichte im neunzehnten Jahrhundert* (4 vols., Freiburg im Breisgau, 1929–1937), subtly differentiates between parliamentary monarchy and constitutional monarchy, noting that the first was the ideal based on the eighteenth-century English model, whereas the second satisfied the "practical politicians" in Germany. Ludwig Beutin, "Das Bürgertum als Gesellschaftsstand im 19. Jahrhundert," in Hermann Kellenbenz, ed., *Gesammelte Schriften zur Wirtschafts- und Sozialgeschichte* (Cologne and Graz, 1963), pp. 305–6, asserts that the middle-class goal was a responsible ministry and a Western European constitution.
3. June 21, 1862, cited in Eugene N. Anderson, *The Social and Political Conflict in Prussia, 1858–1864* (Lincoln, 1954), p. 233.
4. Eduard Lasker, "Wie ist die Verfassung in Preussen gehandhabt worden?" (1861), in *Zur Verfassungsgeschichte Preussens* (Leipzig, 1874), pp. 3–5, 7, 37–38.
5. Article 44 read: "The King's ministers shall be responsible. All official acts of the King shall require for their validity the countersignature of a minister, who shall thereby assume responsibility for them."
6. Lasker, "Die Regentschaft" (1864) and "Der König in der Verfassung" (1863), in *Verfassungsgeschichte*, pp. 133 and 398, 400–408.
7. Ibid., pp. 385–86; RT, March 11, 1867, 1: 126, May 20, 1871, 2: 827, 1003; Lasker, "Welt und Staatsweisheit," *Wege und Ziele zur Kulturentwicklung* (Leipzig, 1881), pp. 27–29; Lasker, *Fünfzehn Jahre parlamentarische Geschichte 1866–1880*, which composes part of *AELN*, pp. 10–12, 23–26.
8. Lasker, "Wort und Tat," in *Wege und Ziele*, pp. 234, 247–56.
9. RT, May 17, 1870, 2: 962, Dec. 5, 1870, 3: 82–83, May 29, 1873, 2: 899, and esp. June 5, 1868, 1: 262–63; Theodore Hamerow, "1848," in Leonard Krieger and Fritz Stern, eds., *The Responsibility of Power: Historical Essays in Honor of Hajo Holborn* (New York, 1967), p. 161; RT, March 11, 1867, 1: 126; LT, May 8, 1867, 1: 88–89; RT, April 3, 1868, 1: 87; Treitschke, "Bund und Reich," in Treitschke, *Zehn Jahre Deutscher Kämpfe. Schriften zur Tagespolitik* (2 vols., Berlin, 1897), 2: 226. EL to Mittnacht, Berlin, Oct. 14, 1870, to Hölder, Berlin, Dec. 15, 1870, ALN (March): 62, 69; Freytag to EL, Munich, Jan. 9, 1871, ALN (Nov.): 192, stating that centralization was not Germanic; RT, June 2, 1869, 2: 1254, where Lasker argued against placing any national power under the Bundesrat; RT, March 8, 1878, 1: 389, where Lasker called again for a central government, but with responsibility deriving from the heads of departments. Still later Lasker stated that one of two ways to prevent war was the growth

of popular power; see EL to Lewis Appleton of the International Arbitration and Peace Association, May 1881, LNP.

10. LT, Nov. 14, 20, 1868, 1: 62–63, 159–62; RT, June 6, 1872, 2: 792–93. On competence see RT, April 19, 1869, 1: 464–68, Dec. 7, 1870, 3: 119, May 29, 1872, 2: 596–98, Nov. 20, 1876, 1: 215. On conflict of Land and Reich see RT, Jan. 14, 1875, 2: 1005; LT, Nov. 21, 1872, 1: 60, Feb. 8, 13, 1872, 2: 676–77, 744.

11. RT, March 11, 1867, 1: 124–25, Dec. 7, 1870, 3: 129; EL to Kiefer, Berlin, Dec. 13, 1870, ALN (Oct.): 67–68.

12. Karl Ludwig Michelet to EL, Berlin, March 16, 1867, HW, 1: 371–72; speech in Magdeburg, Oct. 27, 1867, p. 6, in LNB; RT, March 16, 1869, 1: 86–87, March 8, 1870, 1: 226–27, April 1, 1870, 1: 587–90, April 29, 1872, 1: 205. See Chapter IV for attitudes to Prussian law and police. For comparison, see Ludwig Bamberger, "Alte Parteien und neue Zustände," in Bamberger, *Gesammelte Schriften* (5 vols., Berlin, 1894–1898), 3: 301. Bamberger deplored the feeling, especially strong around Mainz, that Germany would be absorbed into Prussia if Prussia conquered Germany.

13. Bamberger to EL, Versailles, Nov. 22, 1870, EL to Bamberger, Berlin, Nov. 25, 1870, ALN (Sept.): 287–94. The original letters are in the Lasker and Bamberger papers in LNP.

14. EL to Forckenbeck and Bennigsen, Berlin, Oct. 6, 1870, ALN (June): 310; EL to Delbrück, Berlin, Oct. 23, 1870, to Bennigsen, Berlin, Oct. 24, 1870, and to Delbrück, Berlin, Oct. 26, 1870, ALN (July): 69, 71, 72.

15. Enclosed in EL to Delbrück, Berlin, Oct. 26, 1870, ALN (July): 73–77; Simson to EL, Frankfurt a. Oder, Nov. 10, 1870, ALN (Aug.): 161–62.

16. EL to Hölder, Berlin, Feb. 5, 1871, ALN (Nov.): 196.

17. EL to Freytag, Berlin, Dec. 18, 1870, ALN (Oct.): 73–74; RT, Nov. 20, 1871, 1: 381; EL to Forckenbeck, Berlin, Nov. 20, 1870, ALN (Aug.): 173–74; EL to Hölder, Berlin, Dec. 15, 1870, ALN (Oct.): 69; RT, May 27, 1873, 2: 855.

18. See, for example, Koeppel Pinson, *Modern Germany: Its History and Civilization* (New York, 1954), pp. 156–57, and Hajo Holborn, *A History of Modern Germany 1840–1945* (3 vols., New York, 1969), 3: 224; Lasker to Delbrück, Berlin, Sept. 24, 1870 [sic], ALN (May): 180–81. Marquard Barth mentioned the same desire as Lasker in a letter to Hölder, Munich, Aug. 18, 1870, ALN (April): 55–56. The sentiment for simple extension is also found in the address to the king of Bavaria, which Lasker helped draft, ALN (June): 30; LNP contains five separate drafts of the address.

19. EL to Hölder, Berlin, Sept. 26, 1870, to Barth, Berlin, Oct. 2, 1870, to Simson, Oct. 2, 1870, to Forckenbeck and Bennigsen, Berlin, Oct. 6, 1870, ALN (June): 297, 303–4, 312.

20. EL to Barth, Sept. 24, 1870, ALN (May): 185; EL to Delbrück, Berlin, Nov. 1, 1870, ALN (July): 82; EL to Simson, Berlin, Nov. 20, 1870, HW, 1: 486–87. See the report of Delbrück's intentions (identical to Lasker's) in EL to Forckenbeck and Bennigsen, Berlin, Oct. 6, 1870, ALN (June): 310; and Delbrück's defense of parliamentary discussion in Delbrück to EL, Nov. 9, 1870, ALN (Aug.): 166. Hölder agreed completely; see Hölder to EL, Stuttgart, Nov. 28 1870, ALN (Sept.): 185; George G. Windell, *The Catholics and German Unity, 1866–71* (Minneapolis, 1954), pp. 294–95.

21. Lasker, "Die Krisis in Preussen," *Verfassungsgeschichte*, p. 305; LT, Aug. 28, 1866, 1: 137–38; RT, March 11, 1867, 1: 127, May 10, 1869, 2: 711; EL to a friend in 1869, ALN (Dec.): 363; EL to Hölder, Berlin, Dec. 15, 1870, ALN (Oct.): 70. Though it was weak, Lasker considered the Zollparlament important because it was the first step toward representation of all Germany; see *Stenographische Berichte über die Vehandlungen des durch die allerhöchste Verordnung vom 13. April 1868 einberufenen deutschen Zollparlaments* (3 vols., Berlin, 1868–1870), May 1, 1868, 1: 49.

22. Lasker's speech in Magdeburg, Oct. 27, 1867, pp. 7–8, in LNB; RT, April 5, 1871, 1: 174, Feb. 28, 1870, 1: 114. See also Anderson, *Social and Political Crisis*, p. 279; RT, April 5, 1867, 1: 565, March 13, 1869, 1: 58, April 5, 1867, 1: 554; EL to Diez, Berlin, Feb. 22, 1871, ALN (June): 52–53; Treitschke, "Die Freiheit" (1861), in Treitschke, *Historische und politische Aufsätze* (4 vols., Leipzig, 1886–1897), 3: 42.

23. Ziegler to Rodbertus, June 30, 1866, in Ludwig Dehio, "Die preussische Demokratie und der Krieg von 1866. Aus dem Briefwechsel von Karl Rodbertus mit Franz Ziegler," *Forschungen zur brandenburgischen und Preussischen Geschichte* 39 (1927): 258–59; Unruh's diary, 1867, in Heinrich Ritter von Poschinger, *Fürst Bismarck und die Parlamentarier* (3 vols., Breslau, 1894–1896), 1: 342; "Vertrauliche Programm," Berlin, June 1867, in *AELN*, pp. 159–60; EL to Berthold Auerbach, Berlin, Feb. 11, 1867, HW, 1: 368; LT, Nov. 3, 1879, 1: 393. Also see Anderson, *Social and Political Crisis*, pp. 274–75; T. S. Hamerow, *Restoration, Revolution, Reaction: Economics and Politics in Germany, 1815–1871* (Princeton, 1958), p. 215; and Hamerow, *The Social Foundations of German Unification, 1858–1871*, vol. 1, *Ideas and Institutions* (Princeton, 1969), pp. 300–301.

24. LT, Nov. 20, 1872, 1: 31; LT, Nov. 26, 1873, 1: 99–106, for the attack on the Center party; *Frankfurter Zeitung*, Oct. 30, Nov. 28, 30, 1873; LT, May 26, 1876, 3: 1750–52; Martin Philippson, *Max von Forckenbeck* (Dresden, 1898), p. 276, who reasoned similarly; August Bebel, *Die Parlamentarische Tätigkeit des deutschen Reichstages und der Landtage von 1874–1876* (Berlin, 1876), pp. 74–76; *Frankfurter Zeitung*, Aug. 22, 1877; Ludwig

144   Notes to pages 70–77

Bamberger, *Deutschland und der Sozialismus* (Leipzig, 1878), p. 35; "Eduard Lasker," *Preussische Jahrbücher* (1884): 202–203. For a pithy description of the *Dreiklassensystem*, see Otto Pflanze, *Bismarck and the Development of Germany: The Period of Unification, 1815–1871* (Princeton, 1963), pp. 220–21; also Walter Gagel, *Die Wahlrechtsfrage in der Geschichte der deutschen liberalen Parteien 1848–1918* (Düsseldorf, 1958), pp. 52–54.

25. RT, March 13, May 13, 1869, 1: 42–43, 969.

26. Theodor von Bernhardi, *Aus dem Leben Theodor von Bernhardis* (9 vols., Leipzig, 1897), 6: 193; LT, May 8, 1867, 1: 87–88; RT, Feb. 5, 1874, 1: 31. Eugen Richter relates that Saxony did pay a *Diäten* and that the Saxon deputies, including Bebel, brought their wives to Berlin; see Eugen Richter, *Jugend Erinnerungen* (Berlin, 1892), p. 190. Saxony also became an early base for the Social Democrats.

27. Lasker, "Der König in die Verfassung," *Verfassungsgeschichte*, p. 414; Otto Elben, *Lebenserinnerungen, 1823–1899* (Stuttgart, 1931), p. 166. See Lasker's speech in Sonneberg on May 22, 1881, p. 13, in LNB; he still felt the *Volk* were liberal. See *Frankfurter Zeitung*, Dec. 31, 1873, for an early criticism of Lasker's reluctance to work among the people or with the press; he was convinced, according to the paper, that the Reichstag was his only medium.

28. Lasker, "Die Krisis in Preussen," *Verfassungsgeschichte*, p. 319. See Hamerow, *Social Foundations*, 1: 374–78, for an excellent discussion of this point vis-à-vis the election returns. EL to H. B. Oppenheim, Berlin, Oct. 17, 1865, HW, 1: 263; Martin Spahn, "Zur Entstehung der nationalliberalen Partei," *Zeitschrift für Politik* 1 (1907–1908): 429; Julius von Hennig to EL, Berlin, Sept. 30, 1868, HW, 1: 426. Hamerow, *Social Foundations*, 1: 380, supports this viewpoint.

29. RT, May 23, 1870, 1: 1124, April 17, 1871, 1: 249, Oct. 18, 1878, 3: 356; Lasker's speech at Frankfurt am Main, Sept. 29, 1879, pp. 11–12, LNB; RT, May 10, 1880, 2: 1311, Jan. 14, 1882, 1: 642; Lasker, *Fünfzehn Jahre*, pp. 139–40; *Frankfurter Zeitung*, Jan. 5, 1875. Also see RT, Dec. 18, 1876, 2: 865, for a similar comment about public response to the new penal code.

30. Eduard Lasker, *Erlebnisse einer Mannes-Seele*, ed. Berthold Auerbach (Stuttgart, 1873), p. 75. But Adalbert Wahl, *Beiträge zur Geschichte der Konfliktszeit* (Tübingen, 1914), pp. 44–45, connected Lasker's confidence in the *Volk* with Rousseau.

31. LT, Nov. 19, 1867, 1: 27; RT, June 6, 1868, 1: 288; LT, Oct. 25, 1872, 3: 1610–12. See also Gerhard Lowenberg, *Parliament in the German Political System* (Ithaca, N.Y., 1966), p. 10; Lowenberg, *Synoptische Darstellung der Geschäftsordnung des Deutschen Bundestages und ihrer Vorläufer*, Wissenschaftliche Abteilung, Deutschen Bundestag (Bonn, 1961); RT, May 29, 1867, 1: 456–57; EL to Bennigsen, Berlin, Nov. 7, 1870, to Simson, Berlin, Nov. 9, 1870, and to Delbrück, Berlin, Nov. 10, 1870 (in the evening), ALN (Aug.): 160, 161, 163; EL to Simson, Berlin, Nov. 9, 1872, HW, 2: 64–65.

32. For Lasker's position on freedom of speech in the German and Prussian assemblies, see RT, March 29, 1867, 1: 439–41; LT, Nov. 27, 1867, 1: 100–103, Jan. 8, 1868, 2: 695. Lasker's major speech on nonprosecution was in the Reichstag on April 3, 1868, 1: 86–88. See also LT, Nov. 3, 1869, 1: 304, and RT, Dec. 16, 1874, 2: 742–47, for the Majunke case; RT, March 4, 1879, 1: 261–69, May 5, 1881, 2: 946–47, June 16, 1882, 1: 523.

33. RT, April 5, 1867, 1: 554. The confederal power in the Bundesrat also affected budget control, but only in the direction of negating increased budgets; that is, it had no power to overturn the Reichstag's right of budget rejection. Lasker worried about possible antinational use of this confederal right as early as 1867, but it was never an issue. See RT, March 11, 1867, 1: 126.

34. RT, April 9, 1867, 1: 647; "Vertrauliche Programm," Berlin, June 1867, in *AELN*, p. 160. George Windell, "The Bismarckian Empire as a Federal State, 1866–1880: A Chronicle of Failure," *Central European History* 1 (Dec. 1969): 299, states that the government never challenged parliament's right to control the budget, but it is necessary to add that no budgets were ever rejected and that the liberals never used that right to do anything more than embarrass the administration. Before 1884 it was not even used as a political tool against Bismarck.

35. RT, Oct. 18, 1867, 2: 479, Nov. 29, 1871, 1: 614–18, Feb. 16, 1874, 1: 86–90.

36. EL to Franz von Stauffenberg, Berlin, April 3, 1874, and to Konrad Listemann, Berlin, April 8, 1874, HW, 2: 103, 105–6; Helmut Böhme, *Deutschlands Weg zur Grossmacht. Studien zum Verhältnis von Wirtschaft und Staat während der Reichsgründungszeit, 1848–1881* (Cologne, 1966), pp. 380–81; RT, April 9, 1880, 1: 580–82.

37. Lasker's speech in Frankfurt am Main, Sept. 29, 1879, p. 34, LNB; RT, March 8, 1881, 1: 199–202.

38. LT, Nov. 21, 1866, 2: 611–12, Jan. 30, 1867, 3: 1805–6, Dec. 9, 18, 1869, 2: 1081, 1318–19, Feb. 1, 1868, 3: 1305–7 (on the *Welfenfond*); RT, Nov. 4, 1871, 1: 131–33, June 13, 1872, 2: 974 (on the necessity of Reichstag approval for government sale of real estate).

39. LT, Nov. 14, 1868, 1: 61–62, Oct. 12, 1869, 1: 48–49.

40. RT, Nov. 29, 1871, 1: 613; LT, Feb. 15, 16, 17, 19, 1872, 2: 782–83, 806, 815, 834, 843, 865. See also RT, April 8, 1872, 2: 58, for a review of Prussian misuse of accounting in the *Konfliktszeit*; RT, June 8, 1872, 2: 850, for an attack by Lasker on government piecemeal budget presentation. See Max von Forckenbeck to Stauffenberg, Berlin, May 17, 1878, HW, 2: 193–94, on the government's lack of contact with the House; in twelve years Forckenbeck had

not once been told ahead of time of the dissolution of the Reichstag. See Fraenkel, "Vorbelastungen," p. 336.

41. RT, March 27, 1867, 1: 365–67, 392, 401, a series of speeches on the same day. In September 1866 Lasker ridiculed the attempt to make ministerial responsibility a prerequisite for the indemnity, which in effect was an agreement not to enforce the responsibility of the ministers. See LT, Sept. 3, 1866, 1: 183–84.

42. LT, May 8, 1867, 1: 90.

43. RT, March 11, 1867, 1: 126–27; EL to Kiefer, Berlin, Dec. 13, 1870, ALN (Oct.): 67–68. Also see RT, Sept. 28, 1867, 2: 135.

44. LT, Feb. 1, 1868, 3: 1308; RT, April 22, 1868, 1: 160–61.

45. RT, April 16, 1869, 1: 409–11.

46. RT, March 10, 1867, 1: 51–54, March 13, 1877, 1: 129–30; EL to Stauffenberg, Berlin, Oct. 9, 1877, HW, 2: 187–88; Bennigsen to his mother, Berlin, Oct. 22, 1877, ABRB (1906): 262–63. Also see Bennigsen to EL, Hannover, June 30, 1878, AELN, pp. 165–66; Hintze, "Das preussische Staatsministerium im 19. Jahrhundert," in Hintze, Gesammelte Schriften, 3: 603; Dietrich Sandberger, Die Ministerkandidatur Bennigsens, Historische Studien, no. 187 (Berlin, 1929), pp. 79–126; also see RT, Feb. 23, March 9, 1878, 1: 158–59, 415–16, for later and almost pointless uses of the argument that the burden of office was too great.

47. LT, Nov. 30, Dec. 1, 1866, 2: 784–88, 851. See Chapter VI for the Wagener case.

48. Irmgard Loeber, Bismarcks Pressepolitik in den Jahren des Verfassungskonfliktes, 1862–1866 (Munich, 1935), pp. 14–16, 23–31, 45–47, 52–53; Irene Fischer-Frauendienst, Bismarcks Pressepolitik (Münster, 1963), pp. 157–58.

49. LT, April 7, 1865, 2: 1038, Nov. 23, 1866, 2: 649–50; Spahn, "Entstehung der nationalliberalen Partei," p. 381, citing the Vossische Zeitung, May 17, 1866.

50. LT, Dec. 7, 1868, 1: 539; RT, Oct. 30, 1871, 1: 70–74.

51. LT, Jan. 20, 1874, 1: 716–17, Jan. 31, 1877, 1: 193. One of Lasker's few complaints about the official press between 1867 and 1878 was an occasion in 1869 when the Provinzial Korrespondenz described him as "democratic"; Lasker protested that it was used to mean "radical," which was contrary to his intention. See LT, Oct. 20, 1869, 1: 140.

52. Moritz Busch, Tagebuchblätter (3 vols., Leipzig, 1899), 1: 24–26.

53. Frankfurter Zeitung, Jan. 19, 1874; Friedrich Zabel to EL, Montreux, April 7, 1874, EL to Stauffenberg, Berlin, April 3, 1874, HW, 2: 104, 102–103; Frankfurter Zeitung, Jan. 6, 1876.

54. Wolfgang Pack, Das parlamentarische Ringen um das Sozialistengesetz Bismarcks, 1868–1890 (Düsseldorf, 1961), pp. 47–66, 95–97, is the best analysis of the government press war. Pack had access to files of the Norddeutsche Allgemeine Zeitung, the Kreuzzeitung, the Provinzial Korrespondenz, and the National Zeitung for the entire period, as well as the more easily obtainable papers like the Frankfurter Zeitung. See Frankfurter Zeitung, July 17, 1878, which also cites the same impression from the Berliner Autographische Correspondenz; Erich Forester, Adalbert Falk, sein Leben und Werken als Preussischer Kulturminister (Gotha, 1927), pp. 488–89 (July 2, 1878). Ballhausen, Bismarcksche Erinnerungen, p. 84ff. (Feb. 11, 1876), cited in Otto von Bismarck, Die Gesammelten Werke (15 vols., Berlin, 1924–1935), 8: 168, predicted the National Liberals would lose.

55. LT, Feb. 8, 1879, 2: 1233–34; RT, March 18, April 22, 1880, 1: 484–85, 846; Lasker speech in Sonneberg, Oct. 9, 1881, p. 11, LNB. See also Bamberger, Forward to the fourth edition of the article "Die Sezession," late Jan. 1881, p. 47. Bamberger was horrified by the chancellor's blatant attacks on individuals. Ludwig Bergsträsser, Geschichte der politischen Parteien in Deutschland (Berlin and Leipzig, 1926), p. 136, compares Bismarck's action in and after 1878 with his use of the miners' strike in 1889.

56. "Politische Übersicht," Frankfurter Zeitung und Handelsbericht, Jan. 14, 1880, p. 1; Herbert von Bismarck to Rantzau, Kissingen, July 27, 1879, in Walter Bussmann, ed., Staatssekretär Graf Herbert von Bismarck aus seiner politischen Privatkorrespondenz (Göttingen, 1964), pp. 88–90 (Herbert discusses how Lasker should be treated in the press). See also Siemens to his son-in-law Gorz, Dec. 1, 1882, in Karl Helffereich, Georg von Siemens (3 vols., Berlin, 1923), 3: 167–68; Norman Rich and M. H. Fisher, The Holstein Papers (4 vols., Cambridge, 1955–1963), 2: 67–69, 72, (instructions, Feb. 2, 1884), and 87 (Bismarck's maxim, Feb. 22, 1884).

57. See Bernhardi, Aus dem Leben Bernhardis, 6: 173, for an interesting conversation with General Alvensleben on the usefulness of constitutions in drawing people into public life. See Heinrich von Treitschke, "Das constitutionelle Königthum in Deutschland," in Treitschke, Historische und politische Aufsätze, 3: 499, on the strength of the English aristocracy in true self-government outside Parliament.

58. LT, Oct. 19, 1869, 1: 114–19; Lasker speech in Frankfurt am Main, Dec. 29, 1873, reported in an Extra Beilage of the Neuen Frankfurter Presse, Jan. 1, 1874, p. 3, LNB; LT, Feb. 10, 1875, 1: 160, 170–71.

59. RT, March 21, 1867, 1: 296; LT, Feb. 10, 1869, 2: 1559–60; RT, March 11, 1874, 1: 301.

60. RT, March 20, 1869, 1: 201; LT, Oct. 19, 1869, 1: 115, Jan. 10, 1870, 3: 1370.

61. LT, Oct. 19, Nov. 11, 1869, 1: 114–15, 439, Nov. 20, 1872, 1: 31.

62. LT, Oct. 19, 1869, 1: 115–17, March 16, 21, 1872, 3: 1304–5, 1447–48, 1486, Nov. 20, 1872, 1: 30, April 28, 1874, 2: 1300, March 4, 1878, 1: 312; Lasker speech in Frankfurt (see note 58 above), p. 4.

63. LT, Feb. 5, 10, 1875, 1: 83, 161, March 4, 1876, 1: 443–48.

VI. The Crisis of Liberal Economics

1. T. S. Hamerow, *Restoration, Revolution, Reaction: Economics and Politics in Germany, 1815–1871* (Princeton, 1958), pp. 238–55; Hamerow, *The Social Foundations of German Unification, 1858–1871*, vol. 1, *Ideas and Institutions* (Princeton, 1969), pp. 33–34, 44–47, 51, 55, 71–72, 78; Gustav Stolper, *German Economy, 1870–1940* (New York, 1940), pp. 36, 61, 71.

2. Peter Molt, *Der Reichstag vor der improvisierten Revolution* (Cologne and Opladen, 1963), p. 39; David S. Landes, "Technological Change and Development in Western Europe, 1750–1914," in *The Cambridge Economic History of Europe* (Cambridge, 1965), vol. 6, pt. 1 p. 458; Hans Rosenberg, *Grosse Depression und Bismarckzeit. Wirtschaftsablauf, Gesellschaft und Politik in Mitteleuropa* (Berlin, 1967), pp. 47–48.

3. For an interesting discussion of the connection between the modern capitalist economy and the rise of democracy, see Seymour M. Lipset, *Political Man: The Social Basis of Politics* (New York, 1963), pp. 44, 68, 71.

4. Peter Stearns, *European Society in Upheaval* (New York, 1967), pp. 200, 212, 236–38, 290, 294, 300; Hamerow, *Social Foundations*, 1: 92–93, 64–66. See Lenore O'Boyle, "The Middle Class in Western Europe, 1815–1848," *American Historical Review* 71 (1966): 826–27, for a discussion of the problem involved in use of the term "middle class." See also Shepherd Clough, *Economic History of Europe* (New York, 1947), pp. 564–66; Hans Ulrich Wehler, *Bismarck und der Imperialismus* (Cologne and Berlin, 1969), pp. 44–45, for expansion of trade.

5. Gottfried Waldstedt, "Eduard Lasker, Biographische Skizze," Berlin, 1873, p. 10. See Chapter V for Lasker's attitude toward universal suffrage.

6. Lasker, "Polizeigewalt und Rechtschutz in Preussen" (1861), in Lasker, *Zur Verfassungsgeschichte Preussens* (Leipzig, 1874), p. 197; Lasker's speech in Magdeburg, Oct. 10, 1868, pp. 22–23, LNB. See Guido de Ruggiero, *The History of European Liberalism*, trans. R. G. Collingwood (1927; reprint Boston, 1959), p. 359, for a concise statement of this element of liberal belief in the importance of legal opportunity. Lasker was elected *Syndikus* of the Verein zur Wahrung Kaufmannischer Interessen (Association to Protect Commercial Interests) in 1865; see Sigmund Meyer to Lasker, Dec. 8, 1865, including formal notice from the Verein also dated Dec. 8, in LNP.

7. Helmut Köster, "Aus Laskers politische Frühzeit" (Ph.D. diss., University of Leipzig, 1924), pp. 225–27, citing Lasker to Gröning, Bremen, June 11, 1870; Ludwig Beutin, "Das Bürgertum als Gesellschaftsstand im 19. Jahrhundert," in Hermann Kellenbenz, ed., *Gesammelte Schriften zur Wirtschafts- und Sozialgeschichte* (Cologne and Graz, 1963), p. 299.

8. Eduard Lasker, "Der Mensch," in Lasker, *Wege und Ziele zur Kulturentwicklung* (Leipzig, 1881), pp. 335, 337–40, 350, 390–91, 392, 395, 399.

9. Lasker, "Welt- und Staats-Weisheit," *Wege und Ziele*, pp. 9–10, 16, 37–39.

10. EL to Stauffenberg, Berlin, Sept. 12, Oct, 9, 1877, HW, 2: 186–188. Stearns, *European Society in Upheaval*, p. 167, writes that the middle class was pragmatic and followed no specific economic theories, a description easily applied to Lasker.

11. LT, Dec. 17, 1866, 2: 1200–1202. Eugene N. Anderson, *The Social and Political Conflict in Prussia, 1858–1864* (Lincoln, 1954), p. 316, writes that the upper bourgeoisie regarded cooperatives as a means of preserving the middle-class character of the handworkers, that is, of preventing them from becoming a proletariat.

12. RT, April 17, 1877, 1: 548–49. Letters to Lasker in LNP indicate that he was still actively involved in the struggle to protect the handworkers in 1878 and 1879; see Oppenheim to EL, June 20, 1877, and Rickert to EL, Jan. 24, 1879.

13. RT, Sept. 24, Oct. 14, 1867, 1: 89, 394–95, June 17, 1868, 1: 542.

14. RT, Oct. 10, 1867, 2: 345–46; LT, Jan. 16, 1879, 1: 645–47.

15. For Lasker's attitude toward workers and politics, see his letter to Gröning of June 11, 1870, in Köster, "Laskers politischer Frühzeit," pp. 225–27; Karl Erich Born, "Sozialpolitische Probleme und Bestrebungen in Deutschland von 1848 bis zur Bismarckschen Gesetzgebung," *Vierteljahrschrift für Sozial-, Wirtschaft-, und Kulturgeschichte* 46 (1959): 42–43; RT, April 17, 1872, 1: 80–82.

16. RT, Feb. 20, 1874, 1: 135–44.

17. RT, April 17, 1877, 1: 545–50.

18. LT, Sept. 19, 1866, 1: 408.

19. LT, Jan. 7, 1867, 3: 1381–83; RT, April 4, 1870, 2: 647.

20. Lasker probably meant that the bonds sold because of the money possibly to be made on the lottery rather than because of confidence in the ability of the government or firm to amortize the bonds; he regarded the practice as a gamble.

21. RT, May 18, 1870, 2: 1005–6, April 24, 1871, 1: 360–61. See also a similar clash on the *Invalidenfonds*, RT, May 3, 1873, 1: 474–75.

22. RT, Nov. 17, 1874, 1: 175–83, Jan. 25, 1875, 2: 1273–79. See also Helmut Böhme, *Deutschlands Weg zur Grossmacht. Studien zum Verhältnis von Wirtschaft und Staat während der Reichsgründungszeit. 1848–1881* (Cologne, 1966), pp. 352–53.

23. RT, April 13, Nov. 7, 1871, 1: 216–17, 173; LT, Dec. 19, 1872, 1: 406–9.

24. LT, Jan. 14, 1873, 1: 536–38; Ludwig to Anna, Feb. 7, 1873, Bamberger Nachlass, Berlin. See also Gordon Mork, "The Prussian Railway Scandal of 1873: Economics and Politics in the German Empire," *European Studies Review* 1 (1971): 35–48; LT, Feb. 7, 1873, 2: 934–50. For von Roon, see ibid., p. 951. For a good, brief description of the scandal see Fritz Stern, *Gold and Iron. Bismarck, Bleichröder, and the Building of the German Empire* (New York, 1977), p. 242.

25. *Frankfurter Zeitung*, Feb. 10, 1873, lead article; also Feb. 14, 16. Ludwig to Anna, Berlin, Feb. 14, 1873 (expressing fear of Lasker's zeal), Feb. 21, 1873 (on Lasker's lack of knowledge of the world), Feb. 28, 1873 (commenting that Lasker was sick of overwork), and May 4, 1873 (on the differences of character between the two men), Bamberger Nachlass, Berlin. *Frankfurter Zeitung*, Oct. 15, 1873. See also the congratulatory letters to Lasker: Adolf Stahr to EL, Berlin, Feb. 8, 1873, Eduard Stephani to EL, Leipzig, Feb. 10, 1873, HW, 2: 74–76; also the letters in LNP, including a formal inquiry from a representative of Romania requesting advice on Strousberg's railroad activity there.

26. Ivo Lambi, *Free Trade and Protection in Germany, 1868–1879*, (Wiesbaden, 1963), pp. 73–84; LT, May 12, 1874, 3: 1657; Walter Steglich, "Beitrag zur Problematik des Bündnisses zwischen Junkern und Bourgeoisie in Deutschland, 1870 bis 1880," *Wissenschaftliche Zeitschrift der Humboldt-Universität zu Berlin* 9 (1959–1960): 333–36; Andreas Dorpalen, *Heinrich von Treitschke* (New Haven, 1957), p. 206; Lasker's brochure, "Berechtigung und einige Worte an unbefangene Leser," 1876, p. 10, LNB.

27. Martin Spahn, "Zur Entstehung der nationalliberalen Partei," *Zeitschrift für Politik* 1 (1907–1908): 457, describing Lasker as doctrinaire in 1866–1867; Fritz Stern, "Money, Morals and the Pillars of Bismarck's Society," *Central European History* 3 (March–June 1970): 61–62; Hans-Joachim Schoeps, "Hermann Wagener—Ein konservativer Sozialist. Ein Beitrag zur Ideengeschichte des Sozialismus," *Zeitschrift für Religions- und Geistesgeschichte* 8 (1956): 196, stating that Lasker did nothing worse than many others, including his friends. See Otto Glagau, *Des Reiches Noth und der neue Culturkampf* (Osnabrück, 1879), pp. 22–27.

28. Lasker, "Berechtigung und einige Worte," pp. 6–7; Wilhelm Wehrenpfennig to Johannes Miquel, Berlin, Sept. 28, 1876, HW, 2: 158–60, concluding that if Lasker could not satisfy him, Miquel should appeal to a court of arbitration of the National Liberal party. To my knowledge no such action occurred, and Lasker and Miquel remained on friendly terms.

29. *Frankfurter Zeitung*, April 7, 1873, lead article. Some individuals were fatally damaged by the scandal. Wagener lost his entire public career; Strousberg, his fortune and his business honor. See H. B. Strousberg to EL, Feb. 7, 1876, LNP, for a nine-page complaint about his treatment.

30. LT, May 10, 1873, 3: 1875; RT, April 4, 1873, 1: 213–24.

31. LT, May 15, 1873, 3: 1934–35, Jan. 12, 1874, 1: 513–14. For the *Kreis*, see LT, April 28, 1874, 2: 1300; for the *Seehandlung*, see LT, Dec. 9, 1868, 1: 580–82.

32. Waldemar Graf von Roon, *Denkwürdigkeiten aus dem Leben des Generalfeldmarschalls Kriegministers Grafen von Roon* (3 vols., Berlin, 1905), 3: 349–50, on the special commission; see p. 348, Wilhelm to Roon, Feb. 9, 1873, for the king's decision to act through an executive rather than a parliamentary committee. Also see Roon to Forckenbeck, Berlin, Feb. 5, 1873, in Forckenbeck Nachlass, Zentrales Staatsarchiv Merseburg, LT, May 12, 1874, 2: 1649–56, May 16, 1874, 3: 1744–49.

33. RT, Nov. 24, 1875, 1: 314; LT, March 29, 1876, 2: 887–98; Viktor Böhmert to EL, Stuttgart, April 2, 1876, and Beilage zu no. 199, Oct. 14, 1876, HW, 2: 145–47, 160–61; Heinrich Ritter von Poschinger, *Fürst Bismarck und die Parlamentarier* (3 vols., Breslau, 1894–1896), 1: 69 (Feb. 1, 1873, report of a parliamentary dinner at which Bismarck told Lasker that his attack came as close to Bismarck as the hairs on his head); Lasker, "Berechtigung und einige Worte," pp. 11–12; August Bebel, *Die Parlamentarische Tätigkeit des deutschen Reichstages und der Landtage von 1874–1867* (Berlin, 1876), pp. 55–56; Lasker speech in Frankfurt am Main, Sept. 28, 1879, pp. 36–37, LNB; Stolper, *German Economy*, p. 72; Rosenberg, *Grosse Depression*, p. 64.

34. RT, Dec. 3, 5, 1881, 1: 192–93, 223–24. For a thoughtful consideration of this era see Böhme, *Weg zur Grossmacht*, esp. pp. 387–91.

35. Böhme, *Weg zur Grossmacht*, p. 211; Werner Schunke, *Die preussischen Freihändler und die Entstehung der Nationalliberalen Partei*, Leipziger Historische Abhandlungen 41 (Leipzig, 1916), pp. 2–4; Gustav Schmoller, "Hermann Schulze-Delitzsch und Eduard Lasker," *Jahrbuch für Gesetzgebung, Verwaltung, und Volkswirtschaft im Deutschen Reich* 8 (1884): 273; Dietrich Sandberger, *Die Ministerkandidatur Bennigsens*, Historische Studien no. 187 (Berlin, 1929), p. 31. Even de Ruggiero suggests that free trade leads naturally to private monopoly and support by in-

dustry (the interests) of an oppressive (protectionist) state; see de Ruggiero, *European Liberalism*, pp. 421–24.

36. LT, Dec. 11, 1871, 1: 49–54, Feb. 22, 1872, 2: 912–19.

37. LT, Feb. 18, 1876, 1: 97–98; Bebel, *Parlamentarische Tätigkeit*, p. 51; RT, Feb. 23, 1878, 1: 156–62; Helmut Steinsdorfer, *Franz Freiherr Schenk von Stauffenberg (1834–1901) als ein bayrischer und deutscher Politiker* (Munich, 1959), pp. 36–37.

38. RT, March 28, 1881, 1: 551–57; Lasker, "An die Wähler," end of September 1881, pp. 7–8, LNB.

39. Clough, *Economic History of Europe*, p. 653.

40. See especially Ivo Lambi, *Free Trade*, pp. 113ff., 131ff., 170–71, 207–25. Kenneth Barkin, *The Controversy over German Industrialization 1890–1902* (Chicago, 1970), pp. 32–37; see especially p. 35, where he writes that the shift to protection, "while of great consequence, is not the watershed in modern German history pictured by some historians," and p. 37, "after 1879 liberal economists were regarded as the outcasts whose vague theoretical solutions were no longer in tune with the problem of a developing nation." John Stuart Mill, *On Liberty* (1859; New York, 1963), pp. 219–20, stated that restraints on trade are within the competence of the state but that they are wrong "solely because they do not really produce the results which it is desired to produce by them."

41. Böhme, *Weg zur Grossmacht*, pp. 355–59, 370–73, 489–93, 499–503.

42. EL to Karl Baumbach, Berlin, April 1, 1879, HW, 2: 233–34.

43. RT, May 8, 1879, 2: 1043–57. The *Frankfurter Zeitung*, May 10, 1879, thoroughly covered his speech and liked his ideas, but wondered how revisionist he would prove to be.

44. RT, May 8, 1879, 2: 1047, 1051–52 (calling it a policy of turning possessor against nonpossessor); see p. 1049 for his comment on beer. RT, May 28, 1879, 2: 1509–12, July 5, 1879, 3: 2064–67; see especially 3: 2066 for use of figures from Laspeyres, which, Lasker said, showed prices rising five to six cents on the pound from a three-cent-per-pound tariff. RT, July 5, 1879, 3: 2064–75.

45. RT, May 8, 1879, 2: 1052–54. See also Lasker's speech in Frankfurt am Main, Sept. 29, 1879, pp. 11, 17, LNB; EL to Franz von Stauffenberg, Aug. 10, 1880, HW, 2: 341–42, stating that he agreed to the program for the *Austritt* but wanted it clear that he opposed indirect taxes and tariffs; Lasker's speech in Sonneberg, May 22, 1881, pp. 2, 8, LNB. See EL to Baumbach, Berlin, April 1, 1879, HW, 2: 233–34, and his speech in Sonneberg (p. 8), stating that other countries had already retaliated in kind; Lasker, "An die Wähler," p. 7.

46. RT, May 8, 1879, 2: 1049; EL to Karl Baumbach, Berlin, June 6, 1879, HW, 2: 242; Lasker speech in Sonneberg, May 22, 1881, p. 2, LNB.

47. RT, May 8, 1879, 2: 1047–49, 1055–56; EL to Baumbach, Berlin, June 6, 1879, HW, 2: 242. See also Lasker's speech in Frankfurt am Main, Sept. 29, 1879, p. 17, LNB, for his attitude to the separation of agricultural and urban interests.

48. RT, March 28, 1881, 1: 558. Lasker speech in Sonneberg, May 22, 1881, pp. 3–4, 12–13; speech in Frankfurt, Sept. 29, 1879, p. 35; Lasker, "An die Wähler," late Sept. 1881, pp. 5–6, all in LNB.

49. Schmoller, "Schulze-Delitzsch und Lasker," pp. 273–74; Rickert to EL, Zoppot, Aug. 16, 1880, HW, 2: 347, on Lasker's and the National Liberal party's differences on free trade; EL to Miquel, Berlin, Aug. 1, 1879, HW, 2: 261; Böhme, *Weg zur Grossmacht*, 553, citing Auswärtige Amt Bonn, Deutschland, 103, vol. 2. Wilhelm von Kardorff tried to convert Lasker to protection in 1875, and a former political opponent from Thuringia, Felix Freiherr von Stein, indicated that if Lasker were at all favorable to the issue he would get the votes of the agrarians in his second Meiningen electoral district. Gustave Godeffroy wrote Lasker in February 1877 that the elimination of the iron tax would be disastrous and enclosed some anti-free trade articles from the *Berliner Borsen Zeitung* for his perusal. In July 1878 Lasker told an election audience in Camburg that he was not an enemy of industry and that he was prepared to accept moderate protective tariffs. But it is possible that he changed his mind due to other political rather than economic pressures. RT, May 27, 1873, 2: 854–57; Kardorff to EL, Wabnitz, June 6, 1875, and Freiherr von Stein to EL, Gr. Kochberg bei Rudolstadt, June 22, 1876, HW, 2: 150–52; Godeffroy to EL, Feb. 12, 1877, LNP; Lasker's speech in Camburg on July 3, 1878, printed in the *Camburger Wochenblatt*, July 8, 1878, p. 2, LNB. See also Martin Philippson, *Max von Forckenbeck* (Dresden, 1898), p. 314.

50. Walter Vogel, *Bismarcks Arbeiterversicherung; ihre Entstehung im Kräftespiel der Zeit* (Braunschweig, 1951), pp. 19, 24–25; Otto Quandt, *Die Anfänge der Bismarckschen Sozialgesetzgebung und die Haltung der Parteien (Das Unfallversicherungsgesetz 1881–1884)*, Historische Studien 344 (Berlin, 1938), pp. 9, 16, 19, 26–27; Evelyn A. Clark, "Adolf Wagner: From National Economist to National Socialist," *Political Science Quarterly* 15 (1940): 393; William O. Shanahan, *German Protestants Face the Social Question* (Notre Dame, 1954), pp. 266–69, for discussion of some conservatives' (including especially Hermann Wagener's) willingness and interest in social legislation as early as the 1850s.

51. LT, Feb. 22, 1868, 3: 1844; Lasker's speech in Magdeburg, Oct. 10, 1868, p. 15, LNB; RT, April 29, May 9, 1871, 1: 464–66, 608–11; Schmoller to von Sybel, Halle, July 29, 1872, HW, 2: 56–57.

52. Schmoller to EL, Halle, Aug. 11, 1872, Oppenheim to EL, Aug. 19, 1872, EL to Oppenheim, Pontresina, Aug. 24, 1872, Oppenheim to EL, Danzig, Aug. 29, 1872, EL to Oppenheim, Innsbruck, Sept. 7, 1872, HW, 2: 57–59.

53. Bamberger to EL, Baden-Baden, Sept. 26, 1872, Lasker to Schmoller, no date or place, draft form, HW, 2: 60–61. See also Elise Conrad, *Der Verein für Sozialpolitik und seine Wirksamkeit auf dem Gebiet der gewerblichen Arbeiterfrage* (Zurich, 1906), pp. 57–58, 64–65.

54. See, for example, the series of articles in the *Frankfurter Zeitung* in spring and summer 1872, especially April 9, July 17, 19, 20, 21, 1872; Gustav Schmoller, "Über Grundfragen des Rechts und der Volkswirtschaft," *Jahrbücher für National Oekonomischen Statistik* (1875), p. 101, cited in Lambi, *Free Trade*, p. 127; Brentano to Schmoller, Nov. 10, 1875, in Walther Goetz, "Der Briefwechsel Gustav Schmollers mit Lujo Brentano," *Archiv für Kulurgeschichte* 30 (1941): 146; Brentano to EL, Breslau, Nov. 12, 21, 1875, HW, 2: 138–39; Brentano to Schmoller, Breslau, Jan. 30, 1876, in Goetz, "Briefwechsel," p. 154; Brentano to EL, Jan. 30, 1876, HW, 2: 143–44.

55. RT, March 4, May 2, 1878, 1: 313, 989.

56. RT, April 2, 1881, 1: 724–30.

57. RT, May 31, June 1, 15, 1881, 2: 1458–59, 1482, 1487, 1747–51.

58. Lasker, "An die Wähler," late September 1881, pp. 3–5, LNB. In May, Lasker had predicted, correctly, that Bismarck would fail to win Social Democratic support and that both sides would be disappointed; see RT, May 31, 1881, 2: 1460. He repeated this argument on Oct. 9, 1881, in Sonneberg in a public speech, pp. 14–16, 18–19, in LNB.

59. RT, Jan. 10, 18, 1882, 1: 512–14, 720–27.

60. RT, May 16, 1882, 1: 236–37, April 21, 1883, 3: 2026–29.

61. Bamberger, in his funeral eulogy of Jan. 28, 1884, pp. 25–26, commented that Lasker was partially a state socialist. Treitschke, "Die Lage nach den Wahlen," Nov. 10, 1881, in Treitschke, *Deutsche Kämpfe: Neue Folge. Schriften zur Tagespolitik* (Leipzig, 1896), pp. 160–61. In his last letter from America to Bamberger, Lasker praised the free-trade system of the United States; see EL to Bamberger, Nov. 2, 1883, LNP.

VII. Lasker and the Collapse of the National Liberal Party

1. Coverage by the *Frankfurter Zeitung* for this period is excellent. See June 14, 1878, for the reference to the *Schleswiger Nachrichten*; June 18, 19, and 24 in general; June 26 for the slogan "Hinweg mit aller Laskerei"; and July 5 for the analysis of the National Liberal party and its wings, including the significance of the Meiningen election pitting Lasker against Herbert Bismarck.

2. EL to Stauffenberg, Berlin, June 30, 1878, HW, 2: 208–9; Ludwig von Cuny to Bennigsen, July 7, 1878, and Mosle to Bennigsen, July 19, 1878, in ABRB (1907): 148, nn. 1, 2; Stephani to Bennigsen, Dresden, July 14, 1878, in ibid., pp. 78–81; Hermann Oncken, *Rudolf von Bennigsen. Ein deutscher liberaler Politiker* (2 vols., Stuttgart, 1910), 2: 375; *Frankfurter Zeitung*, Aug. 9, 10, 1878, on election results; EL to Stauffenberg, Freiburg (Baden), Aug. 3, 1878, HW, 2: 211–12; Heinrich Ritter von Poschinger, *Fürst Bismarck und die Parlamentarier* (3 vols., Breslau, 1894–1896), 3: 12–13, citing K. Braun, "Physiologie". Braun was pessimistic and convinced that the government press was out to get Lasker. Elben's letters from the South were very pessimistic; see Elben to EL, Jan. 1, 19, and March 9, 1877, LNP.

3. Hölder Tagebuch, Stuttgart, Aug. 8, 1878, in Poschinger, *Fürst Bismarck*, 2: 288–89; Bamberger to Stauffenberg, Interlaken, Aug. 13, 1878, EL to Stauffenberg, Murren (bei Interlaken), Aug. 13, 1878, HW, 2: 216–18; Friedrich Boettcher, *Eduard Stephani. Ein Beitrag zur Zeitgeschichte, insbesondere zur Geschichte der Nationalliberalen Partei* (Leipzig, 1887), p. 221; Hölder Tagebuch, Berlin, Oct. 8, 14, 17, 1878, in Poschinger, *Fürst Bismarck*, 2: 294–99; EL to Stauffenberg, Berlin, Nov. 14, 1878, HW, 2: 226.

4. The *Frankfurter Zeitung*'s review of news included statements to this effect from the *Norddeutsche Allgemeine Zeitung* on May 15, 1879, the *Deutschen Volkswirtschaftlichen Correspondenz* on May 16, 1879, and the *Kölnische Zeitung* and *Grenzboten* on July 26, 1879; Hölder Tagebuch, Berlin, May 2, 15, 21, 1879, in Poschinger, *Fürst Bismarck*, 2: 342–43, 345–46, 348 (on Bennigsen's vacillation); Stauffenberg to EL, Risstissen, June 4, 1879, Bamberger to Stauffenberg, Berlin, June 5, 1879, Forckenbeck to EL, Badeweiler, June 9, 1879, EL to Stauffenberg, Berlin, June 29, 1879, EL to Miquel, Berlin, June 29, 1879, HW, 2: 240–41, 243, 246–47, 250; Hölder Tagebücher, July 11, 1879, in Poschinger, *Fürst Bismarck*, 2: 359; EL to Stauffenberg, Berlin, July 15, 1879, EL to Miquel, Berlin, July 16, 1879, Stauffenberg to EL, Risstissen, July 23, 1879, Forckenbeck to Stauffenberg, Berlin, July 27, 1879, HW, 2: 252–53, 254–55, 256, 257; Julius Rodenberg, "Briefe an Eduard Lasker," *Deutsche Rundschau* 38 (1884): 456, later related that Lasker had stated that the National Liberal party was split as early as May 1879.

5. EL to Miquel, Berlin, Aug. 1, 1879, to Stauffenberg, Berlin, Aug. 2, 1879, and to Richard Schumann, Berlin, Aug. 3, 1879, HW, 2: 260–62, 265–66. On the margin of a printed appeal of Aug. 25, 1879, to the party to organize for the coming election, Heinrich Rickert asked Lasker what his plans were (LNP).

6. Oppenheim to EL, Berlin, Aug. 30, 1879, Miquel to Benda, Osnabrück, Aug. 5, 1879, Miquel to Bennigsen, Osnabrück, Oct. 3, 1879, HW, 2: 273–74, 266–67, 225; *Frankfurter Zeitung*, Oct. 1, 4, 1879, on Lasker's candidacy in Frankfurt am Main; Miquel to Benda, Osnabrück, Oct. 25, 1879, Stauffenberg to EL, Berlin, Aug. 30, 1879, HW, 2: 280, 273–74; Boettcher, *Stephani*, pp. 226, 237–38. Also see Lasker's speech in Frankfurt on Sept. 29, 1879, pp. 1–44, LNB.

7. EL to Stauffenberg, Berlin, Dec. 6, 1879, Forckenbeck to Stauffenberg, Berlin, Oct. 6, 1879, HW, 2: 281, 275–76; *Frankfurter Zeitung*, Jan. 7, March 5, 1880; Friedrich B. M. Hollyday, *Bismarck's Rival: A Political Biography of General and Admiral Albrecht von Stosch* (Durham, N.C., 1960), p. 193. See Rickert to EL, July 16, 1879, hoping that the atmosphere of the parliament would change with the end of the session; Aug. 18, on organization; Oct. 2, asking where he wanted or planned to run; Aug. 5, advising against Stettin, Danzig, and Posen, but suggesting Breslau; Oct. 13, giving birthday greetings and hoping that the people would see the light soon; and Nov. 12, on the problem of Unruh's resignation. On July 6, 1880, Rückert sent a clipping to Lasker from a local Meiningen paper that argued that no one wanted to support Lasker. The Rickert and Rückert correspondence is in LNP.

8. EL to Stauffenberg, Berlin, March 12, 1880, Bamberger to Stauffenberg, Berlin, March 12, 1880 (11 o'clock in the evening), Forckenbeck to Stauffenberg, Berlin, March 14, 1880, EL to his supporters, March 1880, EL to the Executive Committee, Berlin, March 15, 1880, the Executive Committee to EL, Berlin, March 18, 1880, HW, 2: 299, 300, 301–2, 307–11, 303, 306–7; Berthold Auerbach to Jakob Auerbach, Berlin, March 19, 1880, in Jakob Auerbach, ed., *Berthold Auerbach. Briefe an seinen Freund Jakob Auerbach* (2 vols., Frankfurt am Main, 1884), 2: 427. Stephani expected formal separation of the whole group, but Lasker left alone; Boettcher, *Stephani*, pp. 261–63.

9. Stauffenberg to EL, Risstissen, June 1880, EL to an unnamed colleague (a draft), June 1880, Bamberger to EL, Interlaken, July 14, 1880, EL to Stauffenberg, Berlin, July 15, 1880, HW, 2: 317, 321–22, 326–28. Forckenbeck predicted a union with the other liberals in a united liberal party; Forckenbeck to EL, Nov. 14, 1877, LNP.

10. See the *Frankfurter Zeitung* for July 24, 1880, and for almost all of early July; Rickert to Lasker, Zoppot [bei Danzig], July 19, 1880, HW, 2: 331.

11. EL to Albert Haenel, [July or August 1880], Müller to EL, Gotha, [July or August 1880], HW, 2: 336–38.

12. Rickert to EL, Zoppot bei Danzig, Aug. 5, 1880, EL to Stauffenberg, Berlin, Aug. 10, 1880, Stauffenberg to EL, July 1880, HW, 2: 338–40, 341–42, 323–24; Forckenbeck to Rickert, Berlin, Aug. 11, 1880, in ABRB (1908): 284–86.

13. Rickert to EL, Zoppot, Aug. 12, 13, 1880, HW, 2: 343–45; *Frankfurter Zeitung*, Aug. 14, 19, 1880. LNP contains 100 items of Rickert-Lasker correspondence, of which fully 99 were from Rickert to Lasker, most dealing with the details of party organization. A good illustration of Rickert's talent for political party organization may be found in a circular forwarded by the National Liberal Central Campaign Committee on Nov. 6, 1878, in LNB. The circular is concise, helpful, encouraging; it emphasizes the establishment of contacts with local newspapers on the one hand and with the party in Berlin on the other.

14. EL to Baumbach, Berlin, Aug. 15, 1880, EL to Stauffenberg, Berlin, Aug. 15, 1880. Baumbach to EL, Sonneberg, Aug. 15, 1880, HW, 2: 345–46, in which he agreed to join the *Austritt* and had already heard from Rickert by letter. Rickert to Bennigsen, Zoppot, Aug. 17, 1880, in ABRB (1908): 286–88; *Frankfurter Zeitung*, Aug. 24, 1880. See also Martin Philippson, *Max von Forckenbeck* (Dresden, 1898), p. 329. Baumbach to EL, Sonneberg, Aug. 26, 1880, HW, 2: 351, wanted Lasker to come to speak immediately after the announcement; see ibid., pp. 355–56 for Lasker's draft of the declaration of *Austritt* and pp. 356–57 for its final form. The declaration is also more easily available in Wilhelm Mommsen, ed., *Deutsche Parteiprogramme* (Munich, 1964), pp. 156–57. The *Frankfurter Zeitung* of Aug. 31, 1880, announced the formal *Austritt*.

15. See Ludwig Bamberger, "Die Sezession," Berlin, late summer 1880, in Bamberger, *Gesammelte Schriften* (5 vols., Berlin, 1894–1898), 5: 72, for mention of Bismarck's fear of the elite in the Liberale Vereinigung; Richter to EL, Berlin, Sept. 7, 1880, HW, 2: 360.

16. Stephani to Bennigsen, Leipzig, Sept. 7, 1880, Benda to Miquel, Rudow, Sept. 9, 1880, Bennigsen to Rickert, Hannover, Sept. 13, 1880, Rickert to Bennigsen, Zoppot, Sept. 16, 1880, in ABRB (1908): 288–89, 290–91, 292, 293.

17. Gustav Lipke to Stauffenberg, Berlin, Sept. 21, Oct. 12, 1880, HW, 2: 366–67, 368. Lipke was not concerned about Lasker's trip to Italy since he was too close to the Progressives anyway. Baumbach to EL, Sonneberg, Nov. 22, 1880, Bamberger to EL, Dec. 14, 1880, on the purchase of the *Tribune*, HW, 2: 371, 372. Also see for the *Tribune*, Paul Lindau, *Nur Erinnerungen* (2 vols., Stuttgart and Berlin, 1919), 2: 97, and Th. Barth to Carl Schurz, Dec. 31, 1883, Carl Schurz Papers, Reel 79, #1753d in the Library of Congress; Treitschke, "Zur inneren Lage am Jahresschlusse," Dec. 10, 1880, *Preussische Jahrbücher*, in Treitschke, *Deutsche Kämpfe: Neue Folge. Schriften zur Tagespolitik* (Leipzig, 1896), p. 127, and "Der Reichstag und die Parteien," June 15, 1880; Stauffenberg to EL, Munich, Feb. 10, 1881, HW, 2: 375. See also Philippson, *Forckenbeck*, pp. 338–40. Richter and Parisius both corresponded with Lasker in later 1880 and 1881, but relations were strained by electoral competition, and no real political cooperation resulted. See Richter to EL, Nov. 6, 1881, protesting against a Liberal Union representative in Hamburg

who announced his support publicly for the National Liberal candidate, and Parisius to EL, Sept. 9, 14, 1881, on local but not national cooperation, all in LNP.

18. *Frankfurter Zeitung*, Oct. 20, 1880, quoting from the *Weserzeitung*; Nov. 24, 1880, and May 30 and June 5, 1881, on the all-liberal party. Treitschke in "Zur inneren Lage," p. 127, saw the problem of the Liberal Unionists and opined that they had waited too long to secede.

19. Eduard Lasker, *Fünfzehn Jahre parlamentarische Geschichte 1866–1880*, in *AELN*, pp. 5–9.

20. EL to Bennigsen, Berlin, Sept, 3, 1881, in Oncken, *Bennigsen*, 2: 470; Bennigsen to EL, Hannover, Sept. 5, 1881, Benda to Bennigsen, Rudow, Sept. 5, 1881, EL to Bennigsen, Berlin, Sept. 14, 1881, in ABRB (1908): 54–56.

21. Lasker speech in Sonneberg, Oct. 9, 1881, pp. 1–3, in LNB.

22. Bennigsen to Benda, Hannover, Nov. 5, 1881, EL to Bennigsen, Berlin, Nov. 8, 1881, Bennigsen to EL, Hannover, Nov. 11, 1881, EL to Bennigsen, Berlin, Nov. 14, 1881, in Oncken, *Bennigsen*, 2: 476–77, 478–79. Also see EL to an unnamed correspondent, no date, containing a similar reference to the Free Conservatives, HW, 2: 387–88; and see Bamberger, "Die Sezession," p. 58.

23. RT, Nov. 28, 1881, 1: 58–59, 61ff., 72. See, for example, Karl Schrader to EL, Berlin, Aug. 1, 1882, and Bamberger to EL, Interlaken, Sept. 6, 1882, HW, 2: 391–92.

VIII. Eduard Lasker and German Liberalism

1. The most thoughtful consideration of this subject may be found in James J. Sheehan, *German Liberalism in the Nineteenth Century* (Chicago and London, 1978), pp. 2ff.

2. Heinrich A. Winkler, *Preussischer Liberalismus und deutscher Nationalstaat. Studien zur Geschichte der deutschen Fortschrittspartei 1861–1866* (Tübingen, 1964), pp. 123–24, states this argument most clearly and forcefully.

3. The best recent explication of this argument about Bismarck is Lothar Gall's *Bismarck. Der weisse Revolutionär* (Frankfurt am Main, Berlin, Vienna, 1980).

4. Margaret L. Anderson makes this point in her excellent work, *Windhorst: A Political Biography* (Oxford, 1981), esp. pp. 168–69 and 191 with reference to Lasker.

5. See Ludwig Bamberger, *Bismarcks Grosses Spiel. Die Geheimen Tagebücher Ludwig Bamberger*, ed. Ernst Feder (Frankfurt am Main, 1932), pp. 271–73; EL to Bennigsen, London, Royal Hotel, June 14, 1883, in Hermann Oncken, *Rudolf von Bennigsen, Ein deutscher liberaler Politiker* (2 vols., Stuttgart, 1910), 2: 499–500. Also see John Gunther, *Taken at the Flood: The Story of Ablbert D. Lasker* (New York, 1960), pp. 17–22 for Morris's life and pp. 22–24 for Eduard, much of which is inaccurate.

6. The trip is described in Richard W. Dill, *Der Parlamentarier Eduard Lasker und die parlamentarische Stilentwicklung der Jahre 1867–84* (Erlangen, 1958), pp. 200–201; also EL to Bamberger, Nov. 2, 1883, in LNP.

7. Dill, *Stilentwicklung*, pp. 201ff.; Stanley Zucker, *Ludwig Bamberger: German Liberal Politician and Social Critic, 1823–1899* (Pittsburgh, 1975), p. 252, and Chapter I.

Bibliographical Note

There are only a few easily obtainable treatments of Eduard Lasker in English. Veit Valentin, "Bismarck and Lasker," *Journal of Central European Affairs* 3 (Jan. 1944): 400–15, examines the relations between those two strong-willed individuals; Louis Snyder, "Bismarck and the Lasker Resolution," *Review of Politics* 29 (Jan. 1967): 41–64, tells the fascinating story of Bismarck's refusal to transmit the condolences of the American House of Representatives to the Reichstag and the resulting political and diplomatic uproar; Gordon R. Mork, "The Making of a German Nationalist: Eduard Lasker's Early Years, 1829–1847," *Societas* 1 (1971): 23–32, argues that Lasker's early years formed his "national" thinking; James F. Harris, "Eduard Lasker and Compromise Liberalism," *Journal of Modern History* 42 (Sept. 1970): 342–60, treats Lasker's political tactics. Richard W. Dill, *Der Parlamentarier Eduard Lasker und die parlamentarische Stilentwicklung der Jahre 1867–84* (Erlangen, 1958), focuses on the style of politics in these years, thus avoiding the important issues and using only the available published sources. Helmut Köster, "Aus Laskers politische Frühzeit" (Ph.D. diss., University of Leipzig, 1924), is much better, though limited in the depth of its treatment by lack of materials and a too narrow focus on the early years. Paul Wentzcke, "Glaubensbekenntnisse einer politischen Jugend. Beiträge zum Lebensbild Ludwig Aegidis und Eduard Laskers," in Wentzcke, ed., *Deutscher Staat und deutsche Parteien. Beiträge zur deutschen Partei- und Ideengeschichte. Friedrich Meinecke zum 60. Geburtstag dargebracht* (1922; reprint Aalen, 1973), pp. 87–92 and Wentzcke, "Aus Eduard Laskers sozialistischen Anfängen," *Archiv für die Geschichte des Sozialismus und der Arbeiterbewegung* 11 (1925): 207–14, are valuable, but limited in scope and depth. Also see James F. Harris, "Eduard Lasker, 1829–1884: An Analysis of the Political Ideas of a Left-Wing Liberal" (Ph.D. diss., University of Wisconsin, 1968), pp. i-vi, 1–307, which provides a general description of Lasker's life and analyses of his parliamentary activity.

Far more valuable than any of the above for the reader interested in examining Lasker's ideas at close range are the politician's own speeches, writings, and letters. Eduard Lasker spoke so frequently and at such great length in the three parliamentary bodies of which he was a member that their minutes constitute a mine of valuable information over the course of his career. His speeches were candid, well-prepared, usually dispassionate, and extremely honest. See *Stenographische Berichte über die Verhandlungen des Reichstages* (Berlin, 1867, et seq.), *Wörtlicher Berichte über die Verhandlungen des preussischen Abgeordnetenhauses* (Berlin, 1865, et seq.), and *Stenographische Berichte über die Verhandlungen des durch die allerhöchste Verordnung vom 13. April 1868 einberufenen deutschen Zollparlaments* (3 vols., Berlin, 1868–1870). The minutes from the Customs Parliament are the least useful, while the Reichstag provides more material on foreign policy and, after 1870, national policy than the more local Prussian Landtag. It should be noted that, in terms of sheer quantity, Lasker's parliamentary speeches are the single largest source for his ideas and actions.

Lasker's literary efforts were mixed. His journalistic productions are useful when they discuss politics or the state, as in *Zur Verfassungsgeschichte Preussens* (Leipzig, 1874), which simply republished, with some changes, articles that had originally appeared in Oppenheim's *Deutsche Jahrbücher für Politik und Literatur* in the 1860s or in *Fünfzehn Jahre parlamentarische Geschichte 1866–1880*, in *Aus Eduard Laskers Nachlass* ed. Wilhelm Cahn (Berlin, 1902), pp. 1–136. But Lasker's writing became fuzzy, amorphous, and lacking in content when devoted either to literature, as in *Erlebnisse einer Mannes-Seele*, ed. Berthold Auerbach (Stuttgart, 1873), in which he treated his misfortunes in love in uninspired and heavily romantic prose, or to cultural criticism, as in *Wege und Ziele zur Kulturentwicklung* (Leipzig, 1881). Several collections of Lasker's letters exist in published form, the most important of which are to be found in Julius Heyderhoff and Paul Wentzcke, eds., *Deutscher Liberalismus im Zeitalter Bismarcks. Eine politische Briefsammlung* (2 vols., Bonn and Leipzig, 1925), and in Wilhelm Cahn, ed., "Aus Eduard Laskers Nachlass. Sein Briefwechsel in den Jahren 1870–71," *Deutsche Revue* 15 (March-December, 1892). See also Julius Rodenberg, "Briefe an Eduard Lasker," *Deutsche Rundschau* 38 (1884) and Jakob Auerbach, ed., *Berthold Auerbach. Briefe an seinen Freund Jakob Auerbach* (2 vols., Frankfurt am Main, 1884). Letters are also available along with reminiscences of all kinds in the memoirs of Lasker's friends and enemies; most notably, see Ludwig Bamberger, *Gesammelte Schriften* (5 vols., Berlin, 1894–1898), and especially Bamberger, *Bismarcks Grosses Spiel. Die Geheimen Tagebücher Ludwig Bambergers*, ed. Ernst Feder (Frankfurt am Main, 1932). Other sources for Lasker are Hermann Oncken, *Rudolf von Bennigsen: Ein deutscher liberaler Politiker* (2 vols., Stuttgart, 1910), and Heinrich Ritter von Poschinger, *Fürst Bismarck und die Parlamentarier* (3 vols., Breslau, 1894–1896), which contain the diaries of Julius Hölder and Hans Viktor von Unruh along with scraps of valuable material intermixed with several decades of gossip. Hermann Oncken, ed., "Aus den Briefen Rudolf von Bennigsens," *Deutsche Revue* (1904–1909 in 35 separate segments), contains many letters from, to, and about Lasker.

Unpublished letters may be found in the following depositories: for Lasker, Bamberger, Bennigsen, and Stauffenberg, the Zentrales Staatsarchiv in Potsdam; for Berthold Auerbach, the Schiller National-museum in Marbach; for Bamberger, the Stiftung Preussischer Kulturbesitz in Dahlem; and for Lasker, the Leo Baeck Institute, New York City, and the Brandeis University Library, Waltham, Massachusetts. Individual letters may also be found in the Carl Schurz collection in the Library of Congress Manuscripts Division, the Paul Lindau Papers in the Bundesarchiv in Koblenz, and the Andrew Dickson White Papers in the Cornell University Library, Ithaca, New York. The largest collections of Lasker materials are in the Brandeis and Potsdam archives. The Brandeis collection consists mostly of printed materials, such as campaign speeches and legislation, along with correspondence directed to Lasker from persons who are usually unknown and unimportant. Potsdam holds the most important correspondence between Lasker and his political allies. This collection provided the basis for the Heyderhoff and Wentzcke publication of letters from liberal political leaders of the nineteenth century. Only a few important letters were not published, and the remainder are significant primarily for filling in the details of Lasker's life.

The notes to the chapters record the sources used in this analysis of Eduard Lasker. It should be noted that they list only materials actually used and do not include the entire body of works consulted. Though I examined many more sources than cited in the text, I have refrained from noting any that did not add to my treatment of the immediate problem. Those who seek the full bibliographical information for any work cited can consult the index, which incorporates a reference to each use of every work cited in this book. The first reference will give complete bibliographical information.

Index

This index combines the usual substantive headings with entries for each of the sources used in the writing of the book. English alphabetical usage has been employed in alphabetizing this index. Consequently, German words containing diacritical marks such as "Lückentheorie" are alphabetized "u" rather than "ue" as is normally the case in Europe. Readers should note that libraries, archives, and catalogues in this country as well as in Europe vary in use of this convention. The first entry for all titles carries complete bibliographical information.

ABRB. See Oncken, H., "Aus den Briefen".
Accident insurance law, 104. See also law.
Address to King Ludwig of Bavaria, 26, 67, 143n.18
"Address", 136n.35
AELN. See Cahn, Wilhelm, ed., *Aus Eduard Laskers Nachlass.*
Aeternat, 74, 75
Agitation, Reichstag roll-call votes on, 58, (Table 4.2). See also Press, press (governmental).
Agricultural tariffs, Reichstag roll-call votes on, 101, 102 (Table 6.3). See also tariffs.
Albers, Detlev, "Reichstag und Aussenpolitik", 137n.51
Allgemeine Zeitung des Judentums, 13, 15, 134n.52
Alliance Israelite Universelle, 14
ALN. See Cahn, Wilhelm, ed., "Aus Eduard Laskers Nachlass".
Alsace and Lorraine, 8, 31, 34, 63, 137n.47, 137n. 56
annexation of, 29
Alvensleben, General, [prob. Gustav von, 1803–81], 145n.57
Amtsblatt, 81. See also press (governmental).
Amtsblätter, 79. See also press (governmental).
Anderson, Eugene N., 42
Social and Political Conflict, 132n.28, 135n.9, 138n.5, 140n.2, 142n.3, 143n.22, 143n.23, 146n.11
Anderson, Eugene N., and Pauline R. Anderson, *Political Institutions*, 132n.26, 138n.11, 140n.33
Anderson, Lee F., et al, *Legislative Roll-call Analysis*, 119 (Table 8.1n)
Anderson, Margaret L., *Windthorst*, 151n.4
Angermann, Erich, *Robert von Mohl*, 138n.3
Annexations, in 1866, 23. See also Austro-Prussian war.
"Announcement", 21

Anschluss, 19
Anti-Jesuit law, 13, 50, 117, 118
Anti-Semitism, 14. See also Glagau, Perrot.
Antisocialist laws
and Bismarck, 50
first, 50, 107, 119
and Lasker, 13, 70
and NL, 31, 82, 117
and penal code, 49
second, 36, 41, 50, 118
Lasker's speech for it, 72
and protective tariff bill, 97
and workers' associations, 91
Appleton, Lewis, letter to, 143n. 9
Article 44 (Prussian Constitution), 142n.5. See also constitutions, of Prussia.
Asher, Dr. A., "Über Lasker's Aufenthalt", 132n19, 133n.46
Assassination attempts (1878), 50, 72, 79, 107. See also Hödel.
Assembly, state. See Landtag.
Assembly of German Representatives (1866), 70
Assessor, 5
Association for Social Politics, 102, 103. See also *Verein für Sozialpolitik*.
Auerbach, Berthold (1812–82), 10, 11, 14, 21, 69, 109
letters from, 133n.35, 136n.29, 150n.8
letters to, 134n.58, 143n.23
Auerbach, Jakob ed., *Berthold Auerbach*, 105n.8, 133n.35, 136n.29
letters to, 133n.35, 136n.29, 150n.8
"Aufruf an das deutsche Volk", 136n.31, 136n. 35
Ausfeld, Carl (1814-?), 77
Austria, 66. See also Blum, R., Bohemia, Fröbel, Hartmann, Lasker, Olmütz, Revolutions of 1848, Vienna.
and Frederick the Great, 3
as a Great Power, 17
and Italian nationalism, 6

and Prussia, 7, 19, 20, 32, 39, 136n. 40
and Schleswig-Holstein, 7
and Schwarzenberg, 5
and South Germany, 22
Austro-Prussian war (1866), 19, 22, 47
Austritt, 150n.14. See also secession.

Baden, 8, 24–28, 40, 136n.28. See also
    Bismarck, O., Lasker.
"Die badischen Frage", 136n.29
Baehr, Otto, Dr. (1817–95), 10
    letter from, 133n.37
Baerwald, Hermann (1828–1907), 14
    letter from, 134n.50
    letter to, 134n.58
Bagehot, Walter (1826–77), 133n.39
Ballhausen, Lucius von, *Bismarcksche
    Erinnerungen*, 145n.54
Bamberger, Ludwig (1823–99)
    and anti-Semitism, 14
    and Austria, 21
    banking practices, 92
    and Bismarck, 40
    and Hans Blum, 132n.14
    and Catholics, 28
    and compromise, 39
    as a Jewish politician, 94
    and Lasker, 10, 12, 93, 120
    and South Germany, 27, 65
    and NL, 38, 109
    and government press, 83
    and Prussia, 143n.12
    and secession, 110, 112
    and universal suffrage, 69
    and *Verein für Sozialpolitik*, 103
    "Alte Parteien", 135n.16, 135n.17,
        143n.12
    Bismarcks Grosses Spiel, 131n.3, 131n.5m
        133n.38, 133n.48, 134n.60, 151n.5
    Deutschland und der Sozialismus,
        143–44n.24
    Eduard Lasker, 133n.29, 133n.33,
        133n.35, 149n.61
    "Kandidaten Rede", 139n.24
    "Die Sezession", 135n.16, 150n.15,
        151n.22
    "Über Kompromisse", 139n.23, 140n.34
    "Vertrauliche Briefe", 139n.27
    "Vorwort", 145n.55
    letters from 136n.38, 137n.46, 143n.13,
        147n.24, 147n.25, 149n.3, 149n.4,

149n.53, 150n.8, 150n.9, 150n.17,
    151n.23
    letters to, 137n.52, 143n.13, 149n.61,
        151n.6
Bamberger, Anna, letters to, 147n.24, 147n.25.
    See also Bamberger, Ludwig.
Bank, German state central, 92
Baumbach, Karl Adolf (1844–96), 97, 110, 111
    letter from, 150n.14
    letters to, 148.n42, 148n.45–148n.47,
        150n.14
Baumgarten, Hermann (1825–93), 22, 25–27, 40
    letters from, 135n.20, 136n.29, 136n.37,
        136n.38
    letters to, 136n.38
    "Selbstkritik", 139n.24
Barkin, Kenneth, *German Industrialization*,
    148n.40
Baron, Salo W.
    "The Jewish Question", 131n.6
    "The Revolution of 1848", 133n.49
Barth, Marquard (1809–85), 26, 67, 143n.18
    letters from, 137n.47, 143n.18, 150n.17
    letters to, 141n.12, 143n.19, 143n.20
Bavaria. See also Munich.
    and Austria, 136n.40
    and Catholics, 64
    and Lasker, 26–27, 65
    and the Liberal Group, 38
    and the N. Ger. Confed., 8
    and Stauffenberg, 50
    and unity, 25, 28, 66
    and France, 25
Bebel, August (1840–1913), 25, 39, 69, 96, 97,
    142n.45, 144n.26
    Aus meinem Leben, 142n.45
    Parlamentarische Tätigkeit, 142n.45,
        143n.24, 147n.33, 148n.37
Becker, Josef, "Aufnahme Badens", 136n.26
Benda, Robert von (1816–99), 108, 111, 112
    letters from, 150n.16, 151n.20
    letters to, 150n.6, 151n.22
Bennigsen, Rudolf von (1824–1902)
    and agitation, Reichstag votes on, 58
        (Table 4.2n)
    and Alsace-Lorraine, 29
    and Bismarck, 19
    and death penalty, RT votes on
        (Table 4.1n)
    and *Diäten*, RT votes on, 71 (Table 5.1n)
    and elections, 28
    and federal executive, RT votes on, 80

(Table 5.5n)
and Hannover, 38
and immunity in parliament, RT votes on,
    74 (Table 5.2n)
and Lasker, 26–27, 65, 67, 70 , 83, 119
and Luxembourg, 22
and military budget bills, RT votes on, 75
    (Table 5.3n)
and ministerial responsibility, RT votes on,
    78 (Table 5.4n), 77
and NL, 10, 40, 41, 79, 107, 139n.30,
    140n.30
pres. of Nationalverein, 7, 18
and press, RT votes on, 59 (Table 4.3n)
retirement of, 108, 113
and Liberal Union, 108, 111, 112
and secret funds, LT votes on, 82
    (Table 5.6n)
and tariffs, RT votes on agricultural tariffs,
    102 (Table 6.3n)
on iron tariffs, 100 (Table 6.2n)
and trade unions, 90
and J. Volk, 139n.18
and workers' freedom, RT votes on, 91
    (Table 6.1n)
and workers' insurance, RT votes on, 105
    (Table 6.4n)
letters from, 133n.36, 135n.7, 135n.20,
    136n.38, 137n.46, 137n.48, 139n.24,
    139n.26, 145n.46, 150n.16, 151n.20,
    151n.22
letters to, 135n.9, 135n.20, 136n.32,
    136n.37, 143n.14, 143n.19, 143n.20,
    144n.31, 149n.2, 150n.6, 150n.14,
    150n.16, 151n.20
Berdahl, Robert M., "New Thoughts on German
    Nationalism", 134n.1
Bergmann, Eugen von, Entwicklung deutscher,
    polnischer und jüdischer Bevölkerung,
    131n.7, 131n.8
Bergsträsser, Ludwig, Geschichte der politischen
    Parteien, 139n.18, 139n. 27, 139n.29,
    145n.55
Berlin, 25, 28, 109
    and Brentano, 103
    city court of, 5, 141n.34
    Lasker eulogy in, 15
    as capital, 65
    federal court of, 48
    and Lasker, 5–6, 89, 93, 120
    migration to, 2
    and NL, 36, 107

and Progressives, 8
and Prussian national assembly, 3
Berlin Committee for Russian Jews, 14
Berlin Handworkers Association, 88
Berliner Autographische Correspondenz, 50,
    145n.54
Berliner Bank, 95
Berliner Börsen Zeitung, 148n.49
Bernhardi, Theodore (1802–87), 70
    Aus dem Leben, 144n.26, 145n.57
"Berthold Auerbach und der Antisemitismus",
    134n.63
Bettelheim, Anton, Berthold Auerbach, 131n.10
Beushausen, Gertrud, Zur Strukturanalyse,
    138n.5, 138n.13, 139n.16
Beutin, Ludwig, "Das Bürgertum", 142n.2,
    146n.7
Biedermann, Karl (1812–1901), 49
    letter from, 141n.17
Biron, Prince, 93, 95
Bismarck, Herbert von (1849–1904), 145n.56,
    149n.1
    letter from 145n.56
Bismarck, Otto Fürst von (1815–98), 53, 93
    antisocialist bill, 51
    and Baden, 24–25
    and Bennigsen, 108, 140n.30
    Chancellor, 1
    violator of Prussian constitution, 54, 62–3,
        70
    and constitutional assembly in 1870, 67
    and German Confederation, 8
    and falsification of history, 115
    and Lasker, 9, 14, 49, 96, 104, 113, 120
    and Lasker's role in South Germany,
        27–28, 65
    and Lasker's exposure of railroad scandal,
        95, 147n.33
    and liberalism, 18, 42
    Minister-President of Prussia, 6
    and ministerial responsibility, 77–78
    and NL, 31, 33, 41, 43
    national policy supported by Lasker, 19,
        22, 40, 68, 116
    and NL ministers, 40–41, 79
    opposition to, 112
    political development of, 18, 107
    power of, 20, 30, 39
    and press, 72, 79, 81–83
    and Reichstag, 50
    and Schleswig-Holstein, 7
    and secession, 110

and *Septennat*, 117
and Social Democrats, 50, 149n.58
and social insurance, 102
and protective tariffs, 41, 97–99
and unification, 17, 115
and *Zollverein*, 23, 139n.30
Black Forest, 10
Bleichröder, Gerson von (1822–93), 133n.33
Bloch, S., *In der Heimat*, 134n.63
Block, Hermann, *parlamentarische Krise*,
138n.4, 140n.32
Blum, Robert (1807–48), 3
Blum, Hans, 132n.14
Die deutsche Revolution, 132n.14
Vorkämpfer der deutschen Einheit, 132n.14
Blum, Wilhelm, letters from, 136n.27
Bluntschli, Johann Kaspar (1808–81), letter to,
136n.29
Bohemia, 3. See also Austria.
Böhme, Helmut, *Weg zur Grossmacht*,
139–40n.30, 144n.36, 147n.22, 147n.34,
147n.35, 148n.41, 148n.49
Böhmert, Viktor (1829–1918), 18, 19
letters from, 135n.9, 147n.33
letter to, 135n.7
Bonaparte, Charles Louis Napoleon, III
(1808–1873), 8, 22. See also France.
Borchardt, Julian, *Aus Geschichte*, 138n.4
Born, Karl Erich, 90; "Sozialpolitische
Probleme", 146n.15
Boettcher, Friedrich, *Eduard Stephani*, 133n.37,
139n.24, 149n.3, 150n.6, 150n.8
Brandenburg, Erich, 18
"Parteiwesen", 134n.2, 134n.5
50 Jahre National-liberale Partei, 138n.4,
138n.10
Braun, Karl (1822–93), 9, 103
"Physiologie", 149n.2
Braunschweig, 107
Bray-Steinburg, Count Otto (1807–99), 27
Bremen, 87
Brentano, Lujo (1844–1931), 41, 103
letters from, 139n.28, 149n.54
Breslau, 2, 3, 8, 109, 150n.7
as educational center, 2
Jewish community of, 13
population of, 3
Breslau Rabbinical Seminary, 13
"Breslau Opposition", 131n.13
Breyer, Richard, "Die Stadt Posen", 131n.8
Brinton, Crane, et al., *History of Civilization*,
142n.1

Brockhaus Publishing Co., 6
Brockhaus, E. B. [prob., 1829–1914], letters
from, 133n.40
Brussels, 137n.56
Budgetary control, 22, 73. See also constitu-
tions, military bills.
Bürtgertum, 89
Bund, [Norddeutsche], 24. See also confedera-
tion, N. Ger.
Bundesrat, 27, 30, 64, 67, 70, 77, 78, 144n.33
Bundesstaat, 64
Bunsen [prob. Georg von, 1824–96], 136n.38
Busch, Moritz (1821–99), 81
Tagebuchblätter, 136n.29, 136n.38,
139n.26, 145n.52
Bussmann, Walter
"deutschen Liberalismus", 140n.33
ed., *Herbert von Bismarck*, 145n.56

Cahn, Wilhelm, ed.
Aus Eduard Laskers Nachlass, [cited as
AELN; for full citation see
Abbreviations, p. xvi], 133n.31,
145n.46
"Aus Eduard Laskers Nachlass", [cited as
ALN; for full citation see
Abbreviations, p. xvi], 136n.31,
136n.33, 136n.34, 136n.37–136n.40,
136n.42, 137n.43–137n.48, 141n.12,
142n.9, 143n.11, 143n.13–143n.22,
144n.31, 145n.42
Camburg, 148n.49
campaign speech in, 46
Camburger Wochenblatt, 140n.5, 141n.21,
148n.49
Camphausen, Otto von (1812–96), 41
Cantor, Norman, *Western Civilization*, 142n.1
Capital punishment, 72. See also death penalty.
Carlowitz, Albert, (1802–74), 21
Catholics, 9, 21, 37, 38, 68, 81
in the south, 67
Catholic Church, 13, 49
Censorship in Prussia, 5. See also press.
Center party
anti-liberal, 28
and Bismarck, 9
and Bennigsen, 112
growth of, 33, 116
and "interest" politics, 99
Lasker's fear of, 31
and NL, 42

and police, 53
size of, 34 (Table 3.1), 35 (Table 3.2), 36
   (Table 3.3)
and universal suffrage, 69
Central Europe, 3, 23, 31
Chairman, German Convention of Deputies,
   letter to, 135n.8
Chancellorship, 64. See also confederation, N.
   Ger.
Civil Law (German), 60
Civil War, 4. See also United States.
Clark, Evelyn, "Adolf Wagner", 148n.50
Clough, Sheperd, *Economic History*, 146n.4,
   148n.39
Cohn, Tobias, "Eduard Lasker", 131n.4,
   133n.49, 134n.52
Cohn, Wilhelm, 4, 132n.17
   letters to, 132n.19, 132n.20
Commerce, Minister of in Prussia. See
   Itzenplitz.
Compromise, 39
Confederation, German, (pre 1866), 7
Confederation, North German, 19. See also
   Bund.
Conflict Era, 6, 39, 53, 63, 68, 79, 115, 117.
   See also *Konfliktszeit.*
Congress of Berlin (1878), 14
Conrad, Elise, *Verein für Sozialpolitik*, 149n.53.
   See also Association for Social Politics.
Conservative party,
   and elections, 5, 8
   and government, 99
   growth of, 34, 116
   and Lasker, 9, 53
   and Liberal Union, 110
   occupational composition of, 38
   and the Swindle Era, 94
   size of, 34 (Table 3.1), 35 (Table 3.2), 36
      (Table 3.3)
Constitutions
   analysis of, 61
   convention (1867), 8, 21, 34, 40, 84
   German theories of, 61–62
   of the North German Confederation, 31,
      72, 77, 115
   of Prussia (1850), 5, 62–63, 72. See also
      Conflict Era, *Konfliktszeit.*
   of the Second Reich (1871), 72
   a western European product, 61
Cornelius, Max, ed., *Treitschke's Briefe*,
   133n.37, 135n.9
Craftsmen, 87

Cromwell, Oliver (1599–1658), 19
Cuny, Ludwig von (1833–98), letter from,
   149n.2
"Curiosum", 134n.63

Danish war (1864), 19
Danzig, 87, 109, 150n.7
Death penalty, 68, 118. See also capital punish-
   ment, Lasker.
   abolition of, 56
   Reichstag roll-call votes on (Table 4.1), 57
Dehio, Ludwig
   "Die Taktik der Opposition", 135n.9
   "Benedikt Waldeck", 135n.9
   "preussische Demokratie", 143n.23
Delbrück, Rudolf von (1817–1903), 26, 41, 65,
   66, 68. See also *Reichskanzlei,*
   Reichskanzleramt.
   letter from, 143n.20
   letters to, 136n.38, 143n.14, 143n.15,
      143n.18, 143n.20, 144n.31
Demeter, Karl, "Die soziale Schichtung", 137n.1
Democrats, 42, 115, 117
   hatred of Bismarck, 63
Denmark, 7
Depression of 1873, 9, 93
Deutsche Bund, 7. See also Confederation
   (German).
Deutsche Jahrbücher für Politik und Literatur,
   6, 46, 53, 62
Deutsche Korrespondenz, 111
Deutsche Rundschau, 7
Deutsche Volkspartei, 81
Deutsche Volkswirtshaftlichen Correspondenz,
   149n.4
Diäten, 40, 70, 73, 106, 144n.26
   Reichstag roll-call votes on, 71
Dickens, Charles (1812–70), 10
Diest-Daber, Otto von (1821–1901), 93, 94, 96
Diez, letter to, 143n.22
Dill, Richard W., *Der Parlamentarier Eduard
   Lasker*, 151n.6, 151n.7
Discriminatory laws, 56
Dohm, Ernst (1819–83), 10
Dorpaelen, Andreas
   "Emperor Friedrich III", 140n.33
   Treitschke, 147n.26
Dreiklassensystem, 69, 144n.24. See also elec-
   toral system (Pr.).
Duboc, Julius (1829–1903), "Ein dunkler
   Philosoph", 133n.40

Duncker, Max (1811–86), 19, 25, 26
    letters from, 135n.8, 136n.38
    letters to, 135n.15, 136n.29, 136n.37,
        136n.38

East Prussia, 1
Eastern Europe, 31
Eckardt, Julius von (1836–1908),
    Lebenserinnerungen, 133n.40
"Eduard Lasker"
    (*Preussische Jahrbücher*), 133n.35,
        144n.24
    (*Allgemeine Zeitung des Judentums*),
        134n.63
Ager, Akiba (Rabbi of Posen), 2
"Eisenacher Erklärung", 134n.6
Eisfeld, Gerhard, *Die Enstehung*, 138n.4
Elben, Otto (1823–99), 10, 26, 27, 28, 149n.2
    letters from, 136n.41, 149n.2
    letters to, 136n.39, 137n.43, 137n.45
    Lebenserinnerungen, 133n.36, 136n.39,
        144n.27
Elections
    to the Prussian Landtag (1855), 5 (1858),
        5 (1866), 20, 21
    (of 1879), 108
    to the Reichstag (1881), 14
Election Committees, 35, 138n.6
Electoral districts (N. Ger. Confederation and
        Second Reich), 69
    Berlin No. 1, 7, 135n.10
    Berlin No. 2, 8
    Berlin No. 4, 135n.10
    Meiningen, 99
Electoral system in Prussia, 5. See also
    Dreiklassensystem.
Engelberg, Ernst, *Deutschland*, 140n.2
Engels, Friedrich (1820–95), letter to, 133n.41
England, 30. See also London.
    constitution of, 61, 115
    legal process in, 52–53
    and ministerial government, 78
    Lasker's trip from, 119
    security of, 21
Era of Conflict. See Conflict Era
Erlangen, 111
Eulenburg, Friedrich, Count von (1815–81),
    135n.15
Extra Beilage, (*Neuen Frankfurter Presse*),
    137n.53
Extraterritoriality, 49

Falk, Adalbert (1827–1900), 82. See also
    Kulturkampf.
Federal Executive, Reichstag roll-call votes on,
    80 (Table 5.5)
Feilchenfeld, Florina, letters to, 133n.49,
    141n.24
Feilchenfeld, Hugo
    "Gedächtnisrede", 141n.24
    letters from, 133n.49, 141n.24
Fischer-Frauendienst, Irene, *Bismarcks
    Pressepolitik*, 137n.52, 145n.48
Flemming, Count von, (1813–84), 25
    letter to, 136n.29
Forckenbeck, Max von (1821–84), 65, 67
    and Alsace-Lorraine, 29
    and Bismarck, 40
    and immunity, 73
    and Lasker, 10, 108
    and Liberal Union, 38, 109–10, 150n.9
    and Luxembourg, 22
    and ministerial responsibility, 77
    and NL ministers, 41, 79
    and Reichstag, 144–45n.40
    and South Germany, 26
    letters from, 135n.20, 136n.33, 136n.37,
        37n.48, 139n.27, 144n.40, 149n.4,
        150n.6, 150n.8, 150n.9, 150n.12
    letters to, 137n.48, 143n.14, 143n.17,
        143n.19, 143n.20, 147n.32
Forester, Erich, *Adalbert Falk*, 145n.54
Fortschrittspartei, 18
Fraktion. See National Liberal party caucus.
Fraktionen (parties in Reichstag or Landtag), 35
France, 19. See also Bonaparte, Nice.
    hostile to Germany, 17, 20
    intervention by, 24
    Lasker's fear of, 21
    legal system of, 52
    and Bavaria, 136n.40
    and Luxembourg, 22
    and Prussia, 8, 25, 32, 40
Francke [prob. Karl Philipp, 1805–70], letter to,
    135n.8
Franco-Prussian war, 23
Fraenkel, Ernst, "Historische Vorbelastungen",
    140n.34, 142n.2, 145n.40
Frankfurt am Main, 3, 23, 30, 32, 69, 81, 109
Frankfurter Zeitung, 133n.40
    antisocialist law, 50–51
    and compromise, 40
    and indemnity bill, 21
    and Lasker, 9, 72, 94, 109

and Lasker's southern policy, 25–26
and Lasker's exposure of railroad scandal,
    93
and Liberal Union, 111
and NL, 107
and government use of the press, 82–83
and H. Rickert, 110
and L. Sonnemann, 81
and universal suffrage, 69
citations, 134n.58, 135n.17, 135n.18,
    39n.20, 139n.24, 140n.30 141n.20,
    141n.21, 141n.23, 141n.24, 143n.24,
    144n.27, 144n.29, 145n.53 145n.54,
    147n.25, 147n.29, 148n.43, 149n.1,
    149n.2, 149n.4, 149n.54, 150n.6,
    150n.7, 150n.10, 150n.13, 150n.14,
    151n.18
Frankl, P., and S. Maybaum, Geistliche Reden,
    134n.63
Frantz, Constantin (1817–91), Der
    Nationalliberalismus, 134n.57
Frederick II, The Great, King of Prussia
    (1712–86), 3
Frederick William IV, King of Prussia
    (1795–1861), 5
Freedom, 20, 21, 22
Freedom of association, 90
Freemasons, 4
Free Conservative party, 113, 151n.22
    and Bismarck, 41
    and Hohenlohe, 9
    and NL, 42
    size of, 36, (Table 3.3)
Free trade, 9
Freiburg im Breisgau, 2
Frenzel, Karl (1827–1914), 10, 103, 133n.39
Freytag, Gustav (1816–95), 19, 66
    letters from, 137n.45, 142n.9
    letters to, 135n.9, 137n.45, 143n.17
Fricke, Dieter, ed., Die bürgerlichen Parteien,
    138n.4
Friedberg, Bernhardine, 7, 23
Fries, Hugo Friedrich (1818–1905), 77
Fritsche, F. W. (1825–1905), 141n.24
Fröbel, Julius, (1805–93), 3
    Ein Lebenslauf, 132n.14

Gagel, Walter, Die Walhrechtsfrage, 144n.24
Gall, Lothar, "Elsass und Lothringen 1870",
    137n.49
    Bismarck, 151n.3

Galveston (Texas), 2, 4, 14, 119. See also
    United States.
Gambetta, Léon (1838–82), 25
Geheime Fonds, 81
Gelber, N. M., "Intervention", 134n.59
Gemeinde (community), 69, 72, 84
    of Jarotschin, 1
General Accounting Office, 76
"The General and Secret Suffrage", 138n.6
Generalregister, [for full citation, see
    Table 4.1n], 57 (Table 4.1n), 58
    (Table 4.2n), 59 (Table 4.3n), 71
    (Table 5.1n), 74 (Table 5.2n), 75
    (Table 5.3n), 78 (Table 5.4n), 80
    (Table 5.5n), 91 (Table 6.1n), 100
    (Table 6.2n), 102 (Table 6.3n), 105
    (Table 6.4n), 119, 138n.12
German Empire, 115. See also Reich, Second
    Reich.
German Freethinking party, 113
German Imperial party, 34 (Table 3.1), 35
    (Table 3.2)
German Workers' Association, 2
German Yearbook for Politics and Literature.
    See Deutsche Jahrbücher für Politik und
    Literatur.
Germany, 1
    constitutional development of, 61
    depression of 1873, 93
    disunity of, 18
    legal system, 52
    and ministerial responsibility, 72
    and Prussia, 21, 24
    and revolution, 46
Giles, Ferdinand, 137n.56
Gillis, John, Prussian Bureaucracy, 132n.17,
    138n.11
Glagau, Otto (?–1892),
    attacks on Lasker, 94
    Des Reiches Noth, 134n.57, 147n.27
Gneist, Rudolf von (1816–95), 21, 53, 60,
    141n.30
Godeffroy, Gustav (1817–93), 148n.49
    letter from, 148n.49
Goethe, Johann Wolfgang von (1749–1832), 11
Goetz, Walther, "Briefwechsel Gustav
    Schmollers", 139n.28, 149n.54
Gorz, letter to, 145n.56
Gottschall, Rudolf von, Aus meiner Jugend,
    131n.13
Great Britain. See England.
Grenzboten, 149n.4

Groening, Albert (1839–1903), letter to, 146n.7,
    146n.15
Group Schauss-Volk. See Liberal Group.
Gründer (Swindlers), 96
Gründungsprogramm, 135n.21
Gunther, John, *Taken at the Flood*, 132n.19,
    151n.5

Habeas Corpus, law of, 53
Haenel, Albert (1833–1918), 83, 110, 113
    letter to, 150n.11
Hahn, Ludwig Ernst (1820–88), 82
Hall of Mirrors, 8
Hallowell, John H., *Decline of Liberalism*,
    140n.1
Hamburg, 87, 150n.17
Hamburger, Ernst, "Jews in Public Service",
    132n.17
Hamerow, Theodore S.
    "1848", 142n.9
    Social Foundations, vol. 1, *Ideas
        and Institutions*, 132n.25, 134n.5,
        138n.5, 143n.23, 144n.28, 146n.1,
        146n.4
    Restoration, 143n.23, 146n.1
Handworker Association, 6. See also Berlin.
Hannover, 23, 38, 107, 112
Harms, Paul, *Nationalliberale Partei*, 138n.4
Harris, James F.
    "Eduard Lasker", 133n.49, 141n.18
    "Compromise Liberalism", 135n.15,
        139n.21
Hartmann, Moritz (1821–72), 3
    Revolutionäre Errinnerungen, 132n.14
Hasselmann, Wilhelm (1844–?), 141n.24
Heffter, Heinrich, *Selbstverwaltung*, 140n.2
Heine, Heinrich (1797–1856), 10
Helfferich, Karl, *Georg von Siemens*, 133n.37,
    145n.56
Hennig, Julius von (1822–77), 10, 71, 77
    letter from, 144n.28
Heppner, Aron and Izaak Herzberg, eds., *Aus
    Vergangenheit*, 131n.2
Herrenhaus, 72
Herzfeld, Hans, *Johannes Miquel*, 138n.3
Hess, Adalbert, *Das Parlament*, 137n.1
Hesse-Darmstadt, 8, 136n.28
Hesse-Kassel, 23, 26, 27
Heyderhoff, Julius and Paul Wentzcke, eds.,
    Deutsche Liberalismus, [for full citation,
    see Abbreviations, p. xvi], 133n.37,

134n.58, 135n.8, 135n.10, 135n.17,
    135n.20, 136n.28–136n.29, 136n.38,
    136n.40, 137n.45, 139n.27, 139n.29,
    140n.32, 141n.17, 142n.45, 143n.12,
    143n.20, 143n.23, 144n.28, 144n.31,
    144n.36, 144n.40, 145n.46, 145n.53,
    146n.10, 147n.25, 147n.28, 147n.33,
    148n.42, 148n.45–148n.47, 148n.49,
    148n.51, 149n.2, 149n.3, 149n.4, 149n.5,
    149n.53, 149n.54, 150n.6–150n.15,
    150n.17, 151n.22, 151n.23
Heydt, August Freiherr von der (1801–74), 73,
    79
Hinschius, Paul (1835–98), 107
Hintze, Otto, 17
    "Machtpolitik", 134n.2, 142n.2
    "Liberalismus", 134n.2
    "Rechtsstaat", 140n.2
    "preussische Staatsministerium", 145n.46
Hirsch, Rabbi Samson Raphael (1808–88), 13
Hödel, Max (1857–78), 50
Hohenlohe-Schillingsfürst, Prince Chlodwig zu
    (1819–1901), 9, 10, 41, 42
    Denkwürdigkeiten, 133n.33, 133n.39,
        136n.38, 140n.31
Holborn, Hajo, *Modern Germany*, 140n.2,
    143n.18
Hölder, Julius von (1819–87)
    and Bavaria, 27
    and centralization, 66
    and Lasker, 107
    and NL, 39
    and new party name, 108
    and Imperial railroad bill, 95
    and ultramontanes, 28
    and National party, 26
    and union with north, 29
    letters from, 136n.27, 136n.36, 136n.39,
        137n.46, 137n.47, 143n.20
    letters to, 136n.36, 136n.37, 137n.47,
        142n.9, 143n.16, 143n.17, 143n.18,
        143n.19, 143n.21
Hollyday, Frederick B.M., *Bismarck's Rival*,
    150n.7
Holstein, Friedrich von (1837–1909), 29, 83
Honoratioren, 33
Houndsditch (London), 4. See also England.
House of Representatives. See United States.
House Rules (N. Ger. Reichstag), 72
Hoverback, Leopold Freiherr von (1822–75), 21
Huber, Ernest R., ed., *Dokumente*, 36
    (Table 3.3n), 79

Hungry forties, 87
Hüsgen, Eduard, *Ludwig Windhorst*, 140n.30

Income, per capita, 87
Indemnity Bill, 20, 31
International Arbitration and Peace Association,
    31, 143n.9
Invalidenfonds, 147n.21
Iron Chancellor, 77. See also Bismarck, Otto
    von.
Iron Tariff, Reichstag roll-call votes on, 100
    (Table 6.2). See also tariffs.
Israelitische Wochenschrift, 15, 134n.63
Italy, 6, 20, 21, 24
Itzenplitz, Heinrich Graf von (1799–1883), 93

Jacoby, Johann (1805–77), 7
Jarotschin (Jaroczyn), 1, 2, 5, 15
    population of, 1
Jesuits, 49
Jews, 38, 49, 68
    emancipation of, 13
    attacks on Lasker, 50
    and law, 56
    press, 15
    of Romania, 14
Joachim, Joseph (1831–1901), 10
Jörg, Joseph Edmund (1819–1901), 25, 30
Jüdische Presse, 15, 134n.63
Justizgesetz, 48

Kalkoff, Hermann, *Nationalliberale
    Parlamentarier*, 139n.13, 139n.19
Kapp, Friedrich (1824–84), 10
Kardorff, Wilhelm von (1828–1907), letter from,
    148n.49
Karlsruhe, 25
Kellenbenz, Hermann, *Gesammelte Schriften*,
    142n.2
Keller, Gottfried (1819–90), 10
Kiefer, Friedrich (1830–95), 25, 26, 28, 29,
    136n.28, 136n.40
    letters from, 136n.28, 136n.29, 136n.34,
        136n.40, 137n.43, 137n.48
    letters to, 143n.11, 145n.43
Kinkel family, 132n.20
Kinkel, Gottfried (1815–82), 4, 11
    letter from, 132n.20
Kinkel, Johanna, 4, 12

Kleines Statistisches Taschenbuch, 131n.8
Kober, Adolf, "Jews in . . . 1848", 131n.10
Kölnische Zeitung, 149n.4
Königsberg Hartungsche Zeitung, 62
Königgrätz, 62
Konfliktszeit, 6, 53, 144n.40. See also Conflict
    Era.
Köster, Helmut, "Aus Laskers politische
    Frühzeit", 131n.10, 132n.15, 132n.17,
        132n.18, 132n.22, 132n.29, 146n.7,
        146n.15
Kreis, 72, 147n.31
Kreisblätter, 79
Kreisordnungen, 69, 84
Kremer, Willy, *Der Soziale Aufbau der
    Parteien*, 137n.1
Kreuzzeitung, 82, 93, 145n.54
Krieger, Leonard, *German Ideas of Freedom*,
    45, 140n.2
Krohn and Salomon, 4
Kulturkampf, 79, 105. See also Center party,
    Falk, May laws.
    and anti-Jesuit law, 49
    and Lasker, 13
    and liberals, 117
    and NL, 40

Laboulaye, Edouard René Lefebvre de
    (1811–83), 133n.39
Lafrey, 133n.39
Lambi, Ivo, *Free Trade*, 147n.26, 148n.40,
    149n.54
Landes, David S., "Technological Change",
    146n.2
Landrat, 53, 83–85
Landtag (Prussian), 1, 9, 23, 47
    and administration, 76
    elections to, 20–21
    immunity of members of, 54
    and indemnity bill, 3
    and Jews, 50
    and Lasker, 7, 10, 19, 24, 45, 77, 94
    and Lasker on cooperatives, 89
    and Lasker defeated in election (1879), 98
    and the Liberal Union, 38
    and NL, 117
    opposition to government by, 6, 62
    party distribution in, 33, 36 (Table 3.3)
Lasker, Albert D. (1880–1952), 4, 132n.19
Lasker, Daniel (1800–52), 2, 4
Lasker, Eduard (1829–84)

analyst of the Prussian state, 46
and annexation of Alsace and Lorraine, 29
and anti-Semitism, 14, 96, 134n.58
and antisocialist laws, 50–51
and Association to Protect Commercial
    Interests, 146n.6
and Association for Social Politics, 103
and Baden, 24–25
on banking and currency, 92, 146n.20
and Bavarian autonomy, 27, 65
and bill of rights, 55
birth, 1
and Herbert von Bismarck, 50, 149n.1
and Otto von Bismarck, 7, 21, 96, 147n.33
as Bismarck opponent, 9, 41, 72, 98
as Bismarck supporter, 8, 22, 116
and Bleichröder, 133n.33
"Breslau Opposition", 132n.13
and budgetary power, 22, 73
and the Bundesrat, 64, 66, 68, 142n.9
for a centralized state, 21, 64, 83
childhood, 1–2
and the Constitution of Prussia (1850),
    62–63
and constitutionalism, 62–63, 67, 85
death of, 1, 9, 15, 83, 120
and death penalty, 56–57 (Table 4.1n)
decline in popularity of, 117
and Diäten, 70, 71 (Table 5.1n)
and diplomacy, 30, 40
early political activity, 6–8
and economics, 88–89, 92, 95–96
and the executive, 77, 79–90 (Table 5.5n)
and elections in Prussia (1878ff), 108–09,
    111
elections in the Reich, 81, 83
on electoral districts, 69
and freedom of association, 90
and free trade, 96, 99, 102
and the Geheime Fonds, 81, 82
    (Table 5.6n)
goals in the early 1850s, 4
and governmental press, 82, 145n.51
Gunther's treatment of, 148n.44
illness, 14
and immunity for members of parliament,
    73, 74 (Table 5.2n)
and Indmenity Bill, 21
as a Jew, 2, 12–14, 49, 94, 141n.18
and Friedrich Kiefer, 136n.28, 136n.40
and the Kulturkampf, 43–49
on language as the basis of civilization, 88

on law, 45
on uniformity of law, 46–48
and "special laws", 49–50
on legal codification, 47–48
and law enforcement, 51
as legal theorist, 46
for a national legal system, 48, 51
on legal process, 47, 52
as a lawyer, 4–5
as legal reformer, 55–56, 60
and Leonhardt, 54, 141n.34
and Lippe, 54, 79
on judicial patronage, 55
on legal reciprocity, 49
and liberalism, 113, 116
and the Liberal Union, 38, 110
and liberal unity, 107–08, 110–112
in London, 4, 5
and Luxembourg, 22
and the middle class, 72
on military budget bills, 30, 74, 75
    (Table 5.3n)
on militray bill of 1867, 73
on military bill of 1874, 74–75
and ministerial responsibility, 77–78
and Miquel, 147n.28
and national priorities, 20, 22, 32, 48,
    64–65, 83
and the NL party caucus, 10, 33, 37
and NL ministers, 41, 79
and NL left wing, 43, 107
criticism of NL by, 98, 109
and NL split, 107–08, 137n.52, 149n.4
resignation from NL, 98, 109
and the navy, 109, 135n.22
opposition to government, 40, 53, 83
as a parlamentarian, 9–10, 15, 46, 68
and peace, 31, 136n.32, 137n.56
and the police, 52–54, 84
and press laws, 55–57, 58 (Table 4.2n), 59
    (Table 4.3n)
on manipulation of the press, 79, 82, 83,
    149n.2
and exposure of railroad scandal, 9, 92–95
and parliament, 27, 55, 64, 68, 85
non-political characteristics of, 6, 9–11,
    133n.39
and the Progressives, 113, 150n.17
and the Rechsstaat, 45–46
and the revolutions of 1848, 3, 132n.14
and secession from NL, 109–111, 150n.14
and annexation of Schleswig-Holstein, 7

and self-government, 72, 83–84
and socialism, 73, 89, 139n.16
and state socialism, 91, 102, 104–05
  (Table 6.4n)
and South Germany, 25–26, 28, 66
controversy over concessions to the south
  in 1866, 27–28, 65–66
critical of special interests, 85, 94, 99
and state ownership of industry, 76
and tariffs, 97–99, 100 (Table 6.2n),
  148n.44
and taxes, 23, 64, 96, 98
and Karl Twesten, 19
for unification, 17, 18, 115
and progressive nature of unity, 23–24,
  30–31
and the United States, 14, 109, 113, 119,
  149n.61
and universal suffrage, 69, 72, 141n.9
opposed to universal suffrage in locality,
  69, 72, 84
and the Volk, 70
and war, 19, 25, 135n.17
and workers, 88–89, 103
for workers' freedom, 90, 91 (Table 6.1n)
and Zollparlament, 143.21
Publications:
  "After the Peace", 20
  "An die Wähler", 148n.38, 148n.45,
    148n.48, 149n.58
  "Announcement", 20
  "Berechtigung", 94, 147n.26, 147n.28,
    147n.33
  "Cosmopolitan and National Wisdom", 63,
    88, 142n.7, 146n.9
  "Erklärung", 135n.14, 135n.16
  Erlebnisse einer Mannes-Seele, 11, 12,
    132n.21, 133n.42–133n.47, 144n.30
  Fünfzehn Jahre, 72, 11, 133n.31, 142n.7,
    144n.29, 151n.19
  "The Future of the German Empire", 31,
    137n.54
  "Justification and a Few Words to a
    Disinterested Reader". See
    "Berechtigung".
  "Justizgesetze", 60, 142n.45
  "Der König in der Verfassung", 142n.6,
    144n.27
  "Die Krisis in Preussen", 143n.21, 144n.28
  "Die Mahnung", 135n.12
  Means and Objectives of Cultural
    Development, 88

"Der Mensch und seine Geschlecht",
  140n.4, 146n.8
"Police Power", 53
"Polizeigewalt". See "Police Power".
"Die Regentschaft", 142n.6
speech in Camburg, 140n.5, 141n.21,
  148n.49
speech in Frankfurt am Main, 140n.30,
  141n.24, 144n.29, 144n.37, 145n.58,
  145n.62, 147n.33, 148n.45, 148n.47,
  148n.48, 150n.6
speech in Magdeburg, 136n.23, 143n.12,
  143n.22, 146n.6, 148n.51
speech in Sonneberg, 144n.27, 145n.55,
  148n.45, 148n.46, 148n.48, 149n.58,
  151n.21
"The Struggle over the Judicial Code".
  See "Justizgesetze".
"Die Thronrede", 135n.15
Verfassungsgeschichte, 132n.27, 140n.3,
  141n.25, 141n.29
"Welt und Staatsweisheit". See
  "Cosmopolitan and National Wisdom".
"Wie ist die Verfassung. . .", 142n.4
"Wort und Tat", 132n.14, 140n.5, 142n.8
Letters from: 132n.19–20, 134n.58,
  35n.10, 136n.32–34, 136n.37,
  136n.39–40, 137n.43–46, 137n.48,
  137n.52, 140n.32 141n.12, 142n.9,
  143n.9, 143n.11, 143n.13–23, 144n.28,
  144n.31, 144n.36, 145n.43, 146n.7,
  146n.10, 146n.15 148n.42, 148n.45,
  148n.46–47, 148n.49, 148n.52,
  149n.2–3, 149n.5, 149n.53, 149n.61,
  150n.7–9, 150n.12, 150n.14, 150n.17
  151n.6, 151n.20
Letters to: 132n.20, 132n.29, 133n.39–41,
  134n.50 135n.11, 136n.27–29,
  136n.36–38, 136n.40, 136n.42,
  137n.43, 137n.46–48, 137n.52, 138n.8,
  139n.27, 139n.29, 141n.17, 141n.28,
  142n.9, 143n.12, 143n.13, 143n.15,
  143n.20, 144n.28, 145n.46, 145n.53,
  146n.6, 146n.12, 147n.25, 147n.33,
  148n.49, 148n.52, 149n.2, 149n.4–5,
  149n.54, 150n.6–7, 150n.9–15,
  150n.17, 151n.17, 151n.20,
  151n.22–23
Lasker, Jizchock. See Lasker, Eduard.
Lasker, Max, 2, 4, 12
Lasker, Morris (1840–1916), 1, 4, 14, 119,
  151n.5

Lasker, Rebecca (? –1839), 2
"Laskers Beziehung zu Frankfurt", 133n.34
Lasker-Rickert-Forckenbeck Group, 109
Lasker-Rickert Group, 109
Laspeyres, Eteinne (1834–1913), 98, 148n.44
Lassalle, Ferdinand (1825–64), 12
Laubert, M., "Stadt Posen", 131n.6
Laufs, Adolf, "E. Lasker und der Rechsstaat",
    140n.2
Law, 45. See also accident insurance, anti-
    Jesuit, antisocialist, civil, discriminatory,
    and May laws.
    English common, 60
    on corporations (1869), 94
Left Center party, 36 (table 3.3)
Leipzig, 31, 48
Leo Baeck Institute Archives, 132n.19, 134n.61,
    141n.24
Leonhardt, Gerhard A. W. (1815–80), 54,
    141n.26, 141n.34
Lesse, Theodore Wilhelm (1827–1904), 110
Liberal economic theory, failure of, 116
Liberale Gruppe. See Liberal Group.
Liberal Group, 38, 76, 139n.17
    religious composition of, 38
Liberal Imperial party, 34, (Table 3.1), 35
    (Table 3.2), 108
Liberal party, 99
Liberal reform, 20
Liberal tactics of compromise, 115
Liberale Vereinigung. See Liberal Union.
Liberal Union, 34 (Table 3.1), 35 (Table 3.2),
    36 (Table 3.3), 38, 76, 80, 98, 111, 116,
    119, 139n.17, 150n.17, 151n.18
    attack on NL, 111
    and elections of 1881, 112
    newspaper, 111
    political and geographical composition of,
    38
    and Progressives, 111, 113
Liberalism, 19, 22, 53, 72, 88, 115
Liberals, 9, 19, 21, 94
    hatred of Bismarck, 63
Ligue International de la Paix, 137n.56
Lindau, Paul (1839–1919), Nur Erinnerungen,
    150n.17
Linder, Dr. Otto (1820–67), 132n.13
Lipke, Gustav (1820–89), 150n.17
    letter from, 150n.17
Lippe, Leopold Graf zur (1815–89), 52, 54, 79,
    141n.26
Lipset, Seymour Martin, Political Man, 146n.3

Listemann, Konrad, letter to 144n.36
Loeber, Irmgard, Bismarcks Pressepolitik,
    145n.48
Löwenthal, Dr., 2
London, 4, 12, 14, 137n.56. See also England.
Lottery Bonds, 92
Lowenberg, Gerhard
    Bundestages, 144n.31
    Parliament, 144n.31
LT. See Wörtliche Berichte.
Lübeck, 87
Lückentheorie, 54, 70
Luxembourg, 22

MacKendrick, Paul, et. al., Western Civilization,
    142n.1
Magdeburg, 23, 109
Main River, 26
Mainz, 28, 38
Malinckrodt, Hermann von (1821–74), 53
Manteuffel era, 54, 61
Manteuffel, Otto von (1805–82), 5
Marquardsen, Heinrich (1826–97), 26, 28
    letters to, 136n.34, 136n.39, 137n.43,
    137n.45–46
Marx, Karl (1818–83), 11
    letter from, 133n.41
    and Friedrich Engels, Briefwechsel,
    133n.41
Masonic Order, 132n.19. See also freemasons.
May laws, 49. See also Falk, Kulturkampf.
Mayer, E.W., "Parteikrisen", 135n.9, 135n.17
Mayer Gustav
    Briefe . . . Lassalle, 131n.5
    "Trennung", 134n.3
Mecklenburg, 2, 12, 13
    Duke of, 95
Meiningen, 8, 83, 110–12
Meinecke, Friedrich, "Zur Geschichte", 134n.5
"The Members of the Reichstag", 138n.11
Merryman, John Henry, Civil Law Tradition,
    140n.1, 141n.13 141n.26, 141n.28,
    142n.40, 142n.46
Meyer Sigmund, letters from, 146n.6
Michaelis, Otto (1826–90), 103, 135n.17
Michelet, Karl Ludwig (1801–93), letter from,
    143n.12
Mietsteuer, 97
Military alliances, with S. Germany, 20
Military bills
    of 1867, 73, 117–18

of 1871, 40, 74
of 1874, 36, 40, 74, 75, 118
Reichstag roll-call voes on, 75 (Table 5.3)
seven-year military budget, 43. See also
Septennat.
Military law, 49
Military suffrage, 69–70
Mill, John Stuart (1806–73), 46
On Liberty, 140n.6, 148n.40
Ministerial responsibility, 77, 145n.41
Reichstag roll-call votes on, 78 (Table 5.4)
Miquel, Johannes von (1828–1901), 11, 38, 39,
41, 78, 94, 97 99, 108, 137n.52, 147n.28
letters from, 133n.40, 137n.52, 150n.6
letters to, 140n.32, 147n.28, 148n.49,
149n.4, 149n.5, 150n.16
Mittnacht, Hermann Freiherr von (1825–1909),
letters to, 136n.40, 142n.9
Möcke, Dr., 132n.13
Mohl, Robert von (1799–1875), 10
Lebenserinnerungen, 133n.35, 133n.36
Molt, Peter, Der Reichstag, 137n.1, 146n.2
Moltke, Helmut Graf von, General (1800–91),
30
Mommsen, Wilhelm
"Parteigeschichte", 134n.2
Parteiprogramme, 134n.6, 134–35n.6,
139n.24, 141n.7, 150n.14
Johannes von Miquel, 138n.3
Mork, Gordon R.
"Making of a German Nationalist", 131n.4,
131n.7
"Prussian Railway Scandal", 147n.24
Morley, John (1838–1923), 139n.23
Mosle, [prob. Alexander, 1827-?], letter from,
149n.2
Mount Sinai Hospital, 14
Müller, E. A. (1813–77), 110
letter from, 150n.11
Munich, 26, 67

Napoleon III (Charles Louis Napoleon Bonaparte
(1808–73), 8. See also France.
Napoleonic Wars, 61
National Assembly
of Germany (1848), 3
of Prussia (1848), 3, 61
National Party (Württemberg), 26
National Liberal Party, 36, 38, 85, 147n.28.
See also Lasker.
and antisocialist law, 50–51

"Aufruf", 25
and Bismarck, 39, 42, 83, 116
central campaign committee, 150n.13
decline of, 112, 117
and Diäten, 70
and electoral districts, 69
electoral problems in 1878, 50, 82, 107–08
founding of, 7–8
and free trade, 96, 148n.49
goals of, 25, 39
as a governmental party, 40–41, 81
and immunity, 73
internal disunity of, 33, 41, 94
for Kulturkampf, 40, 42
Lasker as leader of, 1, 14
left wing of, 10, 82, 95, 107, 109,
139n.20
success of 117–19
and military bill (1874), 73–75, 82
and ministerial responsibility, 77–78
and NL ministers, 40, 79, 139n.26
Fraktion. See party caucus.
party caucus, 10, 35–36
and political alliances, 42, 113
power in parliament, 9, 33, 41–42, 94
and agitation and press cases, 56–57
program of, 22, 40, 69, 73, 141n.7
and Progressives, 111
in Prussian Landtag, 10
affected by railroad scandal, 95
religious composition of, 37, 139n.14
secession of left wing, 110–11
secession of right wing, 108
size of, 34–36, 42
social composition of, 37–38, 139n.13
and treaties with South Germany, 66
split in, 57, 69–70, 107, 149n.4
and Stauffenberg, 107
studies of, 33
and tariffs, 96, 99
and Verein für Sozialpolitik, 103
and workers' freedom, 90
National Liberal Executive Committee
and Lasker, 97, 109
and the Liberal Union, 38
as strongest element in NL, 36
united on press laws, 56
purpose of, 35
membership, 36, 38, 138n.7
social composition of, 37–38
size of, 37
and treaties with South Germany, 66

and tariffs, 99
and workers' freedom, 90
letter from, 150n.8
letter to, 150n.8
Nationalverein, 6–7, 18–19, 49
National Zeitung, 20, 37 (Table 3.4n), 82, 103,
    145n.54
Nees von Esenbeck, Christian (1776–1858), 3,
    132n.16
Neuen Frankfurter Presse, 145n.58
New Era, 5–6, 18, 45, 116
New York, 1, 14, 119–20. See also United
    States.
Nice, 14. See also France.
Nipperdey, Thomas, *Organisation*, 137n.1,
    138n.2, 138n.9–10, 139n.18
North America, 64. See also United States.
North Germany, 8
North German Confederation, 8, 13, 20–21, 23,
    47–48, 61, 65–68, 70, 73, 77, 115
North German liberals, 29
North German Reichstag, 24
North German constituent assembly, 47
Norddeutsche Allgemeine Zeitung, 82–83,
    145n.54, 149n.4
Northern liberals, 27
Northern Pacific railroad, 119
Northern Railroad Corporation, 95
Noyes, P. H. *Organization and Revolution*,
    131n.8, 131n.12, 132n.16

O'Boyle, Lenore
    "The Middle Class", 138n.11, 146n.4
    "Liberal political Leadership", 137n.1,
        138n.12
Ochiltree, Thomas Peck (1837–1902), 1
    "The Late Dr. Eduard Lasker", 131n.1
    Resolution of, 1
Occupations, multicoding, 138n.12
Oder River, 2
Oder Strasse, 3
Oetker, Friedrich (1808–81), 10
    letters to 133n.37, 135n.20
Old Liberal Center party, 36 (Table 3.3)
Old Testament, 56
Olmütz (1850), 19, 31. See also Austria.
Oncken, Hermann
    "Aus den Briefen Rudolf von Bennigsen"
        [cited as ABRB; for full citation see
        Abbreviations, p. xvi], 133n.36,
        134n.4, 135n.7, 135n.9, 135n.20,

136n.38, 137n.46, 139n.24, 139n.26,
    145n.46, 149n.2, 150n.12, 150n.14,
    150n.16, 151n.20
"Bennigsen", 140n.30
Rudolf von Bennigsen, 134n.6, 136n.32,
    136n.37, 138n.3, 140n.32, 149n.2,
    151n.5, 151n.20, 151n.22
Oppenheim, Heinrich Bernhard (1819–80), 6–7,
    19–20, 23, 29, 37 (Table 3.4n), 41, 53,
    70, 103
    literary advice of, 133n.39
    "The Price of Victory", 29, 137n.49
    "Der Siegespreis". See "The Price of
        Victory".
    letters from, 133n.39, 135n.10–11,
        139n.29, 146n.12, 148n.52, 150n.6
    letters to, 135n.10, 141n.17, 144n.28
Oppler, Adolf, letters from 133n.40–41

Pack, Wolfgang, *parlamentarische Ringen*,
    145n.54
Palmer, R.R. and Joel Colton, *History of the
    Modern World*, 142n.1
Parisius, Ludolf (1827–1900), 11, 150n.17
    letter from, 151n.17
Parliament
    immunity of members, 72–73
    powers of, 72
    Reichstag roll-call votes on, 74 (Table 5.2)
    weakness of, 73
Particularism, 23, 27, 99
    of Prussia, 19
"Party", concept of, 34–35
Patriots, 28
Penal Code, roll-call votes, 48
Perles, J. "Geschichte der Juden in Posen",
    131n.7
Perrot, Franz (1835–91), 96, 103. See also
    anti-Semitism.
    attack on Lasker, 94
    Bismarck und die Juden, 134n.57
Pflanze, Otto
    Bismarck, 132n.28, 144n.24
    "Juridicial and Political Responsibility",
        140n.1
Philippson, Ludwig (1811–89), 13, 15
Philippson, Martin
    "Forckenbecks erstes Debut", 135n.20
    Max von Forckenbeck, 143n.24, 148n.49,
        150n.14, 150n.17
Pikart, Eberhard, "Die Rolle der Parteien",

140n.34
Pinson, Koeppel, *Modern Germany*, 143n.18
Poles, 8
Police, 85
  in Prussia, 53
Polish party, 34 (Table 3.1), 35 (Table 3.2), 36
  (Table 3.3)
"Politische Übersicht", 145n.56
Pontresina, 10
Popular vote, 33
Poschinger, Heinrich Ritter von (1845–1911), 41
  Fürst Bismarck, 133n.33–34, 139n.29–30,
    140n.30, 143n.23, 147n.33, 149n.2–4
  Hans Viktor von Unruh, 137n.43
Posen
  city of, 31–32, 150n.7
  population of, 3
  Grand Duchy of, 3
  province, 1, 8
  migration of Jews from, 2
Poznan. See Posen.
Prämienanleihen (lottery bonds), 92
Press, 15
  legal status of, 56
  offenses, 59
Press (governmental)
  attacks on NL enemies, 81
  and the Baden affair, 25, 136n.29
  and Lasker, 30–31, 82, 145n.51, 149n.2
  and second antisocialist bill, 50
  studied by Pack, 145n.54
  use of in 1878, 81, 83
Preussische Jahrbücher, 6, 41, 69
Prince-Smith, John (1809–74), 103
Principles of Pragmatic Politics, 17. See also
  Rochau, A. L. von.
Progressives
  and Alsace and Lorraine, 29
  in Berlin, 8
  central committee of, 67
  in Conflict Era, 6, 39, 46, 116
  for constitutional unity, 18
  in 1881 Reichstag election, 5, 34, 112
  and Lasker, 7, 9, 113
  and the Liberal Union, 109, 111
  and the NL, 42, 81, 112, 117
  national wing of, 21
  pessimistic after 1866, 115
  size of, 34–36
Prosch, Carl Friedrich Wilhelm (1802–76), 13
Provinzial Korrespondenz, 81, 145n.51,
  145n.54. See also press (governmental).

Prussia, 1. See also constitutions, of Prussia.
  as absolutist, 31, 46
  and Austrian war, 20, 40
  and balance of power, 22
  dynastic change in 1858, 45
  electoral system, 70
  and Germany, 143n.12
  and Jews, 4
  judicial system, 47, 52
  and Lasker, 5
  and ministerial responsibility, 72–73, 77
  over-represented in NL, 38
  and N. Ger. Confederation, 8, 61, 65
  and Poles, 3
  reform of 21, 23
  and railroads, 76
  and Schleswig-Holstein, 7
  southern opposition to, 26–27, 30
  and unification, 18
Public opinion, 56
Pulzer, P.G.J., *Political Anti-Semitism*, 131n.6,
  134n.56
Putbus, Prince Wilhelm von, and railraod scandal, 93, 95
Puttkamer, Robert von (1828–1900), 83
Puttkamer Era (1880s), 55

Quandt, Otto, *Sozialgesetzgebung*, 148.50

Railroads, 92
Railroad Office (German State), 95
Rantzau, Kuno Graf zu (1843-?), letter to,
  145n.56
Real wages, 87
Realpolitik, 22, 39, 117
Rechtsstaat, 45, 96
Referendar, 5
Regency (Prussian, 1858), 63
Reich, 70. See also Second Reich.
Reichensperger, Peter (1810–92), 21
  letter from, 141n.17
Reichsgründung, 17, 25, 67
Reichskanzlei, 41. See also Delbrück.
Reichskanleramt, 79. See also Delbrück.
Reichstag
  and Alsace and Lorraine, 29
  annual sessions, 76
  and Baden affair, 25
  budget control by, 22, 41, 73
  constitutional assembly of 1867, 8, 39–40,

69
debates. See *Stenographische Berichte*.
Diäten, 70
elections to, 34, 107, 112
and foreign policy, 30
and Jewish emancipation, 13
jurisdiction of, 64
and Lasker, 1, 7, 9, 19, 120
and Lasker speech on police, 54
Lasker speech on workers' freedom, 90
Lasker as candidate for, 30
name of, 23
and National Liberal party, 33, 36–37, 39,
    117
party strength in, 34–35
and press, 56
and railroads, 95
as source of law, 47–48, 63–65
and formation of Second Reich, 25, 66–68
specific sessions of, 48, 99
and Social Democrats, 51
and treaties with South Germany, 27–28,
    66
Reichstagsbureau, ed., *Generalregister*. See
    Generalregister.
Revolutions of 1848, 3, 45, 115
Revolution, rejected by liberals in 1861ff., 62
Rhineland, 87
Rich, Norman H. and M. H. Fisher, eds., *The
    Holstein Papers*, 145n.56
Richelieu, Armand Jean Duplessis, Duke of
    (1585–1642), 19
Richter, Eugen (1838–1906), 67, 96, 111–12,
    144n.26
    Jugend Erinnerungen, 144n.26, 150n.17
    letters from, 150n.15, 150n.17
Rickert, Heinrich (1833–1902), 109–111, 119,
    149n.5
    replaces Lasker as organizer, 110
    letters from, 138n.8, 146n.12, 148n.49,
        49n.5, 150n.7, 150n.10, 150n.12–14,
        150n.16
    letters to, 150n.12, 150n.16
Rickert[Heinrich]-Lasker Letters, 150n.13
Riedel, Emil Freiherr von (1832–1906), 28
    letter to, 137n.44
Ringer, Fritz K., *Decline of the Mandarins*,
    138n.13
Ritter, Gerhard, "Indemnitäts-Vorlage", 135n.18
Rochau, August Ludwig von (1810–73), 17, 22,
    39
    Grundsätze, 134n.2, 139n.22

notes from, 135n.20
Rocker, Rudolf, *Johann Most*, 139n.16
Rodbertus, Johann Karl (1805–75), letter to,
    143n.23
Rodenberg, Julius (1831–1914), 7
    "Briefe an Eduard Lasker", 132n.29,
        133n.39, 133n.41, 149n.4
    Erinnerungen, 132n.20
Rohde, Gotthold, "Posen", 131n.8
Romania, 147.25
Rome, 24
Roon, General Albrecht Graf von (1803–79), 6,
    8, 30, 93–94
    Denkwürdigkeiten, 147n.32
    letter from, 147n.32
Rosenberg, Hans, *Grosse Depression*, 134n.56,
    138n.5, 138–39n.13, 146n.2, 147n.33
Rössler, Konstantin (1820–96), letter from,
    135n.15
Rousseau, Jean Jacques (1712–78), 144n.30
Rubinstein, Anton (1830–94), 10
Rückert, Ludwig (1830-?), 150n.7
    Letter from, 150n.7
Ruge, Arnold (1803–80), 3, 11
Ruge, Richard, letter to, 133n.40
Ruggiero, Guido de *History of European
    Liberalism*, 140n.1, 146n.6, 147–48n.35
Runclin, 133n.39
Russia, 17

Sandberger, Dietrich, *Ministerkandidatur*,
    139n.30, 145n.46, 147n.35
San Francisco, 120. See also United States.
St. Matthias Gymnasium, 2
St. Elizabeths Gymnasium, 2
Savigny, Friedrich Karl von (1799–1861), 60,
    63
Saxony, 87
Schauss, Friedrich von (1832–93), 38, 108
Schauss-Volk Group. See Liberal Group.
Schieder, Theodore
    ed., *Reichsgründung*, 134n.2
    "Das Verhältnis", 140n.2
Schierbaum, Hansjürgen, *Die politischen
    Wahlen*, 137n.1
Schlesische Zeitung (Breslau), 132n.13
Schleswig-Holstein, 107
    annexed, 23
    cause of war, 7
    Lasker for annexation of, 19, 31
    lesson of, for Lasker, 70

Schleswiger-Nachrichten, 107, 149n.1
Schmidt, Julian (1818–86), 10
Schmoller, Gustav (1838–1917), 9, 99, 103
  "Grundfragen", 149n.54
  "Hermann Schulze-Delitzsch", 133n.34,
    147n.35, 148n.49
  letters from, 148n.51, 148n.52
Schnabel, Franz, *Deutsche Geschichte*, 142n.2
Schoeps, Hans-Joachim, "Hermann Wagener",
  147n.27
Schrader, Karl (1834–1913), letter from,
  151n.23
Schraepler, Ernst, "liberalen Bürgertums",
  140n.33
Schroth, Hans-Georg, 42
  Welt- und Staatsideen, 140n.33
Schultze, Johannes, ed., *Max Duncker*, 135n.8,
  135n.15, 136n.29 136n.37, 136n.38
Schulze-Delitzsch, Hermann (1808–83), 67,
  89–90, 96, 102
  letter to, 149n.5
Schunke, Werner, *Die preussischen Freihändler*,
  135n.13, 135n.16, 147n.35
Schurz, Carl (1829–1916), 120
  letter to, 150n.17
Schwarck, 7
Schwarz, Max, *MdR*, 34 (Table 3.1n), 35
  (Table 3.2n)
Schwarzenberg, Fürst Felix von (1800–52), 5
Secession (of NL left wing), 110. See also
  Lasker, Liberal Union, NL.
Second Reich, 1, 8, 17, 33, 61. See also
  German Empire.
Secret Funds, Reichstag roll-call votes on, 82
  (Table 5.6)
Seehandlung, 147n.31
Seeley, Sir J. R., 17
Self-government, 83
Seligman, Jesse, 120
Sell, Friedrich S., *Die Tragödie*, 140n.2
Septennat, 74–75, 82, 117. See also military
  bills.
Sezessionisten. See secession.
Shanahan, William O., *German Protestants*,
  148n.50
Sheehan, James J.
  Lujo Brentano, 138n.3–4
  German Liberalism, 151n.1
  "Political Leadership", 140n.33
Sickness Insurance Bill, 104
Siemens, Werner von (1816–92), 7, 10, 83
  letters from 132n.29, 145n.56

Silesia, 3, 29
Simson, Eduard von (1810–99), 66–67, 72
  letter from, 143n.15
  letters to, 136n.40, 140n.19, 143n.20,
    144n.31
Snell, J. H. and Hans Schmitt, *Democratic
  Movement*, 138n.4
Snyder, Louis, "Lasker Resolution", 131n.1
Social Democratic Party
  and the antisocialist law, 41–42, 50
  and August Bebel, 25, 69
  growth of, 34, 116
  Lasker's defense of, 51
  and press, 57, 81
  popular opposition to, 107
  and National Liberals, 42, 69, 117
  size of, 34 (Table 3.1), 35 (Table 3.2), 36
    (Table 3.3)
Socialists, 8, 9, 49
Socialism, 89
State Socialism, 91
Society for the Legal Protection of German
  Citizens, 141n.28
Society for the Public Good (Leipzig), 31
Sonnemann, Leopold (1831–1909), 81
Sorrows of Young Werther, 11
South Germany
  and Bismarck, 8
  in Bundesrat, 65
  economy of, 87
  and *Zollparlament*, 8
  constitutional development, 61
  legal system, 47–48
  Lasker's position on, 27, 115
  and Prussia, 38, 65
  and unity, 22, 24, 26–27
Der Sozialist, 3
Spahn, Martin, "Zur Entstehung", 135n.9–10,
  135n.13, 135n.16, 144n.28, 145n.49,
  147n.27
Spanish throne controversy, 8
Specht, Fritz and Paul Schwabe,
  Reichstagswahlen, 34 (Table 3.1n)
Speier, Selma, "Jewish History", 133n.49
Spielhagen, Friedrich (1829–1911), 10
Staatenbund, 64
Staatsanzeiger, 79. See press (governmental).
Stahr, Adolf (1805–76), letter from, 147n.25
Stauffenberg, Franz von (1834–1901), 82
  elected in Braunschweig, 107
  damaged by government attacks in 1878,
    50, 83, 107

and Lasker, 89, 108–10
and the Liberal Union, 38, 110
as a minister, 41, 79, 108
and Progressives, 111
and secession, 109
letters from, 149n.4, 150n.6, 150n.9,
    150n.17
letters to, 144n.36, 144n.40, 145n.46,
    46n.10, 148n.45 149n.2–149n.5,
    150n.7–150n.9, 150n.12, 150n.14,
    150n.17
Stearns, Peter, European Society, 146n.3,
    146n.10
Steefel, Lawrence D., Schleswig-Holstein,
    133n.30
Stein, Felix Freiherr von, 148n.49
    letter from, 148n.49
Stein, Ludwig (1859–?), Es werde licht, 134n.63
Steinbrecher, Ursula, Liberale partei
    Organization, 137n.1
Steinsdorfer, Helmut, Stauffenberg, 138n.3,
    148n.37
Steglich, Walter, "Junkern und Bourgeoisie",
    147n.26
Stenographische Berichte. . .des Reichstages,
    [for full citation see Abbreviations, p. xvi],
    citations to, 134n.51–52, 134n.59,
    135n.16, 135n.19–20 135n.22, 136n.28,
    136n.30, 136n.41, 137n.50, 137n.52,
    137n.55, 140n.4–5, 140n.32, 141n.8,
    141n.10–17, 141n.19 141n.22–23,
    141n.28, 141n.30, 141n.32, 141n.35–37,
    142n.7, 142n.9, 142n.39–44, 143n.10–12,
    143n.17, 143n.21–22 144n.25, 144n.29,
    144n.31–38, 144n.40, 145n.41,
    145n.43–46, 145n.50, 145n.55,
    145n.59–60, 146n.12–17, 146n.19,
    146n.21–23, 147n.30, 147n.33–34,
    148n.37–38, 138n.43–49, 148n.51,
    149n.55–60, 151n.23
Stenographische Berichte. . .Zollparlaments,
    143n.21
Stephani, Martin Eduard (1817–85), 10, 107,
    150n.8
    for cooperation with the secession, 111
    letters from, 147n.25, 149n.2, 150n.16
Stern, Fritz
    Gold and Iron, 133n.33, 141n.20, 147n.24
    "Money, Morals", 147n.27
Stettin, 3, 150n.7
Stoltenberg, Gerhard, Der deutsche Reichstag,
    139n.15

Stolper, Gustav, German Economy, 146n.1,
    147n.33
Stosch system, 109
Straub, letters from, 136n.27
Strousberg, Henry Bethel (1823–84), 93,
    147n.25, 147n.29
    letter from, 147n.29
Suffrage, limited in the Kreis, 85
Supreme Court, 48
Switzerland, 64
Sybel, Heinrich von (1817–95), 45, 139n.29,
    141n.18
    letter to, 136n.38, 148n.51
    Founding of the German Empire, 140n.2

Talmud, 2
Tariffs, 72, 98, 118. See also agricultural tariff,
    iron tariff.
    protective, 31, 42, 79, 96–97, 107, 117
Taxes
    income, 97
    inheritance, 97
    non-payment of, 62
    property, 97
Temme, Jadokus (1798–1881), 7
Texas, 1, 119. See also United States.
Tiedemann[-Seeheim], Christoph von
    (1836–1907), 139n.29
Thuringia (Saxon), 8, 50
Toury, Jakob, Die politische Orientierungen,
    134n.62
Trade code, 48
Travel costs, 118
Treaties bet. N. and S. Germany, 27, 67
Treitschke, Heinrich von (1834–96), 139n.18
    and Bismarck, 19, 41
    and Lasker, 10
    legislator's code, 68
    and liberalism, 19–21, 40, 106
    and NL, 107
    and Staatenbund, 64
    "Bund und Reich", 142n.9
    "constitutionelle Königthum", 145n.57
    "Die Freiheit", 47, 140n.6, 143n.22
    "Zum Jahresgang", 139n.24
    "Der Krieg", 135n.11
    "Zum Inneren Lage", 149n.61, 150n.17,
        151n.18
    "Der Reichstag", 150n.17
    "Die Zukunft", 135n.11
    letter from, 135n.9

letter to, 133n.37
Tribune, 111, 150n.17
Trübner, [prob. Karl, 1846–1907], letter from,
    141n.28
Tuttle, Hubert, *German Political Leaders*,
    133n.36
Twesten, Karl (1820–70), 71
    and Bismarck, 40
    and Conflict Era, 77
    and press, 81
    and free speech in parliament, 73
    and Prussia, 19, 135n.17
    "Twestens Entwurf", 139n.24
    letter from, 135n.8

Ultramontanes, 23–24. See also Catholics,
    Center party.
Unification (of Germany), 1, 12, 17, 20, 115
    under Prussia, 25
United States of America, 4, 9, 64, 93, 97, 119.
    See also Galveston, New York, San
    Francisco, Texas.
    House of Representatives, 1
    Lasker's trip to, 13
Unity, 20, 22
Universal Suffrage, 8, 18, 20, 69, 115
University of Breslau, 3
Unruh, Hans Viktor von (1806–84), 26, 69,
    150n.7
    letter from, 134n.6

Varzin, 79
"Vergesst die Freiheit nicht!" 136n.38
Verein zur Wahrung Kaufmannischer Interessen,
    146n.6
"Vertrauliche Program", 135n.16, 139n.25,
    143n.23, 144n.34
Vienna, 3. See also Austria.
Vincke, Georg Freiherr von (1811–75), 68
Virchow, Rudolf (1821–1902), 113
Vogel, Walter, *Bismarcks Arbeiterversicherung*,
    148n.50
Volk, 70, 72
Volk, Joseph (1819–82), 38, 108, 139n.18
Volkspartei, 111
Vorgymnasium, 2
Vossische Zeitung, 132n.13
Voter participation, 138n.5

Wagener, Hermann (1815–89), 79, 90, 93, 95,
    147n.29, 148n.50
Wagner, Adolf (1835–1917), 103
Waldeck, Benedikt (1802–70), 7, 21, 23
Waldstedt, Gottfried, "Eduard Lasker", 146n.5
Wehler, Hans-Ulrich, *Bismarck und der
    Imperialismus*, 146n.4
Wahl, Adalbert, *Beiträge. . .Konfliktszeit*,
    140n.2, 140n.3, 144n.30
War of 1866, 21
Warsaw, Grand Duchy of, 3
Wehrenpfennig, Wilhelm (1829–1900), 10, 56
    letters from, 133n.37, 147n.28
Welfenfond, 144n.38
Wendorff, Hermann, *Zentrums*, 135n.9
Wentzcke, Paul
    "Aus Eduard Laskers soz. Anfängen",
        131n.13
    "Glaubensbekenntnisse", 131n.9, 131n.11,
        131n.12, 132n.14 132n.18, 132n.20,
        132n.23
    "Luxembourger Frage", 135n.20
    "Elsass-Lothringen", 137n.47
Weserzeitung, 111, 151n.18
Westphal, Otto, *Welt- und Staatsauffassung*,
    132n.27
Westphalen, Count Ferdinand von (1799–1876),
    5
White, Andrew D. (1832–1918), 120
White, Dan S., *The Splintered Party*, 138n.4
Wiedemann, letter from, 136n.27
Wilhelm I (of Prussia), 6, 19, 24
    as Kaiser, 50
    as Regent, 2–6
Willichs, 107
Windell, George C.
    Catholics and German Unity, 139n.26,
        143n.20
    "Bismarckian Empire", 139n.30, 144n.34
Winkler, Heinrich A., *Preussischer
    Liberalismus*, 138n.4, 151n.2
Windhorst, Ludwig (1812–91), 24
Woltmann, Dr. Alfred [prob. 1841–80], 136n.23
Workers, 68
    accident insurance, 98
    freedom, Reichstag roll-call votes on, 91
        (Table 6.1)
    insurance, Reichstag roll-call votes on, 105
        (Table 6.4)
World War I, 115
World War II, 115
Wörtliche Bericht. . .preussischen

Abgeordnetenhauses, 82 (Table 5.6n),
    134n.50, 134n.52–55, 135n.15–16,
    136n.24–26, 139n.28, 140n.4–5,
    141n.7–8, 141n.16, 141n.18, 141n.26–27,
    141n.29–31, 141n.33–35, 141n.37–38,
    142n.9, 142n.40–42, 143n.10, 143n.21,
    143n.23–24, 144n.26, 144n.31–32,
    144n.38–39, 145n.41–42, 145n.44,
    145n.47, 145n.49–51, 145n.55,
    145n.58–62, 146n.11, 146n.14,
    146n.18–19, 146n.63, 147n.23–24,
    147n.26, 147n.30–33, 148n.36–37,
    148n.51
Württemberg, 8, 26–28, 38, 66

Zabel, Friedrich (1802–87), 36, 37 (Table 3.4n),
    82, 103
    letter from, 145n.53
Zerissenheit, 31
Zettrach, F., 3
Ziegler, Franz (1803–76), letter from, 143n.23
Zinn, Dr., of medicine, 14
Zollparlament, 8, 66, 143n.21
Zollverein, 23, 96, 99
Zucker, Stanley, *Bamberger*, 138n.3, 151n.7
Zur Verfassungsgeschichte Preussens, 6